ABOUT THE AUTHORS

KEN PORTER

Kenneth Porter was born in Laindon in 1944 in the shadow of St Nicholas Church. The family moved to Langdon Hills in 1963 following compulsory purchase by the then Basildon Corporation. He has lived in the area ever since other than for a five year spell living in Southminster when he first got married to Carol in 1965.

He went to two local schools, first Markham's Chase (now Janet Dukes) and then on to the Laindon High Road school. His only real interest at school was sport and history. On leaving school he managed to get a job at Ford Motor in Dagenham and his short spell there convinced him that he will have to get a qualification, so after several years of study qualified as an accountant, retiring as Company Secretary and Finance Director of a small Public Company.

His main hobby has been playing and coaching cricket (Advance/Level 3 coach). He is currently playing for the Essex over 60's. He has been married to Carol for 46 years and thanks her for all her support throughout the years. They have three children, Craig living and working locally, Kevin and Joanne both living in the French Alps. They are a married and have given them four lovely grandchildren, Kayleigh (10), Kyran (8), Callum (6) and Archie (3).

Since retiring local history has taken up his time and he is involved in two local history groups, writes in parish magazines and gives the occasional talks on the history of Laindon and Basildon. This is his first book he has been involved in but has several more in the pipe line.

STEPHEN WYNN

Stephen is 53 years of age and is currently a serving Police officer. He is married to Tanya, they have no children but they do have four German Shepherd's which keep them both busy and active. Stephen has three children, Luke (25), Ross (24) and last but by no means least, Aimee (12).

He has been intrigued by the story of the German POW camp for many years, first researching it back in the late 1970's but it came to nothing. It was only after he had written and had published three other books that he decided to sit down and actually write a book about the camp. It was while researching information for the book that Stephen and Ken met and decided to write the story together.

He has lived in Basildon since 1963 and attended Lee Chapel Infants school before moving on to Blessed Anne Line School (Now St Anne Line Roman Catholic School) before moving on to Woodlands Secondary school. On leaving school he worked in the City of London for a while on Smithfield Meat Market before joining Essex Police in 1983.

His hobbies include football, history and writing. He supports Leeds United, his home town, and as a young man he played for Colchester United's youth team in the FA Youth Cup.

He has already written and had published, along with his friend and other writing partner Chris Burch, two crime fiction novels which follow the exploits of a fictional Detective, Terry Danvers, as well as a non-fiction book about what parents of serving soldiers fighting in places such as Afghanistan go through emotionally. Both of Stephen's sons are currently serving in the military. On their first tours of Afghanistan, Ross was injured and Luke was shot.

He is currently writing the third novel in the Terry Danvers series as well as working on two other books, one of which is a novel and the other a non-fictional story.

Stephen would like to thank his wife Tanya for her continuing support of his writing and his daughter Aimee for her help in the early days of researching this book.

ISBN: 978-1-84944-173-5

British Library Cataloguing in Publication Data.
A catalogue record for this book is available from the British Library.

Published by UKUnpublished.

UKUnpublished
.CO.UK

www.ukunpublished.co.uk
info@ukunpublished.co.uk

German POW Camp 266 Langdon Hills

By

Ken Porter
And
Stephen Wynn

CONTENTS

To all of the Prisoners of Camp 266

The photograph shows twelve unknown German POW's who stayed at Camp 266 in Langdon Hills sometime between April 1945 and June 1948. It is not known when they arrived or how long they stayed for, nobody knows. Each and every one of them though is representative of those who were there before them and those who came after them.

For those three years they were part of our community. They tended our fields, maintained our roads and helped build some of the very houses that we live in today.

After they were eventually released some chose to stay behind and build a new life here rather than return to the uncertainty of a post war Germany, parts of which were under Russian control.

Some had built up strong friendships amongst the local populous and some had even found love and married, but for all of them their story needs to be told and recorded as a truly historical record so that future generations can understand just a little bit more about the part their local community played in the Second World War.

This is there story.

ACKNOWLEDGEMENTS

While researching this book we have come across many people with very interesting stories to tell and we are grateful that they are allowing us to them along with their photographs. In fact we not able to print all the photographs but we will ensure that they are shown on displays of the history of the area in the years to come. A thank you must go to those who did not have any memories to tell but were able to make introduction for us and those who helped out in interpreting some of the documents. We have endeavour to make reference to all those that have contributed to the book in the relevant places. If we have missed anybody or left out a few of their snippets we apologise.

We must make a special reference to those ex-prisoners of camp 266 and its satellite's for their willingness to be interviewed and in many cases have now become close friends. Our only disappointment is that we should have written the book ten years ago.

We have made every effort to contact copyright holders and apologise for any images or statements that remain the copyright of a third party that we have not properly acknowledged or managed to trace.

PROLOGUES

Stephen

To me it was just a field, an ordinary field that was just the same as any other. There was nothing special about it. It was just another place where we could go to play football and enjoy ourselves on those seemingly never ending long summer evenings that there were most years when I was a kid growing up in Basildon.

There is a small car park at the bottom end of the field, the entrance of which used to be the original way into the camp. There is only enough space for about a dozen or so cars, but fill it up they do. Whole families come up there, get out of their vehicles and go and walk the dogs, have a picnic or start up their own game of football by putting jumpers and other tops down to use as goal posts.

Today's Beacon Field is part of the Langdon Hills CountryPark, looking towards the South East Corner. Ken Porter Photograph- October 2011,

There's nothing left there to today to even suggest it had ever been anything other than just an ordinary field. There's a small concreted area of floor that's situated in the far top right hand corner, but that's all. All those years ago in the late 1960's I didn't have a clue what it had once been nor did I ever give it any thought. When I was a kid my thinking only really went as far as playing football with my mates, what time was dinner and would I be home in time not to get a telling off from my mum?

We were lucky because literarily just at the back of where we all lived we had all of these fields and woods to play in. It was fantastic. We only had to walk for about ten minutes and we were suddenly in Alice of wonderland territory that made being a kid a truly wonderful experience. We had everything we could possibly want. Enough space to play football, climb trees, go bird nesting, play hide and seek, catch newts in the local ponds or just sit around and chat.

This was in a time long before mobile phones and computer games had even been thought of let alone invented. Kids spent so much of their time outside playing it really was a different world back then. For me as soon as I got home from school I had to do my homework and the deal with my parents was the quicker I did it then the quicker I could go out and play and the quicker I got out to play the longer I had before having to be back home again for my tea.

I can't remember when it was or how old I was at the time when I first realised that the field I so often played in for fun as a kid had such a recent history attached to it. It was quite surreal to think that where I spent so much of my childhood playing there had once stood a camp that kept German prisoners of war in its midst.

The buildings that some of them had lived in for four years and had in effect become their homes had long ago being dismantles and taken down. There is now nothing left to show what the field had once been or what part it had played in the history of our town. There is no plaque, no wooden board, no nothing, in fact very little had ever been written about it at all. It was as if somebody had come along and simply erased its very existence. I always wondered why that was so. It was almost if there was a deep rooted dark secret that somebody had decided needed hiding from future generations, my generation, but of course there wasn't. It was simply that nobody had ever felt the need to sit down and write about those days.

Ken and I felt that it was about time that today's generation of our community learnt about the significance of the field and the part that it played in our local history.

As you turn off of the A13 and head in towards Basildon at what is known locally as the Five Bells round about, you turn on to the A176 (Nethermayne) which then heads slightly up hill as you drive towards the local hospital. About a mile up the hill on the left hand side is Dry Street. Turn left there and the road starts to slowly meander its way through the leafy lanes of the Essex countryside.

The road carries on for about six miles passing lush green fields on either side that prove to be a more than suitable eating ground for both cattle and horses alike. The smattering of cottages, bungalows, an old church and farm houses along with their out buildings, only add to the peace and tranquillity of the area.

As each inch you drive takes you further down the road so you have the feeling of travelling back in time as you almost become as one with your surroundings, leaving behind the hustle and bustle of big town life and all the stresses that go with it.

When your journey finally comes to an end as Dry Street forms a T-junction with the B1007, otherwise known as the High Road Langdon Hills, you have to look left and right before moving off. For some this is to ensure that they don't have a collision with other vehicles coming at them from either side. For others it is because they are looking for what remains of Camp 266, the Second World War prisoner of war camp that once housed captured German combatants from 1945 to 1948. If you blink you will miss it because all that remains of it today is a field where the only activities it is used for are picnics, dog walking or an impromptu game of football amongst small groups of friends.

Today the field forms part of the Thurrock & District Country Park and its only claim to fame these days is the large thirty foot high beacon pole that sits in the middle of the field which is lit up on special occasions such as the heralding in of the new millennium back in 2000.

Nothing much has changed in the immediate area over the years since it closed its doors as a prisoner of war camp back in 1948. Anybody returning to the area after many years, English or German wouldn't have any difficulty in recognising the area or the fact that this was where they had once worked and lived. There hasn't been a block of flats or a parade of shops built on the site it had simply been returned to the bosom of good old Mother Nature.

It was originally considered for use as the districts original Council offices. It was initially taken over by the Shell oil company for a while and after it had been knocked down it was also used as a cricket pitch.

Even The Crown public house which sits on the top of Crown Hill as it joins with the High Road is still there although it is now mainly a restaurant with a small bar area where people usually have a drink whilst waiting to be called through to their readied table.

As for me growing up in the area as a kid it had just been an ordinary uncompromising, insignificant field where I once played. For some it had been their place of work for others it was their home and for a few more it was the last place they ever saw on God's green earth, miles away from their homes and loved ones.

KEN

My early childhood was very similar to Stephens, although I was a Laindon boy. I was born under the shadow of St Nicholas Church which stood majestically on its small hill overlooking the area. My parent's bungalow in Pound lane was next to a corn field and with the open space around the church it gave me ample scope to explore and wander at will with no worries to my parents.

Our favourite spot was the playing field of Laindon Park School, known to us in those far off days as 'Donaldson' or 'Donald Duck' named after a previous head school mistress. Here we would play cricket and football, cricket taking preference. It was here that the current head master, Jack Wilson saw me and a few of my mates playing cricket and enquired whether we had any cricket whites as Laindon Cricket Club, who played at the back of the Essex Country Club in Basildon Road just past the school, were short that week. I was thirteen at the time, the following year I was regularly playing cricket for Laindon. Playing the game was to become my life's passion.

Laindon Like the rest of the Basildon district was made up of miles of unmade roads with wooden bungalows with very poor facilities, many only occupied at weekends or as holiday times. Along these roads we would play and go scrumping, looking for the bungalows that were not occupied so to reduce the risk of being caught. We did very little damage if any at all; we might have broken the odd branch as we tried to pick an apple or two.

Langdon Hills however was a far off place for me as a young kid, so it was not very often that I would venture over the railway bridge at Laindon Station to explore the wilds of this part of the parish. When I did it would be to go blue bell picking or a trip to the recreation ground to play on the swings, slides or have a paddle and a picnic.

I did however join the 1st Laindon Scout group that held their meetings at the Old Baptist Hall, then later at the Methodist Church, both of which were in Langdon Hills. Although there may have been a few excursions in to the wilds of Langdon Hills, all these years later, they are not even distant memories. I simply do not remember them. All I know is that in 'Bob a Job week' it was around Laindon that I would travel on my bike to find the odd job of cleaning shoes, cutting the grass, weeding some ones front or back lawn. I have to say I quite enjoyed doing all of this, hard work never frightened me.

My first recollection of the 'Beacon Field' as it is now known was playing for Laindon against Westley Cricket club, whose ground it was in 1959. I was only fifteen years of age at the time. The Pavilion was situated where the large concrete base is now. It was going to be another forty years before I established that this concrete base was the remaining evidence of the Prisoner of War Camp.

Eberhard, one of the German POW's who was held at the camp and whose story you will read later, confirms that this was the base to the camps cook house.

The surviving base of the camp's Cook House and subsequently of Westley Cricket Club Pavilion. – Ken Porter photograph – October 2011.

In fifty years of playing cricket Saturday and Sundays it is not easy to remember all the matches I played in but I do remember this one particularly well. Why because the local papers reported the following week how 'a feature of Laindon's innings was the form of teenager Ken Porter, who defied Westley wicket-hungry attack for over 30 minutes before playing on to Buck' We were all out for sixty, I was the second highest with 9. I had looked forward to playing on this ground because my cricketing hero Trevor Bailey, Essex and England all-rounder had officially opened the ground a couple of years earlier.

The original Beacon Field was actually on the opposite side of Dry Street road behind the back of the Crown Hotel. The current Beacon field only got its name when the current Beacon was erected in 1988 in celebration of the 400th year anniversary of the defeat of the Spanish Armada. The original beacon field was behind the Crown Hotel and was one of many that were erected along the South East Coast as a warning of the approaching Spanish Armada.

I eventually moved with my family to Berry Lane, Langdon Hills in the winter of 1963. The move was bought about by the compulsory purchase of my parent's bungalow in Pound Lane. The irony is that Basildon Corporation was going to develop the area within twelve months. My parent's bungalow is still there and still lived in. Two years later I married and moved to Southminster because the Corporation did not consider me as second generation therefore they did not have any houses to offer me.

I moved back to the Langdon Hills area in 1970, when I found myself in a position to buy my own home there. It was from this time on that I got to know the wilds of Langdon Hills very well. I would spend many hours wandering round the nearby hills with my young children.

History was my favourite subject at school so it was not long before I started to research the history of Laindon and Langdon Hills and of course what fascinated me more than anything was the fact there had been a German Prisoner of War Camp at the top of the hill. It was however going to be another thirty odd years before I came across my first ex POW from the camp, Erwin Hannerman, who had married a local girl and currently still lives in Bulphan and who is now a very close friend of mine.

Although I have managed to establish that my great grandmother worked in service locally at Goldsmith Manor, pre 1900 and I have lived in Langdon Hills, longer than my time in Laindon, I still see myself as a Laindon Boy. Goldsmith Manor lay's on the west side of the Laindon Road on the Southern slopes of Langdon Hills. At the time my grandmother was there it was the country seat of Sir Joseph Dimsdale who was the Lord Mayor of London in 1901.

CHAPTER
(Brief History of the Hills)

Surprisingly one of the things that we have not been able to establish is why the Military chose the summit of the Langdon Hills to establish a German Prison of war camp. The policy of German prisoners being held overseas restricted their ability of being able to escape and get back to Germany. Unlike the allied prisoners in Europe, if they managed to escape and get out of Germany they would quite often have had the help of the local occupied civilians or resistance fighters in an effort to avoid recapture.

German prisoners in England were not in this fortunate position. England was not an occupied country so there would not have been any friendly people willing to help them should they have even managed to escape. However the Langdon Hills camp was surrounded by woodlands and not that far away from the river Thames and the Thames estuary, so any German POW who was willing to attempt an escape had some initial cover to assist them. With the river Thames not that far away they might have been fortunate enough to find a boat to stow away on. So from the outset it does seem a strange place to have a prisoner of war camp.

However as we know the camp did not start taking prisoners until a month before the end of the war and I am sure the prisoners were fully aware of the situation back in Germany. The country was slowly being brought to its knees its infrastructure was being shattered by the continuous allied bombing. If they did actually escape they literally had nowhere to go. Another deterrent would have been the Army camp that was situated less than half a mile away as the road wound its way out towards Horndon-on-the-Hill.

There was only one occasion when three prisoners tried to escape from the camp (More about that later). There were however times when the occasional prisoner did try to escape from other POW camps.

The Chelmsford Chronicle reported on the 2nd November 1945 that Reverend D. R. Holden of Upminster was involved with the recapture of German prisoners who had escaped on the Tuesday from a farm working party at Thorpe-le-Soken. It was Mrs Holden who first spotted the man ravenously eating a piece of bread as she stepped out of her conservatory. She called her husband and the man run off through the churchyard, the Reverend gave chase and managed to catch up with him but in the struggled that followed the escaped POW managed to get away leaving the Reverend holding his coat. He was however detained by local parishioners at the nearby railway station, where he was held until the police arrived. He was in civilian clothes and later a cycle was found hidden in the hedge of the Rectory Garden. I get the feeling he must have been lost because if he was trying to get back home to his family he should have been heading towards the nearest port and that would have been Harwich. All he achieved was to add a few more months on to his captivity.

The Southend District Times and Laindon Recorder reported on the 31st October 1945 about the recapture of Luftwaffe pilot Hans Hather at Leigh on Sea. He had escaped from a POW camp in the North of England and made his way south. It was local workmen who became suspicious and reported their sighting of him to the Police. Initially he claimed that he was an Italian collaborator, but eventually he admitted his identity. More on escapee's later.

Back to the hills, which have often played an important part in the history of the local area. There is a 10,000 year old Mesolithic site on the South Eastern slopes. An Iron age settlement or was it a fort on the South Western slopes just east of the Main Road. The main road itself is a fairly straight road ending up at East Tilbury, where it is believed the Romans landed in Essex from Kent on route to Colchester. We also know that Lord Fairfax and his Parliamentarian troops (Roundheads) travelled along the road on route to take part in the siege of Colchester during the second English civil war in 1648.

Approximately 150 years later the hills were once again in the spot light, this time because of the threat of a French invasion. Following the revolution in France in 1793 the French declared war on both the British and the Dutch. The fighting took place on main land Europe but Britain gradually became aware that Napoleon was considering invading Britain. So between 1805 and 1812, 105 defensive Martello Towers were built along the East Sussex, Kent, Essex and Suffolk Coast.

However, it was not only the coast which had to be defended; defences inland had to be considered as well in case the French did manage to invade us. Various reports were commissioned and the following is what one of the reports had to say of the strategic position of Langdon Hills (referred to as Laindon Hills).

'Laindon Hills are situated near the lower Turnpike Road   (current A13) leading from London to South Shoebury by Stifford & Stanford Le Hope and are about 30 miles distant from the former and 15 from the latter Place.

These hills stand upon a swell of ground that connects them with the Heights of Warley and Billericay and which circumvents the whole of the Flat Country to the westward excepting at the narrow Gorge where the Mardike enters at Stifford Clays.

They are esteemed as high if not the highest ground in the County: have a bold and precipitate descent to the West and sink by more gentle Slops to the East. That branch however that runs by Hawksbury Bush, Vange Hall, Basildon Church and Crays Hill, where it terminates entirely, commands the two Turnpike Roads.

The soil on the sides of these hills is stiff clay which in wet weather is extremely heavy and impassable, towards the summit it partakes more of the Gravel. The enclosures are small with strong fences especially approaching the Crown Public House situated near the top of the Hill. Four roads unite near the Brow and are sheltered by thick woods. There is no reason to apprehend the supply of water would fail, should those hills at any time be occupied by a large force as there is a very good spring in the wood, that constantly runs, a well at the Public House and ponds in the neighbourhood'

Don't you just love the language that report is written in? In some parts I actually found it slightly difficult to understand.

Although there was a beacon position on the hill, the report was concerned that signalling from this elevated spot would be compromised by the woods. It was therefore felt that should it be necessary to communicate from the hill to the forces in the Southern District and at Warley and Danbury. Scaffolding and platform would have to be erected on the roof of the Crown Hotel and the branches of trees lopped off.

The report concluded that Langdon Hills was a strategic positioned and if the area indeed fell into enemy hands the whole of the low country to the West would be at Napoleon's disposal. All that could have then been done would have been to harass his army with light troops and riflemen.

In the end, Nelson and Wellington put paid to Napoleon's ambition to invade, a problem that was not going to rear its ugly head for another 125 years.

Leading up to the Great War (First World War) it was a favourite picnicking spot for the Victorians and Edwardians from the city where they could marvel the surrounding view, a view that had astounded historians over the centuries.

Now there was going to be a Prisoner of War Camp and yes it did cause some concerns. In July 1945 barely three months after it had opened the Chelmsford Chronicle reports that the Billericay Urban Council received a letter from the Ministry of Works proposing to increase the number of German POW's that were being held there to 750 and asked if they had any observations to make on the matter.

As you can imagine a lengthy discussion took place around public health and safety and the fact that the camp immediately adjoins the Langdon Hills public open space, which was used by the public in the summer.

A report that appeared in the Southend District Times and Laindon Recorder on the 11th July 1945 went into greater detail in regards to the Councils concerns and they requested the following assurances from the Ministry of Works.

1.   About the guarding of the Prisoners whilst in the Camp and when being transported to their various places of work.
2.   The sanitary situation at the camp.
3.   The arrangements for medical treatment of prisoners and a guarantee that the local medical practitioners would not be used to treat the German POW's. Would local hospitals be used and under whose medical supervision would they be.
4.   Concerns about the camp being immediately adjacent to the country park and it might become a point of local sightseeing and would this have an adverse effect on the discipline of the camp.
5.   If the proposals were to go ahead would every step necessary be taken to ensure safeguarding the public health and safety?

The council decided that the matter should be made public.

A week later the paper reported that it was the Labour Councillor Charles Leatherland J.P. who had demanded that the matter should be debated in public. He stated that there were some matters that should rightly be debated in private but not this one. He made the point:

"If Germans are to come into the district – especially a district where many of the men folk are away all day and the women and children are left at home – the people are

entitled to know all about it. Moreover the people have a right to be assured that every precaution is taken to ensure public safety. We want to know what kind of prisoners they are, how they will be guarded and what amount of liberty they will have – are they tame Germans or Nazis".

Councillor Leatherland also expressed the view that this was not the proper place to house so many Germans, it being far too close to the centre of population and therefore not fair on the people who lived there.

How many further discussions took place in the weeks that followed we have not been able to establish, but we will see as we read the reports of the local inhabitants that his fears were totally unfounded.

Charles Leatherhead had joined the labour Party in 1921 after serving in the First World War as a Company Sergeant Major of a Machine Gun Battalion.

He moved into the Old Rectory at Dunton in 1934 and was chairman of the Dunton Invasion Committee which reported to the central Laindon Committee who in turn reported to the Billericay area committee.

The then Prime Minister, Harold Wilson, gave him a life peerage in 1964 for his exceptional career in Journalism, politics and public services.

In addition to Buck field being used as a POW camp the house on the opposite of the road in Dry Street, 'Climax' rented out a couple of rooms to one of the British officer.

DO YOU KNOW WHAT TO DO——

IF GERMAN TROOPS REACH DUNTON ?

We hope they will not get here. But if they should, the lives and welfare of us all may depend on whether proper plans have been made in advance to deal with the situation.

The

PARISH INVASION COMMITTEE

(officially constituted by order of the Regional Commissioner)

HAS NOT BEEN IDLE.

It has prepared, or is preparing, plans to deal with :—

Emergency Food Supplies   Welfare of Children
Residents Rendered Homeless.   Casualties
Water Reserves   Emergency Cooking
Gas Attacks   Defence Works

It is co-operating with the Police, Home Guard and Civil Defence Organisations.

The Committee is calling a

PUBLIC MEETING OF RESIDENTS

(Men, Women and Children)
to be held at

DUNTON ENTERTAINMENT HALL,

On Saturday, May 23rd——at 7 p.m.

The business of the meeting will be to :—

1—Hear a report from the Committee on what it has done and what it proposes to do.
2—Strengthen the Committee, and give it a more representative and democratic basis, by electing additional members from the Public Meeting.

We ask you to put aside your private engagements for this one evening, and regard it as one of the duties of good citizenship to attend.

CHARLES LEATHERLAND,
Chairman of the Invasion Committee.

THE "AYWUN" PRESS, LANGDON HILLS.

Climax itself has a long history dating back some one hundred and fifty years, the main part of the building having been built in 1848.

There was a previous building on the site and going back in time before the Crown Hotel which is situated a few hundred yards away, it was a coaching inn known as the 'Crooked Billet.'

Erwin Hannerman, who was one of the German POW's to arrive at the camp on the first day it opened and whose personal story you will read later in the book, became the Batman to the Captain Messenger who lived there with his wife.

CHAPTER
(Chronology of the Second World War)

It's truly amazing when you look at a time line of certain events that occurred before, during and after the 2nd World War. When you look at some of these matters which in some cases took place more than two years before the start of the war, it must have been obvious to most political observers that there was always going to be a war.

There was so much political manoeuvring going on during these years, with alliances been agreed and signed between different countries it was actually becoming confusing. It was a tinder box waiting to explode. Smaller countries were aligning themselves with bigger, more powerful nations for protection just in case they were attacked or threatened with invasion by a neighbouring nation.

In such circumstances it could always take just a relatively minor incident to ignite a war. Because of the agreed alliances between these minnows and giant nations there was always the risk that countries would get drawn into a conflict not of their choosing or wanting but simply because they had aligned themselves with another nation who they had agreed to both protect and support should the need arise.

As early as 1933 when Adolf Hitler was offered the Chancellorship of Germany the writing was already on the wall as to what his intentions were. Within a matter of days of taking up his post it became obvious that he wanted to return Germany to her previous status of military greatness.

At a meeting that took place at the home of General von Hammerstein and which was also attended by other top army Generals and Admirals, Hitler put forward the suggestion that Germany could begin a programme of re-armament which was a clear and direct breach of the Treaty of Versailles.

This was an agreement which Hitler felt was totally unfair and that should never have been signed by Germany in the first place. Many Germans felt that at the time of their surrender they were actually winning the war and that the surrender was based on financial reasons rather than military stratagem. Not only did this cause an air of resentment to fester amongst the general populous but it also allowed the Nazis Party to flourish greatly, with the assistance of Hitler's enigmatic personality.

His nationalistic passion and his ability to verbally whip up a crowd into a frenzy of self-belief for a greater tomorrow had been described as both mesmerising and spell binding.

After the end of the First World War there had been big changes in the social structure of day to day life amongst the masses throughout the United Kingdom. No longer were they prepared to sit back, just accept their lot in life and play second fiddle to members of the elite upper classes. They wanted more out of life. After all it was they who had borne the brunt of the horrors of the war and not the upper classes. There was still a feeling of us and them in many areas of the UK.

Wounded soldiers who quite often came from the countries working classes, on returning home from the war had to make do or were looked after in general hospital wards, taking into account that the National Health Service (NHS) didn't come into existence until 1948, this wasn't always the best.

Wounded officers on the other hand in nearly every case came from the elite upper classes of society. Quite often they had the luxury of recuperating in the grounds and surroundings of a stately home that was located in a nice part of the country and in relative comfort and grandeur.

There had been a revolution in Russia that had seen the Tzar over thrown and both he and his family subsequently murdered by the Bolsheviks. There had been threats of rebellion amongst French troops during the First World War and there was a fear on the international front that Communism would flourish as the masses looked for change from the old world order where the upper classes ruled simply because they had the power and the wealth.

Typically the attitude amongst most senior British politicians of the day was a desire and a focus to keep the status quo in society very much as it always had been before the war, but they also understood how fragile that very status quo was.

Some would say that there was an arrogance amongst the thinking of the British upper classes of the day where as some would equally look upon this as a naivety.

Individuals such as Winston Churchill, who would go on to become one of this country's greatest ever leaders, saw what was coming thankfully all too easily. It was largely due to his insistence that the Royal Air Force was formed early enough to become strong enough to be a force to be reckoned with in time to be able to defeat the might of the German Luftwaffe during the Second World War.

On August the 2nd 1934, President Paul von Hindenburg died. The Chancellor of Germany, Adolf Hitler, assumed the office of Reich President to become the single most powerful man in the country. He requested that the

Wehrmacht oath of allegiance now be sworn directly to him personally and not Germany as a nation.

Churchill Knew that Germany was secretly re-arming herself and that it was only a matter of time before she felt strong enough to strike out at the countries who she felt had wronged her and stolen some of her lands in the immediate aftermath of the First World War. How prophetic his words and warnings would turn out to be.

By now Hitler had given up worrying about what other countries thought of him and Germany. He was doing exactly what he wanted to. He was seeing how far he could go, how far he could push other countries before they responded in kind, but all the time militarily the Germans were becoming stronger and stronger with the passing of everyday.

The first real example of just how far Germany was prepared to take matters took place in February 1936 when Hitler announced that the time was right for Germany to re-occupy the Rhineland which had been made a de-militarised zone at the end of the First World War as part of the Treaty of Versailles.

Less than one month later on the 7th March 1936 Hitler sent in 14,500 of his troops to re-occupy the Rhineland. It then became a case of sit and wait to see what if anything the French would do in retaliation.

Unbeknown to the French and the rest of the watching world Hitler had instructed his troops to withdraw if the French troops put up any resistance. They didn't.

The 'Locarno Pact' which included the 'Rhineland Pact' and which was agreed by Germany, France, Belgium, United Kingdom and Italy in October 1925 was formally signed in London on December 3rd of the same year. The first three signatories of the pact agreed not to attack each other. In the event of any of these three countries breaking their agreement all of the other countries would assist the country that was under attack.

Hitler continued with his acts of intimidation and aggression of neighbouring countries namely, Austria and Czechoslovakia and all the British Government came out with in the way of opposition, was rhetoric as to why they should not intervene in these matters, allowing Hitler and Germany to become even more powerful. This ended with the occupation and invasion of Austria by Germany in an effort to unite the two Germanic speaking nations. Hitler was Austrian by birth.

Hitler had invaded a neighbouring sovereign nation and everybody else had just stood by and watched. Nobody did anything including Great Britain who seemed more intent on appeasing Hitler than helping the Austrians in their time of need.

As far as we are concerned one of the strangest decisions of the entire Second World War was made on the 15th September 1938 when the British Prime Minister Neville Chamberlain visited Adolf Hitler at the Berghof in Germany to discuss the Sudeten Land problem in Czechoslovakia. This showed an amazing arrogance on the part of Chamberlain to think he could discuss the issues of another country and believe he had the right to effectively decide what their fate should be. Chamberlain agreed to Hitler's demand to annex the Sudetenland.

On his return from Germany Chamberlain, when addressing his Government colleagues, came out with the classic line, "Adolf Hitler appears to be a man who could be relied upon when he had given his word." Britain and France urge Czechoslovakia to give the Sudetenland back to Germany stating that neither country would be able to help the Czechs in the event of a German invasion.

On 23rd September 1938 at a meeting in Godesberg Germany, Adolf Hitler presents the British Prime Minister, Neville Chamberlain, with his demands for the parts of Czechoslovakia he wants ceded to him. All of these particular areas were mainly inhabited by a minority German population. The irony of the situation was none of these areas had ever been part of Germany. They had been part of Austria-Hungary which had ceased to be in 1918.

On September 30th 1938 the Munich Agreement, which allows Germany to annex the Sudetenland portion of Czechoslovakia, is signed, by British Prime Minister Neville Chamberlain, French Premier Édouard Daladier, Italian Premier Benito Mussolini, and the German Chancellor Adolf Hitler. Politicians from Czechoslovakia were not invited to the meeting. By now Hitler was certain that Britain wouldn't do anything to stop Germany from taking back the Sudetenland.

Much to everybody's surprise the Czech government refused to accept the proposal that they should give up the Sudetenland. In a political sense Hungary and Poland now become embroiled in the situation when they ask for their own claims on parts of Czechoslovakia to be considered.

Not happy with sending troops into the Sudetenland and taking over Czechoslovakia, Hitler invades Poland. Finally enough is enough for Chamberlain and on the 1st September 1939 the House of Commons passed the National Services Armed Forces Act, conscripting all men who were aged between 18 and 41 years of age into the armed forces.

At 9 am on 3rd September 1939, Sir Neville Henderson, the British Ambassador in Berlin informs the German government that if Germany did not withdraw its armed forces from Poland by 11am that day, a state of war would exist as of that hour between Germany and Great Britain.

Soon after the British ultimatum had been given the French Ambassador in Berlin, Robert Coulondre, delivers a similar ultimatum, but with a 5pm deadline.

Germany ignored Britain's ultimatum and a state of war existed between the two countries. Ironically, although it was Great Britain that ended up declaring war it would appear to have been the Germans strategy to provoke such an act at that time as it was only then that she felt strong enough to win such a war.

It was with this background that the German people had grown up with over the previous six years. It had become a state of mind an indoctrination of the people by the state mechanism, the Hitler Youth movement being a prime example of this. It could not therefore have come as a shock to most German people when war eventually broke out.

We do not suggest for one moment that all Germans liked, sided or agreed with what the Nazis were doing, but I cannot believe that they did not know what the likely outcome was going to be. Because of this we genuinely believe that becoming a Prisoner of War for a young German soldier, sailor or airman must have been quite a shock. One minute they were been told that Germany was going to win the war and that the Third Reich was going to last for over a thousand years and here it was all done and dusted in under six years and they had lost.

Before the end of the first day of war German forces had already captured the town of Czestochova in what was then Upper Silesia (The area where Max Ullrich, one of the personal stories you will read about later in the book came from). This was a war that not all of the countries who were in the same geographically region as the wars main protagonists, wished to become embroiled in, or one that they didn't see was anything to do with them. Quite a few countries were quick enough to claim their countries neutrality including in no particular order, Denmark, Ireland, Spain and Holland, to name but a few.

Australia, who couldn't have possibly been any further away from the troubles which were going on thousands of miles away in Europe, also declared war on Germany. Whether this was out of loyalty to one of its Commonwealth cousins or because of fear of what might happen with Japan in the Pacific Rim is not recorded. Looking at it from today's perspective it does seem somewhat of a strange decision by the then Australian Prime Minister Menzies, as Germany had shown not one single act of aggression or intimidation against them. Add to this that at the same time they had declared war on Germany, they were unable to send any troops to fight in Europe because of their own potential problems with Japan, it appears to be an even stranger decision.

If ever anybody needed reminding that war wasn't nice they had a taste of what it was going to be like very early on in the war. German U-Boat Commanders had been reminded by Admiral Karl Donitz that they should allow the crews of any ships they were going to sink to first get in to lifeboats.

The passenger liner Athenia, was torpedoed and sunk by the German Submarine U-30.

In reality what happened was that the Captain of U-30, Fritz Lemp, opened fire on the ship without realising that it was in fact a civilian liner and not a merchant ship as he had first believed. Lemp went as far as ordering his crew to secrecy. He then had the U-Boats log book re-written to remove any reference to having torpedoed the Athenia.

After the war it was discovered that Admiral Donitz had also been involved in concealing the true facts of what had happened on that fateful day.

U-30 left Wilhelmshaven on 22 August 1939 before World War II began. On 3 September 1939 just 12 days after having left port and only 10 hours after Britain had declared war on Germany, U-30 sank the 13,581 ton British passenger ship SS Athenia about 200 miles west of the Hebrides while she was en route from Liverpool to Montreal, Canada. The SS Athenia was the first ship to be sunk in World War II and out of 1,418 passengers, 112 of them, including 28 Americans, were killed.

Following the attack, the German Ministry of Propaganda having been told by the Kriegsmarine that there was not a single German U-boat in the vicinity of the SS Athenia on the day of her sinking, promptly denied all allegations that a German U-boat was responsible for the sinking of the SS Athenia. Instead, the Germans claimed that the British had torpedoed their own vessel in an attempt to bring the United States into the war on the side of the Allies.

In order to try and calm down the Americans, Joachim von Ribbentrop, the German Foreign Minister, arranged a meeting between Grand Admiral Erich Raeder and the American naval attaché on 16 September 1939.

During the meeting, Raeder assured the attaché that he had received reports from every German submarine that had been at sea at the time of the sinking, "as a result of which it was definitely established that the SS Athenia had not been sunk by a German U-boat". Raeder then asked the attaché to inform the American government. However, not every submarine had returned to port and all U-boats maintained radio silence while at sea.

Intentionally or otherwise what Raeder had told the American attaché was incorrect.

Once U-30 arrived back in port at Wilhelmshaven on 27 September 1939, Admiral Karl Doenitz met Lemp while he was getting off of his U-boat. Doenitz later said that Lemp looked "very unhappy" and that he told the Admiral that he was in fact responsible for the sinking of the SS Athenia. Lemp had mistaken the SS Athenia for an armed merchant cruiser, which he claimed was zig-zagging. Doenitz later received orders that the SS Athenia affair was to be kept a "total secret" and that the High Command of the Navy (OKM) were not to court-martial Lemp as they considered his actions to have been carried out in good-faith.

Any other political explanations about the sinking of the SS Athenia were to be handled by the OKM who would deny any allegations that a German U-boat had sunk the vessel. In order to keep the sinking of the SS Athenia a secret, Admiral Doenitz had U-30's log altered in order to erase any evidence about the true sinking of the SS Athenia.

It was not until seven years later at the Nuremberg trials in 1946 that the truth about the fate of the SS Athenia was confirmed by the Germans.

Early 1940 saw rationing brought in throughout the United Kingdom in an effort to preserve domestic food supplies and to make sure that what we did have would last longer as the feeling of worst to come was never too far away.

The 10th May 1940 saw two major events of the war, Winston Churchill took over from Neville Chamberlain as the British Prime Minister, a position he would go on to keep until after the end of the war. On the same day Germany invaded Belguim, France and Holland in one of the first examples of the Germans military tactic of Blitzkrieg (Lightning war).

A combination of ground troops, tanks and heavy artillery along with effective air support used with devastating speed and tenacity saw them sweep across Western Europe and all that was before them.

The British expeditionary Force, some quarter of a million men along with just over one hundred thousand French troops were rescued from Dunkirk by a combination of the Royal Navy along with commandeered vessels and private boat owners.

Things were not looking good. With France having surrendered in double quick time and now under the control of the Germans, Britain was the obvious next target to be invaded. Before racing across the sea and mounting an invasion the Germans decided that it would be easier and more effective to bomb us in to submission first before deploying tens of thousands of their troops across the Channel. With the tactic having worked against France, Belguim and Holland with stunning efficiency there was no reason for the Germans to believe that it couldn't be repeated against the British.

What would become known as the Battle of Britain, lasted from 10th July to 31st October 1940. In the Luftwaffe the Germans had a very powerful, potent and effective fighting weapon, but Britain not only had the benefits of radar to turn to but the knowledge that if this was a battle that they failed to win then a German invasion across the English Channel would undoubtedly quickly follow.

For some reason best known to the Germans they stopped bombing RAF bases and factories relatively early on in the battle and changed their attacks to some of our major cities. This provided the RAF with the opportunity they needed to fight off the Luftwaffe which in turn then prevented a German invasion of our shores.

In a time of war any military force is going to experience losses. It is simply not possible to engage in any kind of warfare without taking such casualties. As regrettable as they are they are an accepted factor of war, but what aren't so acceptable are the civilian casualties. The Battle of Britain saw some forty thousand British civilian's killed by the German bombing of our cities.

On 22nd June 1941 Adolf Hitler made one of the strangest decisions of his life, whilst still facing a military threat from Britain and her allies in the West, he took the confusing decision to invade Russia in the East, as part of Operation Barbarossa. Fighting a war on two fronts not only meant splitting his forces in two but also brought about logistical nightmares as the need for equipment, machines and food to be moved about all over the place became an issue as well.

Although the initial part of the operation was swift with the Germans moving forward with devastating force, they could not sustain their efforts and momentum. It would appear that the Germans had either not expected to still be fighting when the harsh Russian winter started or had simply not even thought about it. It became blatantly obvious very early on that the German troops were not prepared or equipped to be fighting a winter war against a dogged Russian army defending their mother land to the death, who ceased their opportunity as the German war machine gradually ground to a halt.

In the Pacific the Japanese decided to attack the American fleet at Pearl Harbour in Hawaii. Within a matter of days Hitler came up with another unbelievable decision by declaring war on American.

So now as well as there been fighting all across Europe there was also fighting all across the Pacific region as well which included Asia and Australasia.

15th February 1942 saw the British forces in Singapore, some 25,000 in number, surrender to what turned out to be a much smaller Japanese aggressor.

The bombing by both the Luftwaffe and the RAF of the others major cities continued with ferocity, as both sides openly targeted civilian populations, whilst at the same time heavy fighting in North Africa continued.

1943 really saw a change in the war and what was to be the beginning of the end for the Nazi's, although to start with it was a bit of a mixed bag. After a winter of stalemate in Russia, German forces surrendered to the Red Army in February.

In the first few months of the year German U-Boats still reigned supreme throughout the Atlantic causing mayhem amongst allied shipping, but by May their short lived period of supremacy was over with the effective loss of control of the Atlantic shipping lanes.

A combination of German and Italian forces in North Africa started to sustain heavy losses throughout the region as allied forces started to take more control.

Japan was still on the ascendency in the Pacific especially as it continued its push on in to China.

There was fierce fighting between the Germans and British and American forces from January through till May as they fought for control of Italy. As the German forces dug in at Monte Cassino, rather than risk the unprecedented slaughter of ground troops, allied aircraft bombed the medieval monastery eventually forcing the Germans to surrender.

The D-Day landings began on the 6th June 1944 as 130,000 allied troops landed on the French coast line to begin the effort to rid Europe and the world of the evils of Nazism. Two months later these same troops would be celebrating on the streets of Paris.

Hitler's troubles just kept on getting worst and worst as the Red Army successfully counterattacked the Germans from the East driving them all the way back to Warsaw in Poland, killing, wounding or capturing some 350,000 German soldiers.

The early part of 1945 saw the Russian liberation of Auschwitz revealing at first hand and for the first time the true horrors of the holocaust.

The Blitzing of our major cities had been replaced by the threat of VI and V2 rockets showering down on London and across the South East. In an act or retaliation Churchill allowed the RAF to carry out bombing raids on some of Germany's major cities including Dresden. It was the first time that Britain had knowingly targeted German civilian populations

The race was now on between the allies in the West and the Russians in the East to get to Berlin first. Russia won the race when they reached the capitol on the 21st April 1945. Things then started happening very quickly indeed. Mussolini and his Mistress were hanged by Italian partisans on the 28th April and Hitler committed suicide two days later. Germany's unconditional surrender followed one week later on the 7th May and the war was over, well at least in Europe it was.

The war in the Pacific continued until 14th August 1945 when Japan finally surrendered but only after Atomic bombs had been dropped on both Hiroshima and Nagasaki by the American air force. The original idea had been to invade Japan in an effort to end the war but because it was believed the Japanese would fight to the death in an effort to save their country, the plans were changed because of the amount of casualties it was feared would be incurred.

By the time the fighting was over more than fifty million people had been killed. More than twice as many civilians were killed than there were military personnel.

CHAPTER
(Bomb Alley)

With the Thames, Fenchurch railway line, the A13 and the A127 it is no wonder that the areas of both Laindon and Langdon Hills area were considered to be part of what was known locally as "bomb alley." The Battle of Britain officially started on the 10th July 1940 and went on till the 31st October 1940 and goes down as the official closing date of Fighter Commands defeat of the Luftwaffe in the air over southern England. However by early September Hitler had realised he was not going to defeat Fighter Command and decided to switch his attacks to the major cities of England, not surprisingly, London was one such particular target.

The Blitz, as these bombings became known, started on the 7th September and continued through until the middle of May 1941, when Hitler decided to turn his attentions to Russia, but during this comparatively short period of time, some 60,000 people lost their lives, another 87,000 were seriously injured and 2 million homes were destroyed. As time went on the threat of Invasion disappeared although intermittent bombing raids continued.

It is therefore not surprising then that many dog fights were seen in the skies above the Laindon area even if it was only the planes vapour trails zigzagging across the sky. There were as many as eight aircraft crashed in the Laindon area and because we were in Bomb alley the area received a considerable amount of damage by bombs being jettison by the Luftwaffe on their return from bombing London. Later in the war we were to have many V1 (doodle bugs) and V2's land in the area.

The following are just a few of the stories and accounts covering some of the incidents which took place in the area.

The first major incident which occurred over Laindon, (if we ignore the bombs and incendiary devices that were dropped,) took place on the 5th September 1940 when two spitfires unfortunately collided in mid-air. One crashed in a field opposite Markham's Chase School (now Janet Duke). Markham's school log book records the incident. The pilot of the aircraft was killed.

The initial reports were that the pilot was Robert Barton but on further investigation it is believed the Pilot was in fact Flt. Lt J T Webster who was killed, his unopened parachute pack with the words 'WEBSTER' printed on it was found a few weeks later by a local farmer, Roland Wilson, in a field north of the Arterial Road in the Nevendon area. Roland later handed the parachute into the Nevendon Police who thanked him for his honesty as the silk which the parachute was made from, was a very sought after commodity in wartime Britain. Another eye witness, possibly Percy Calcott, who lived at the Cricketers Pub on the Arterial Road, saw Webster plummet to his death, landing on the north side of the Arterial Road in soft clay. It is understood that the impression left in the ground from the impact of Webster's body hitting the ground could still be seen over a year later.

In 1964, whilst they were excavating a sewer trench in Leinster Road, Laindon, the Basildon Development Corporation contractors recovered a Rolls Royce Merlin Engine believed to have belonged to Webster's aircraft (R6635).

John Terence Webster had joined the RAF in 1938 and was flight commander of No 41 Squadron that had just transferred to Hornchurch two days earlier on the 3rd September. When he died he had recorded 11 confirmed kills and 2 shared.

The other Spitfire, which broke into pieces in mid-air, was initially believed to have been piloted by Squadron Leader H R L Hood DFC, who was not surprisingly known as Robin. At 3pm Hood led 12 Spitfires of 41 Squadron with orders to patrol Maidstone at 15,000ft. It was a slightly hurried affair and the Spitfires were still climbing when they encountered the German aircraft, a combination of He111s, Do17s and Ju88s, which were being escorted by Me109s as they flew up the Thames. Within seconds all hell broke loose and in the pursuing action and confusion, Hood and Webster unfortunately collided with each other at around 3.30pm.

An incident reported at the Essex Record Office has at about the same time an unidentified Germany plane crashing in flames 500 yards north of the A13 near the Gun Inn, Bowers Gifford. One airman was dead in the wreckage, another crew member had reported bailed out before the aircraft crashed. May be it was even brought down by Webster or Hood before their collision.

The question that is still outstanding is what happen to Hood's body, reference to a publication by Philip Harvey on the internet under the title 'His True Fate Revealed' believes that his body is possibly buried at Cannock Chase in a grave recorded 'Unknown' but initially believed to be that of a German.

Philip Harvey also believes that Webster and Hood did not collide but in fact Webster collided with Flt. Lt. Reg Lovett DFC of 73 Squadron which left Castle Camp at 2.55pm in his Hurricane (P3204) with orders to orbit North of Gravesend. Within ten minutes the enemy formation was sighted. 'A' Flight led by Lovett attacked the rear of the formation in the pursuing fight Lovett's aircraft was hit on the port side and as he broke away a Spitfire came upwards almost vertically and they collided. Lovett bailed out and landed thankfully uninjured near Rochford.

Lovett was shot down two days later on the 7th September 1940 and killed. His Hurricane (P3234) crashed near Fritze Farm, Stock near Billericay. Lovett is buried in Hendon Cemetery, aged 26. It is understood that there is or was a plaque in Stock Church in his honour.

The question of whether it was Barton or Webster, Hood or Lovett just goes to show how chaotic the situation was at the time.

Peter Lucas, local reporter during the 1950/60s in his book 'Basildon: Behind the Headline,' mentions that he obtained a small souvenir piece of electrical equipment from the plane marked "Made in Germany." A mystery, how was that ever allowed to happen, one will never know.

If you are interested in reading more on the above conflict why not look up Philip Harvey publication on the web:
www.brew.clients.ch/hood41sqdn.htm

The 15th September 1940 was to be one of the worst days for losses of both aircraft and crews in the Battle of Britain and is the reason why it has since been declared as the Battle of Britain day. Once again the battles raged in the skies above Laindon all morning and at 2.33 in the afternoon Hurricane fighters shot down a Dornier DO17z.2 werk No 3294. It came down in the plotland area of Langdon Hills near Gladstone Road. The area is now known as "Marks Hill Nature Reserve" which is looked after by the Basildon Natural History Society.

Three of the Dornier's crew, Lt. Uemler, Uffz. Maskules and Fw. Vogel were all killed. The fourth member of the crew Uffz. Friebel bailed out and was captured unhurt at Cory Works, Thames Haven. It is understood that the aircraft had released its bombs in the Pitsea/Vange area before it crashed. Thankfully for the people who were living and working in the area the jettisoned bombs did not explode.

The following is a 1998 report by R.J.Collis, an aviation historian who was attached to the British Aviation Archaeological Council.

"On Sunday 15th September 1940 (now celebrated as "Battle of Britain Day) the second of the mass daylight raids against London was plotted by British RDF (Radar Direction Finder) over France as it formed up at about 2.00pm. No fewer than 31 Squadrons of RAF fighters met this second raid of German aircraft. The first two waves of enemy bombers were engaged over Kent and Surrey and were mostly turned away and dispersed. The third wave reached the suburbs of London and was simultaneously attacked by some 300 Hurricanes and Spitfires and incurred heavy loss.

The second formation comprised some 150 Dornier Do 17zs from German units KG2 and KG76 and Heinkel He 111s from KG53. The formation approached on a 10 mile front and British fighters scrambled to meet them between 1.50pm and 2.20pm.

One of the aircraft intercepted during this raid was a Dornier Do 17z-2, Werk-Nr. 3294, 5K + DM from German Luftwaffe unit 4/KG3. The crew of this aircraft, who had been briefed to bomb railway targets in London, comprised: Lt. Kurt Dumler, Uffz. H Maskolus, Fw. A Vogel and Uffz C Friebe (notice different spelling)

The following British pilots are all believed to have carried out attacks on this Dornier before it crashed:

Pilot Officer A E Johnson   46 Sqn Hurricane Stapleford Tawney
Pilot Officer   H P Hill   92 Sqn Spitfire - Biggin Hill
Pilot Officer   D G Williams   92 Sqn Spitfire - Biggin Hill
Pilot Officer R G A Barclay 249 Sqn Hurricane - North Weald
Flight Officer B Van Mentz   222 Sqn Spitfire - Hornchurch
Flight Officer P S Turner   242 Sqn Hurricane - Duxford
Flight Officer J R Hardacre 304 Sqn Hurricane - Hendon

Following incessant fighter attacks, the crew all baled out but three were too low for their parachutes to open and were killed. Only Fw Vogel reached the ground uninjured and was taken prisoner.

At 2.33pm the Dornier, with its petrol tanks in flames, crashed and exploded in Gladstone Road, Langdon Hills. It now seems that in addition to the above, Squadron Leader John Sample of 504 Squadron was the last pilot to attack the Dornier. Afterwards he wrote:

"I started to chase one of the Dornier's which was flying through the tops of the clouds. I attacked him four times altogether. When he first appeared through the cloud, you know how clouds go up and down looking like foam floating on the surface of the water, I fired on him from the left, swung out to the right, turned in towards another hollow in the cloud where I expected him to reappear and fired at him again. After my forth attack he dived headlong into a clump of trees in front of an Essex house. I saw one or two cars parked in the gravel drive in front. I wondered whether there was anyone in the doorway watching the bomber crash. As it hit the ground a tremendous sheet of flame went up."

The remains of the crashed Dornier were first excavated by 2243 (Basildon) Squadron ATC, in the early 1970s with a complete Bramo 323 engine being found at shallow depth along with reduction gear and propeller boss, these items were on display at the Essex Aviation Group Museum at Duxford until late 1999 when the museum folded. The engine is now believed to be in private hands'.

One of the Dornier's propellers - 2nd World War display at Billericay Library 2010. – Photograph by Ken Porter.

Many eye witnesses remember seeing the Dornier racing across the sky just above the bungalows before crashing. It must however be remembered that years after the event the stories of what actually happen are slightly different from each other as you would expect with such a long passage of time between when it happened and now..

One of these eye witnesses was Malcolm Roberts who was a 10 year old boy at the time and living in Osborne Road, Langdon Hills. He sent the following report to Mr Collis;

"I can recall the incident vividly although I was only10 years old at the time. My mother, brother and I were indoors on a dull overcast day when we heard the familiar machine gun fire of a dog fight overhead. My brother who was 14 years old and I ran out into the garden full of the usual excitement until suddenly a Dornier Do 17

appeared from low cloud with one engine on fire. It was shortly followed by a Hurricane from the left side and then a Spitfire appeared from the right, machine guns rattling. The two fighters disappeared into the cloud again and the Dornier turned to the right in a tight turn. Our mother realising the turn would bring it back to us as it dropped altitude rapidly, grabbed us and hauled us back inside to the "safety" of under the kitchen table.

All three of us having just crouched there, heard an almighty thud only a matter of seconds later signifying the bomber had crashed at the top of the road. My brother and I rushed to the scene of the wrecked aircraft which was embedded in a large crater with fire and smashed trees. It had thankfully missed all of the houses. Being a chance of a lifetime we started to collect souvenirs despite the efforts of our local policeman, Sergeant Austin who, with revolver in hand went round threatening us shouting out, "Put it down, put it down".

One item I remember keeping for some time was a piece of expanding pipe which was about 8' long. I kidded myself it was part of a flying helmet (oxygen mask). This changed rather when I was put off by the ether type smell that came from it and having convinced myself it was part of the engine, swapped it at school.

We were not aware of anyone having parachuted from the Dornier although the grim story of a head being seen in a tree might have something to do with this drama. To us boys it was a fantastic day, but not so for the families of these aircrews – such is the horror of war."

Peter Lucas, again in his book, 'Basildon: Behind the Headlines; refers to a report which he received from Mr L W Green who had emigrated to New Zealand in 1948 but at the time he was living in Roseberry Avenue, Langdon Hills. He remembers that when he first saw the German plane it was going so slow in a westerly direction, at first he thought it had stalled. All hell was going on as it was being shot at by British fighters. As it was hit by the gunfire it pivoted round and continued down the length of Roseberry Avenue just above the roof tops and between the houses in St David's Road. Unable to gain height to clear the rising ground east of the High Road, Langdon hills it crashed with an almighty clatter into a tennis court alongside a house in Nightingale Avenue. The occupier of the house had spent many months levelling the ground to make his tennis court only to have it ploughed up by the German plane.

Constance Card also remembers the day well. She remembers it was a cloudy day with patches of blue. Her mother was preparing Sunday Lunch when her father suggested that as they did not have a shelter that they went into their neighbours, Mr Gibbs, because of the considerable amount of fighting going on over head.

There was a burst of gun fire and a German plane came down at the top of the road from where Constance lived. Her husband and Mr Gibbs were the first two on the scene, it had nosed dived in to the garden of a bungalow and the tail of the plane had fallen off in the woods and set fire to the trees. Not a pane of glass was broken in the bungalow. The firemen were soon on the scene but were unable to get water from the pond in Constance's garden because it had dried up due to the hot summer which they had that year, so it took them some time to put the fire out. Constance believed that most of the people in Laindon must have seen or heard the crash because of the numbers that came up to have a look. The army guarded the site for a number of weeks afterwards.

The Thameside Aviation Museum re-excavated the crash site in September 1985, unfortunately nothing was found that could be used for display, so it is a shame that the engine is now in private hands. A pond with a small island now marks the exact spot where the aircraft came down.

Two months later on the 15th November 1940 a squadron of Messerschmitt 109 fighter-bombers took off from Calais, heading towards the dockland area of London. They had 250lb bombs strapped to their underbellies and once these had been released they became fighters again and would be involved in protecting their bombers. It was however quite an uneventful flight and as the bombs fell from the aircrafts it was the job of one pilot, Feldwebel Otto Jarocs, in his Messerschmitt BF 109 to record and mark on his map any bomb damaged which he witnessed on the ground below.

It would appear that he was so engrossed in what he was doing that he got separated from the rest of his flight. He attempted to regain cloud cover and safety but he was spotted and attacked by two Hurricanes from squadron 605 who were based at Croydon. They managed to pump bullets into its wings and rear fuselage. Jarocs managed to make cloud cover again only to leave it over South East Essex and was immediately set upon again by the two Hurricanes. This time his engine was hit and it lost power.

As the 109 pulled up into a stall, Jarocs bailed out and as the Hurricanes circled to record their kill, Jarocs landed by parachute on a shed in the back garden of a house called 'San Joy' in Worthing Road, Laindon. He was captured and taken by the Police to be handed over to the military. He subsequently served six years in prisoner of war camps in Canada.

Jarocs was seen to come down by a number of local people and it has been stated that a nervous member of the 'Home Guard' took a shot at him though in a subsequent interview Otto makes no reference to this fact. I also have difficulty in believing the shooting incident, because my father was in the Laindon Home Guard for a time in the early part of the war and they had only been issued with wooden rifles at the time.

The Laindon Home Guard outside the New Fortune of War Public House on the A127 at Laindon.

Other stories tell us about our women folk coming out after him with pots and pans which leads to one fascinating story about Agnes Monk who lived just one street away in New Century Road. Harry Rossiter, her grandson tells us how one irate ex-east Londoner was "going to carve his bleedin guts out," but Agnes stepped in pushing the woman away and keeping her at bay, until the police arrived, saying he was only doing his job and he had a Mum worrying about him back home in Germany.

In the summer of 1972 a search by David Campbell and Roger Picket was begun to find the actual crash site, locals helped by supplying maps but unfortunately the site could not be found. After the harvest of 1973 another attempt was made, this time with a metal detector. After only a few moments the crash site was found on the 5th September 1973.

The main excavation was carried out with the aid of a mechanical excavator on loan from the farmer of the field. Most of the aircraft had been buried 10 to 12 feet down. The dig went on for seven days and the last item to be removed was the engine on 12th September 1973.

The task of cleaning and preserving the remains, which were in good condition, went on for several months. Approximately ten years on the 29th September 1985 the team carried out a further dig which turned out to be very successful. They found many items including the fuel tank, a compressed air bottle, flares, radiator flaps, seat runners and the control column stick.

Soon after the Essex Historical aircraft Society (EHASH) was formed with their base at the Coal House Fort, Tilbury, where many of the items that were found during the dig can still be viewed.

The excavation team were not just satisfied in finding the aircraft they also wanted to trace the pilot, this they did and in August 1974, Herr Jarocs returned to the scene of his last military engagement and met up with David Campbell. Jarocs left fur flying boot had been found at the scene of the crash and kept as a trophy by the local farmer, unfortunately it did not last and it was thrown away two years before Herr Jarocs return to the UK.

Before returning to Germany, Otto Jarocs gave an interview to Robert Heidemann (RH) a lecturer from Thurrock College. The following is an edited translation by Geoff Williams of Dry Street, also at the time a German Language lecturer from Thurrock College. It appeared in a short publication by the Langdon Hills & District Conversation Society and we thank Geoff for allowing us to repeat it.

'RH: When did you join the Luftwaffe?

OJ: In the Third Reich it was obligatory for all young people to join some Nazi group or other. At the time, I was applying for jobs in the educational service and I had an interest in Morse charting. With a number of friends I wanted to join the S.A. (S.A. – Sturmabteilung a less prominent branch of the Nazi machinery as far as Britain was concerned).

RH: Was this a political or organisation at the time?

OJ: It was already a quasi-political organisation. It was called the German Flying Cub (Deutscher Luftsportverband), but this club was later dissolved and changed to NSFK (National-Sozialistisches Flieger Korps). In this club we interested ourselves in different plane types, with charting courses, with weather observation and with most things that have to do with flying; above all with Morse. Later on everybody had to appear before the military board and I was examined and asked which branch of the services I would like to join. I enjoyed flying and in 1938 I joined the flying school at Oberwiesenfeld, I stayed there for three months and then I returned to teaching for a further three months.

Herr Jarocs then spent a further period of time in training, particularly in night flying and also in flying bigger planes. There was also training in reconnaissance flying, a course which led to promotion to non-commissioned officer (Feldwebel).

With the outbreak of war, Herr Jarocs managed to enter a fighter squadron and in autumn 1939 started fighter training for a period ending in March 1940. After various postings in Germany and retraining in different planes he joined Fighter Squadron (Jagdgeschwader) 26 on the Rhine, near the Dutch border. With the invasion of France Herr Jarocs was station on the English Channel Coast.

OJ: After the invasion of France, on a front that went as far south as Lyons, we were given the unpleasant news that we were to be stationed along the English Channel.

RH: Why was this news so unpleasant?

OJ: Because we had already seen what it was like to fly over water and for a pilot in a plane with a maximum range of one-and-a-half flying hours and only one engine, then flying over water is not exactly pleasant...Before the war it was in fact prohibited.

RH: Where on the French coast were you stationed?

OJ: It was between Cap Gris Nez and Cap Blanc, near Calais.

RH: And from your station in Flanders you took part in the Battle of Britain. How many sorties did you make in this period?

OJ: I flew 71 up to the 1st November 1940, and the sorties after that I didn't count. It must have been a good 90 altogether I suppose. The bad luck with my flying over the channel was that I was in the attacks right up to the 15th November, and a few days later the attacks were suspended. I was actually taken prisoner on the 15th. After the bombers had suffered a lot it was ordered from above that the Messerschmitt 109's should carry bombs. A number of planes were fitted with bomb carrying equipment and in good weather we had to fly out with bombs. Speed and climbing power were significantly impaired by this. These bombs weighed 250 kilos and there was also the armour plating that we had had fitted earlier. We had been carrying bombs I remember for a couple of weeks, but the weather in November was so bad we could hardly carry them. We could only take off with the greatest difficulty.

On this 15th November we were ordered to fly to Calais. In Calais we were loaded with bombs and from there we started for the English coast and flying the north bank of the Thames estuary. As we were being loaded up with the bombs a mechanic told me that he had heard on the radio that the English were no longer bothered about the odd bombs in London and were going about their business despite the bombs.....and that seemed incredible.

Anyway, we flew out on our sortie and because I had been out so often I was given the job of seeing what happened down below. That turned out to be my bad luck. After I had dropped my bomb I looked below and didn't see that I had a 'shadow'. I don't blame myself entirely for this, for it was the job of the group leader to cover any of his comrades and I wasn't covered. When I saw holes in the plane's surface and realised that it was no longer reacting to controls, I thought "now's the time to get out". I flew up into a cloud, a cumulus cloud, nice when you can disappear in them. It was half-past-one, English time and I got out. I had difficulty opening the cockpit at first with the emergency handle but it eventually flew off and I got out. It was a good 12,000 feet up and I pulled my parachute. It was then I lost my left boot."

This left boot was indeed found by a local resident at West Horndon and it remained in this person's possession until 1972. Herr Jarocs's right boot did not last quite so long.

OJ: I heard the plane blow up as it hit the ground below. The Hurricane circled round me whilst I was floating in my parachute and the pilot waved and nodded at me. I drifted north-east and I could see the oil tanks and high tension electric cables and I hoped I'd get over them. I landed on a shed, in a little garden behind a house. A lot of people came, quite friendly and looked. Then a policeman came with a car and he took me to the nearby police station although I am not sure where that actually was.

RH: Were you injured at all?

OJ: I had cut my leg slightly on this shed it was some sort of garage I think. Other than that, no I was not injured. At the police station the policeman took me to his flat on the first floor and I got a cup of tea, a sandwich and a cigarette from his wife. It was a consolation to have friendly people around me. I had a two week old beard then. I had said I would only shave it off when the war was over. You see how optimistic we were.

RH: When were you handed over to the military authorities?

OJ: A British soldier came who spoke German and he took away some things which I had on me. I had no weapons I only had my pocket watch, a handkerchief and a nail clipper. He took the nail clipper away. I didn't mind. Then I went to a military camp, I don't know where it was. I was brought out one night and interrogated by some of the soldiers.
   "Where was I from?" They asked. I didn't tell them. Then they asked me my name, I told them that. They told me that if I said where I was from they would tell my relatives immediately by radio but I still didn't say. Then I was trapped into admitting it, more or less consciously. I was asked,
   "Do you know Sergeant Major Schiffbauer?" I answered, "Is he a prisoner too? "

RH: How many of your comrades from the squadron survived the war?

OJ: Only Schiffbauer and I, just the two of us

RH: How many of you were there in the beginning?

OJ: 12. The last to go were Squadron leader Squadron Leader Seiffert, Sergeant Major Bambers and Sergeant Major Leupold.

OJ: After my interrogation where the connection with Schiffbauer was made I was sent to a prisoner of war camp at Oldham.I was told that it was an old textile mill. There were a lot of prisoners and the accommodation and food were poor. In January 1941 we were sent by a troop transporter to Halifax in Canada. There were English airmen on the boat too, trainee pilots on their way to train in Canada. They would have liked to have been friendly with us but they were not allowed to be.
   One prisoner, Lieutenant Werra (This Lt Werra was the famous "One that got away," whom a film was made of in the 1950s) was able to get hold of a British naval uniform which he wore throughout the voyage on the ship and

he was able to make a number of contacts. It helped that he spoke perfect English.

Once we arrived in Halifax we were fetched from the boat by a heavy guard of big men in their smart uniforms. The press and population said, so we heard, "these Germans look just like us."

During the early period of Herr Jarocs captivity Frau Jarocs was under the impression that her husband was dead. She had been officially informed that Herr Jarocs was missing, believed dead and from Hermann Goring, Commander in Chief of the Luftwaffe she received a savings book containing 2,000 marks for their young daughter Helga. Later, from Herr Jarocs's former commanding officer and then from the Red Cross, she heard that her husband was in fact a prisoner of war. When news came through that her husband was in fact alive Frau Jarocs was not allowed to keep the 2,000 marks. The savings book was declared invalid.

OJ: We then came to a camp that was on Lake Superior and there we had the best accommodation. There was so much food that we couldn't eat everything they gave us. We had running hot and cold water too. In this camp there were both officers and men.

According to the Red Cross conventions this was not permitted. So those like me who were not officers were sent to another camp in Espanola, which was more to the east. It was an old paper factory. The accommodation was not so good but the food was first class. We had a sports ground and the medicinal care was exemplarily. One could go to the dentist's whenever one wanted to and everything was taken care of.

One of my friends, I remember said he wanted to have some fur slippers. He could buy slippers but he wanted fur slippers, prescribed by the doctor. He told the doctor he had cold feet every day and that no matter what they just wouldn't get warm. So he went to the doctor every day and had an examination but before he went, he would put his feet in a bowl of cold water for two hours. He got his fur slippers."

Herr Jarocs spent the rest of the war in captivity. On his release after hostilities ceased he returned to Germany and went back into Education where he enjoyed a successful career, retiring as Headmaster of a secondary school in Munich.

On visiting Britain in 1974 Herr Jarocs saw relics of his former flying machine and chose a couple of souvenirs for himself. His wife also took a souvenir of her husband's plane.

Although it would appear that two hurricanes were involved in shooting down Otto Jarocs, there was one pilot who was credited with the kill and that was Sgt. E.W. Wright from squadron 605 flying out of Croydon. He had survived the Battle of Britain and was awarded the DFM (Distinguished Flying Medal) for his exploits which included six enemy aircraft destroyed, three probably destroyed and a further six damaged. In 1941 he transferred to squadron 232, made flight commander and went to India to fight the Japanese in Malaya.

He was captured in March 1942, remaining in captivity until the end of the War. After the war he flew one of the first groups of Jet fighters to cross the Atlantic from England to America and later commanded two V Bomber bases. He was awarded the DFC (Distinguished Flying Cross) in 1946 in recognition of his gallant and distinguished services rendered during operation against the Japanese. He walked in Winston Churchill's funeral procession, was awarded CBE in 1964 and reached rank of RAF Air Commodore, retiring in 1973. He died on the 5th November 2007 at the age of 88.

Another incident of a German pilot parachuting down that was remembered by many of the locals was the one who landed at the back of Cottis the bakers in Langdon Hills. In a taped interview in 1986 Mrs M Ellul, nee Taylor mentions that on going home from her job with Henbest the tailor in Laindon High Road, she looked up into the sky and saw a parachute coming down. She rode her bicycle as fast as she could over the railway bridge to get her mother, whose house was where the Triangle shops are now. Going back with her mother she saw the pilot land at the back of Cottis.

Similar to the previous incident she records that our women folk were after him with their frying pans etc; but the pilot hid from them in one of the shops until the police came. Mrs Ellul also says that he was wearing what appeared to be an English uniform over his German one. This is something which we have not been able to verify.

Gordon Pope who was in the Laindon Home Guard at the time and living in Emanual Road, Langdon Hills was one of the first on the scene. He reckoned that the pilot actually landed in a chicken run at the back of the shop next to Cottis. As Gordon spoke a little German and the pilot spoke a little English they got on well.

Gordon says that he was quite a nice chap seeing as he was a German, but he cannot remember as reported by others, that our women ran after him with their pots and pans.

Tony Williams who was at school at the time (Langdon Hills Junior School) remembers the incident of the pilot bailing out over Cottis bakery, the children run out of the school to see what was going on. The teachers had a difficult job getting them all back to their classes.

There were many other incidents in the area over the next three to four years but it was in 1944 when it got really frightening again, with first the V1's (doodlebugs-Buzz Bomb) then with the V2's (rocket). The first V1 to hit London was on the 13th June 1944, only seven days after the successful D-Day landings. A New Blitz had begun.

The Basildon district had 18 V1's and 39 V2's land in the area and quite a few of them fell in the Laindon area. This was the worst period of the war for Basildon with more damage and casualties. It was a real scary time, the V1's would fly over with their throbbing engines and everyone would wait with baiting breath for the engines to cut out and fall from the sky, but the deadly V2's fell without warning, creating horrific explosions and huge craters.

Dickens Drive area in Laindon received hits from both the V1's and V2's. The first being a V1 that landed in the Wheatfield off Dickens Drive, on the 10th August 1944 it seriously damaged 36 bungalows, along with St Nicholas Church and its hall.

Imperial War Museum – V1 (Doodle Bug)
    Photograph by Ken Porter

Seventeen people were injured. Then five months later a V2 rocket landed in the same area, again damaging St Nicholas Church and its hall, this time 250 properties were damaged, some had only just been repaired from the previous V1 explosion.

Although she couldn't remember from which explosion, but my mother (Hilda Porter) quite clearly recalls that she instinctively threw herself across the bed to protect me from the flying glass from our bungalow in Pound Lane.

One of the most devastating hits and miraculously escapes came when a V2 landed in the back garden of the home of Ron Cuttler and his wife Rose in Vowler Road, Langdon Hills on 13th November 1944. Ron was a Civil Defence rescue party leader attached to the Laindon First Aid post and was on duty the when the rocket hit. Luckily he always insisted that Rose and the children slept in the shelter when he was on duty.

He had received a call to go to Samuel Road, but when he arrived there was no sign of any activity, so he and his colleagues had a look around and as they drove into Vowler Road he was shocked to see that his house was a pile of rubble scattered over a large area. Houses up and down the road were also damaged and people were milling around wondering what had happen.

They found that the shelter where Ron's family had taken refuge in was covered in mud and though in extreme shock the wardens managed to dig a hole through the top to poke torchlight in and there was his wife who was pregnant with her second child and their 11 year old son, unhurt. The rescuers dug their way up from the crater, into the shelter to get them out. Even the family dog was unhurt he was found drinking water from a puddle.

Four houses were demolished, 21 seriously damaged and 250 other properties sustained slight damage. 60 people were rendered homeless resulting in 4 seriously injured, 17 with slight injuries. Unfortunately an old lady a few doors away died.

Initially it was believed to be V1 as it was only the day before that Winston Churchill officially recognised that a new devastating Rocket was being launched against England, being the'V2'.

The Basildon Rectory was where Reverend Reynolds and his family moved into when he became Rector of Laindon cum Basildon. It was previously known as 'Oliphant's,' which was an old Farm House.

Imperial War Museum
Photograph by Ken Porter

Adrian the reverend's son always understood that the house during the First World War (1914-1918) had been occupied by a German spy named Shroeder who had used a skylight in the roof to signal to German Zeppelins on route to bomb London. He was allegedly caught and interned. (I have not been able to verify this story).

During the Second World War, Adrian again believes that 'Oliphant's' was used as some sort of Landmark for the formations of German bombers. It was a sight he clearly remembers as they flew overhead on their way to London. Maybe the Germans had remembered its location from the 1914-18 war and it might have been this reason why the house seemed to receive so many direct or near hits.

Adrian's sister Hilary's gives her account of her experiences of the war and what happen to the luckless Rectory:

"I remember the bombings during the war; we were under a flight path and were able to stand on the balcony and watch many a 'dog fight'. Not only did we see a German parachute out of his plane, we were also fired at on our way home from school by a plane that appeared to be crashing.

On the 17th September 1940 at around 7.30pm we took our first hit when a German bomb dropped on the Rectory, all very exciting when I saw my windows break and wall crack. My grandmother who was on her way upstairs was held by the blast and when released fell forward and bruised her nose. The crater was very close to the house and the family had a lucky escape. We children had endless fun playing in the crater. Another bomb exploded at the same time in one of the Glebe fields at the end of the drive near Rectory Road. My father returned from a service a few minutes later full of the news, quite oblivious that one had exploded next to the house. On this occasion repairs were quickly carried out and the house made safe.

I also remember that three parachute mines at some time during the war landed in the field behind the Old Rectory in Rectory Road, they were guarded and defused by RAF personnel. Nearly every female in the locality had turquoise parachute (silk) fabric and white silk cord with which they could knit with.

In the last year of the war we were targeted again. It was around 6pm on the 9th January 1945 when a V2 rocket exploded in front of the house just the other side of the drive. Due to the fact we had visitors the night before the family were in the Drawing room where the fire was still going. I had been ill in bed during the day but had been brought downstairs to the drawing room where we were having tea. Fortunately it was the room furthest away from the explosion however we were still lucky not to have been killed because there were great clods of earth and marble from the fireplace raining down on the house. Everything went black and we could smell soot and gas from the gas meter which was fuelled with acetylene gas.

Having gathered our senses, we made our way to Church Road where Mr & Mrs Webb, who ran a poultry farm, very kindly put us up for several days. I was then sent off to stay with our grandparents in Seven Kings, before returning to boarding school for the Easter term. Adrian had to return to boarding school in Surrey the day after the explosion, much to his disgust.

Before the Rectory could be repaired it was hit yet again by another V2, virtually in the same crater on the 11th March at 11pm. This time it rendered it beyond repair and we spent the next four years in Billericay before we were able to move back into a new Rectory which was built on the same site in 1949."

We know that the V2 on the 9th January also damaged the Church Hall and several other properties in Rectory Road, Basildon. Eleven people including three children were injured. The second rocket on the 11th March also damaged many other properties in the vicinity including those that had been previously damaged. This time eight people were injured and five were made homeless. This was to be the last recorded war incident in the area designated later for the Basildon New Town.

The last war incident in the Basildon Borough as a whole was V1 which came down at the Buckwyns Estate, Buttsbury, Billericay on the 25th March 1945.

One of the most bizarre and unfortunate incidents happen sometime in 1944 when a V2 landed in the Laindon area near the Arterial Road (A127) beside a woman who was hanging her washing out. Her bungalow was completely destroyed but she was unhurt. She was however forced to the ground by the blast and that was where her sister found her when returning from shopping. She refused to go to hospital and unfortunately died a few days later from pneumonia, presumably bought on by the shock.

The twist to the story is the series of events that led to the sister going shopping. The sisters had bought a bottle of sauce from a shop on the Arterial Road that was run by the family of Reeves, grandparents of John Joy.

John continues with the story on the BBC web site 'WW2 People's War':

"When the sister tried to open the bottle, they could not so on the morning of the explosion, one of them went to do the shopping and took the bottle back. She explained the difficulty and my grandfather agreed to replace it. He took it from her and placed it on the shelf. When he had provided everything else she wanted, he gave her a replacement bottle of sauce.

When she got home, the women found he had accidentally given her the same bottle. She went back to the shop at once, where my grandfather immediately gave her a replacement. It was while she was away that the V2 fell. If it had not been for my grandfather's momentary carelessness, she might well have been killed."

Many of the bombs and aeroplane shells that fell did not always explode on impact so the authorities were frequently warning people about tampering with any unexploded shells and requested that the authorities should be informed of any unexploded devices. Unfortunately many individuals still ignored these warnings, especially the young.

On the 27th February 1941, seventeen year old Joseph William O'Neil of Langdon Hills brought home an aeroplane cannon shell which had dropped in front of him while he was on duty. Joseph was an auxiliary fireman, employed at East Ham. It would appear that the cannon shell was of a British type which was considered to be very dangerous when unexploded. It would appear that Joseph on the following Saturday with all the family in the front room removed the detonator whilst close to the fire. The shell exploded and seriously injured

Joseph and his mother. Joseph died in Billericay hospital on Sunday 2nd March 1941.

Twenty years later two seven year old boys, Phillip Smith and Harry Hopkins found a live 12 pound anti-aircraft shell in a field in Nightingale Avenue, Langdon Hills. They took it home and put it the door step of Phillip's home. When Mr Smith came home and saw it he immediately removed it and put it in a hole in the garden and phoned the police. While he was on the phone the boys picked the shell up again and put it in the shed. This is where it was when the police arrived. They contacted the bomb disposal squad who successfully dismantled it. The boys thought that Phillips father was a spoil sport.

In the Basildon District, 24 people were killed, 92 seriously injured and 454 slightly injured. Over 6,100 properties were damaged and 149 demolished. Over 18,000 bombs of various types including 8 V1s and 3 V2s were dropped. There were 26 aircraft that crashed which include 9 German planes. 15 German and 7 British airmen were killed. The last aircraft crash in the area was an American Fighter on the 21st January 1945 at Andersons Farm off Lower Dunton Road. The pilot was killed.

CHAPTER
(Prison Camp Design and Structure)

To date, with a few notable exceptions, very little has been written about World War II Prisoner of War Camps in the British Isles. This is surprising given that a large volume of documentary material exists at the Public Records Office, Kew (now The National Archives). Even less work has been undertaken to identify the total population and location of the camps. Incomplete lists have been published in a number of magazines and on the Internet, but often the addresses given have not been sufficiently detailed to permit an accurate interpretation.

However, Dr Anthony Hellen, having undertaken his own research on the subject, provided English Heritage with a list of sites drawn from documentation held at the National Archives and the ICRC Archives in Geneva, to assist with our identification of sites. This was a timely approach as English Heritage staff were at this time considering whether to recommend the scheduling of Camp 93 (Harperley) in County Durham and there was a clear need to establish a national context for making that decision.

Defining exactly what constituted a Prisoner of War camp is difficult because of the immense variety of types, sizes, the classes of buildings used, and the passing years which can all too quickly make memories somewhat confused. After all, we are now talking about a time span stretching back over sixty years.

The number and types of camp varied throughout the war. In addition to the base camps, a large number of smaller hostels and satellite camps were established, with some POW's even been billeted on farms.

Each Prisoner of War camp was allocated an official number during World War II within a prescribed numerical sequence, ranging from Camp 1 (Grizedale Hall, Ambleside) through to Camp1026 (Raynes Park, Wimbledon). This numbering sequence has posed problems for the assessment as some sites have different numbers at different dates (Quorn Camp, Leicestershire – Camp 9 and Camp 183), the same camp number can be used for different locations (Camp 17 – Lodge Moor Camp, Sheffield, and 22 Hyde Park Gardens, London) and some sites have a letter suffix rather than a distinctly different number (Camp 139B Coxhoe Hall, County Durham).

The numbers of each of the camps did not appear to have any real significance to their location but more about which order they were opened in.

Without further documentary evidence to the contrary it is hard to tell whether the inconsistencies in the camps numbering system were the result of deliberate Government policy to be intentionally confusing, or of the fluidity of the situation.

There is certainly documentation held in The National Archives to show that the British were unwilling to release the location of Prisoner of War camps to the Germans due to the fear of possible raids to release them. The Germans on the other hand indicated that they were seeking the information to ensure that they did not bomb the camps by mistake. Mainly because of the mistrust that understandably existed between both sides at the time, it was a situation that was never suitably progressed to the liking of either side.

Not all sites listed within the numbering sequence are true Prisoner of War camps; many are hostels situated some distance away from the parent site, or base camp. These base camps often parented up to several hostels. We are already aware of the hostels that are connected to Langdon Hills.

Yet again, was this Government policy of the day to try and hide the exact number of German POW's that were being held up and down the country from the general populous for propaganda reasons.

During the early part of the war there was no standard design for the POW camps, although the idea of having a common design that could be agreed upon for ease and speed of assembly was most agreeable to those in authority. To begin with, there were not very many camps established and those that there were, served different functions. Some were classed as working camps, some were interrogation centres and some were actual prisons for captured enemy military personnel such as die hard Nazis.

There were also internment camps that were needed for civilians who had been detained who were from enemy countries such as Germany or Italy.

Some of the early camps and locations that were used comprised a mixture of accommodation including pre-existing structures, huts, and tents.

Although contracts for the building of these camps were issued during late 1942 and early 1943 to a number of well-known construction companies, the prisoners built many of these 'Standard' camps themselves, living under canvas until the accommodation was complete.

The most common variety of building used was the 18ft 6in-span Ministry of War Production (MoWP) standard hut, although some sectional timber, Laing, 16-ft and 24-ft span Nissen, British Concrete Federation (BCF) and Orlit huts were used at a number of sites. Contrary to popular belief there were no guard towers at most of these camps, as the prisoners held at the majority of them were usually considered 'low risk' and after 1945 and the end of the war, it wasn't felt that there was any need for them. Many of them even had the barbed wire removed as well.

Due to its more substantial construction, the water tower is often the only structure left at a number of sites that have been demolished. Although there is such a water tower still in place at the back of where Camp 266 was situated, it never actually had anything to do with the POW Camp itself although it was undoubtedly used to supply water for the prisoners who were held there. There is every possibility that the reason for the camp being situated where it was because of the location of the water tower.

By kind permission of Eberhard Fischer.

The Water Tower in the background of this picture is actually just outside of the perimeter of the camp. Notice all of the prisoners washing that is hanging up between the huts. The benches by the front doors were ideal for the prisoners to sit out and enjoy the nice weather.

Even though it was known locally as the Hutted camp the roofs of all of the huts were made or corrugated iron. Each of the huts sat on top of a concrete and brick base which helped keep them dry and damp free.

View of the same Water Tower October 2011. Picture by Ken.

We know that at Langdon Hills, there was a sick bay, a large hall that was used at meal times and for entertainment, kitchens, toilets and bath huts, a reception area and 28 huts that were set out in three rows. These were mainly accommodation huts.

The Langdon Hills camp was predominantly made up of wooden huts, hence its nick name locally as the Hutted Camp.

Junction of the High Road Langdon Hills and Dry Street.

Camp 266 can clearly be seen in the back ground and off to the right of centre. The main entrance to the camp was further down Dry Street and is where a car park is situated today. Notice the military truck in the middle of the photograph (By kind permission of Eberhard Fischer).

Both the MoWP and the Laing living huts were standard in their design being some sixty-feet in length and built in ten six feet bays with windows occupying alternate bays. They had outward opening doors with padlock hasps located in each gable wall.

Photograph by Ken Porter 2011

This is the entrance to Beacon Field today which leads in to a small car park. This is also where the entrance to Camp 266 was located.

The interiors of the huts were open-plan and heated by two cast iron pot-belly stoves. One of the accommodation huts was sub-divided, and providing sleeping quarters for the leader of the camps prisoners and a carpenter's workshop. The variety of hut types used varied. Nissen huts and Laing huts were more frequent in the south east of the country than they were in the north. We are not certain exactly which design Langdon Hills was but I would hazard a guess that it was either a MoWP or one the Laing Huts.

After 1944 and particularly following the surrender of Germany and the return of prisoners from Canada and the USA, many of the camps were hard pressed to hold the sheer number of prisoners that were now coming in to the country.

Strictly speaking no Prisoner of War was supposed to be held under canvas during the winter months, but given the sheer volume of sites where the majority of the accommodation was of this nature, it is clear that some prisoners were held contrary to this rule.

The POW camp at Purfleet by was a good example of where the prisoners lived in tents whilst their captors who were guarding them slept in nice warm, clean wooden huts.

Besides reading to pass away the hours many prisoners utilized their time spent confined in the camps practicing and improving their artistic abilities. This was expressed in many different ways. For some it was drawing, for others it was painting.

One prisoner at the Purfleet camp made a ship in a bottle, which many years later was returned to him in Germany. At the main camp in Tillingham they had a massive concrete ornate water feature that was a sight to behold.

As we have already seen the addresses of most of the camps weren't always recorded correctly, maybe intentionally for security reasons. Documentation would sometimes only carry either the camp number or the name of the nearest town or village.

Camp 266 is an excellent example of this confusion. During War and for years after wards, there was an army camp situated in Old Church Hill, Langdon Hills. The soldiers stationed there were s guards at the POW camp during the years it was open.

For many years the location of Camp 266 was always given as Old Church Hill.

Ariel view of Hutted Camp 266. Taken 11th October 1946.
Kind permission of the English Heritage.

During the mid-1950's Ordnance Survey maps produced the best results for locating some of the camps, with great accuracy, many of which were identified as 'work camps' or 'agricultural workers hostels.'

A typical scene from inside one of the camps huts. Notice the three prisoners playing chess with the heater to their backs.

CHAPTER
(Pictures from ICRC)

Life in the camp for the German prisoners of war was as good as it could possibly be in the circumstances. On the battlefields of Europe they were our sworn enemies where the main business of the day was to try and kill them before they killed you.

Friend and foe worked and lived alongside one another in the leafy lanes of the peaceful and tranquil Essex countryside at camp 266 in Langdon Hills

The below are four pictures that were kindly provided by and reproduced here with permission of the International Commission of the Red Cross (ICRC). The comments that have been attached to each of the pictures are those of the authors and not the ICRC.

(Picture 1.)

We had a good look at this picture very carefully and from the views of the surrounding countryside and the make-up of the buildings that are shown in it, he wasn't happy that it is a photograph of the main Camp 266 at Langdon Hills. To try and clarify this we spoke with Erwin Hannerman who said he

thought that it was of the camp at Tillingham. During our research we managed to acquire a diagram of the same camp which confirms that the above picture is of the Tillingham camp and not of Langdon Hills as was first thought.

The prisoners clearly created their very own Garden of Eden by planting flowers to literary brighten the place up and give it some much needed colour along with a variety of different vegetables to help supplement their own meagre rashers. The centre piece of the garden being a large ornate water feature.

(Pictures 2 & 3.)

Interestingly enough both of these pictures show nearly all of the men reading newspapers, which is a topic which is covered in a lot more detail later on in the book.

It is not known whether the photograph was staged or just happens to be an accurate record of what everyday life was like in the camps where the prisoners just liked to sit about reading during their spare time.

As nobody is actually looking at the photographer (unknown) or paying any interest what so ever about having their picture taken it is more likely that it is in fact a staged photograph. There is a certain irony attached to it I believe, although I do not think for one minute that was the intention. For me it sums up how mundane and routine life had become for the German POW's especially when you consider that for some of them this was to be their life for nearly five years.

It must have been strange waking up each and every morning wondering what the day held in store for you only to quickly realise that it was likely to be the same as it had been the day before, the day before that and the day before that.

The prisoners accommodation, although sparsely decorated was clean, comfortable and tidy. The discipline that goes with being a soldier was apparent in how they looked after their accommodation which for all of them would be exactly how they would keep their own homes back in Germany. Notice the wooden chandelier light fitting and the chess board resting above the open fire place.

During the winter months when it could become extremely cold during the night, sitting close to an open fire in the centre of the room, reading and playing chess and cards to while away the time would have been a very inviting proposition indeed. The winter months of 1947 were particularly severe throughout parts of Essex, including Langdon Hills, with snow fall recorded in some areas as being in excess of six feet high.

The camp was designed to hold a maximum of around seven hundred and fifty POW's but records show that for most of the time it was open it ended up catering for only about a third of those numbers at any one time.

There is evidence to show that in the early days of the camps existence the number of German POW's being held there was quite often in excess of eight hundred. I am sure it was a pattern that was replicated around the country in different camps as overwhelmed guards struggled to cope with the large quantity of German POW's who were flooding into the country. (Picture 4.

The picture shows a young German soldier slowly looking round an exhibition that had been set up in the camp. It appears to be about English Law and the British Constitution. Look at the poster in the foreground with the German word 'Verfassung.' on it, meaning 'Constitution.' Immediately above his head and to the right is another poster. One of the words that can be clearly seen is the German word 'Gesetz.' which means 'Law.' The British Judge looking figure with the long white ceremonial wig can clearly be seen on the poster to the left of the young soldier.

Such displays and classes would have been widely encouraged by the authorities in an attempt to educate the POW's about the British way of life with an emphasis on fairness and justice to all.

For some young men who would have only ever known about Hitler and the Nazis, whilst growing up in a pre-war Germany, it would have been an interesting alternative in a post-war Germany. The concern for the British and allied authorities was that their indoctrination by the Nazis was irreversible.

CHAPTER
(Purfleet Heritage and Military Centre)

The reason for writing this next little piece is just to put a bit of meat on the bones. Purfleet had its very own German Prisoner of War camp during the Second World War which even though it was seen as a satellite camp to what was the main camp at Langdon Hills, it was actually a bigger camp when it came to the actual area that it covered. Although this book is about Camp 266 at Langdon Hills we thought that it was only right and proper that we also included a tiny little bit about Camp 286 at Purfleet.

The Purfleet Heritage and Military Centre is situated in Centurion Way in Purfleet in Essex, which is part of the new Thames Gateway area and sits comfortably on the banks of the river Thames. The centre was set up in 1992 by a group of volunteers who were interested in saving the impressive edifice which houses the museum and is also a scheduled ancient monument grade one listed building having being built way back in 1759.

Just to give you a flavour of how the world was at that time. The famous Guiness brewery was founded in Dublin, Ireland. On January 15th 1759 the British museum opened its doors for the very first time. On May 1st 1759 Josiah Wedgwood founded the Wedgwood Pottery company and King George ll was on the throne of Great Britain.

Great Britain was still embroiled in what became known as the seven year war (1754 –1763) which was fought between the British and French in North America.

George ll was the last English monarch to actually be born outside of the United Kingdom and he was also the last English monarch to lead his troops into battle at the Battle of Dettingen in 1743 during the war of the Austrian succession when Britain and her allies fought and defeated the French.

The building that now houses the Heritage and Military centre is the old number 5 magazine which was once part of the Royal magazine and garrison that once stood on the site. Sadly number 5 magazine the proof house, a clock tower and a section of inner sanctum wall are all that remain of this once great location.

In its heyday the magazine could store 10,400 barrels of gun powder and more if it needed to. The site was eventually sold off to Thurrock council in 1962 by the Ministry of Defence. Along with the rest of the garrison the other four magazines were all demolished with number 5 magazine being used as a storage facility by the council.

The centre houses a wide range of historical artefacts and memorabilia including military ones. In one of the centres alcoves is a small but interesting display about the Second World War prisoner of war camp number 286 which although located in Purfleet it was in fact a satellite camp for the one at Langdon Hills.

The display contains letters, photographs, literature, cap and tunic badges and other such memorabilia which somehow made it feel very personal and human. The camp itself has long since gone and been replaced with flats and houses.

When I first went to visit the centre back in April 2011 I was hoping to find some bits that would be directly connected to what day to day life was like back at Camp 266 in Langdon Hills, but alas it was not to be. It did however give me an insight into life in that camp which was interesting because they did both have things in common with each other, with numerous prisoners having stayed at both of the camps.

It did strike me that most prisoners would have preferred the more luxurious conditions of Langdon Hills with its wooden huts for accommodation rather than the large tents that they had to live in at Purfleet. The winter months in particular could not have been a pleasant experience.

Remember that there was no such thing as Health and Safety back in 1945.

CHAPTER
(A Prisoners Lot)

All in all the day to day life of a German prisoner of war at Camp 266 wasn't that bad at all when everything was taken into account. They had a roof over their heads. A warm bed to sleep in and they were safe and secure. They had newspapers and books to read, a garden where they could grow flowers and vegetables. Most of the prisoners were allowed out under the supervision of guards from the camp to do work mainly on the surrounding farms which they were duly paid a wage for. The ones who were not allowed out were the diehard Nazis who it was felt could not be trusted at all.

German prisoners of war were actually given the same weekly food rations as British soldiers were which happened to be more than the civilian population were provided with. I don't know if this was common knowledge or not at the time.

However, some people did question the amount of rations that these men were receiving. The Chelmsford Chronicle by way of example reported in May 1945 that one of the questions put to the Brains Trust at Wickham Bishops was, 'Should German Prisoners of War in this country continue to receive double that of the civilian rations.' The discussion that followed with only one dissenting voice felt that as the country had pledged to comply with the Geneva Convention, Britain should not break her word, even though it seemed unjust to the British civilians.

The other consideration in all of this also had to be was what rations were British soldiers who had been taken prisoner by the Germans, receiving?

I am therefore slightly amazed by the lengths some families went in helping the POW's considering their rationing was in fact better than those of the local inhabitants. So why did the locals feel obliged to feed them whenever possible. Could it be that rationing was not quite the hardship we are led to believe. For city folk it might have been a problem but those living in the country with their large gardens were able to supplement their rations with home grown vegetables and the keeping of animals, such as chickens, ducks, rabbits and goats etc.

For example I know that my grandfather (Frederick Pitts) kept a goat. Although my grandfather and grandmother would drink the milk the children would not and that included my mother. So any surplus milk my grandfather either exchanged for cow's milk or took it to the local butcher and exchanged it for meat.

The individual weekly food ration for a German prisoner of war held in a Camp in the UK was as follows;

42 ozs of meat. (Not known what type of meat that it was.)
8 ozs of bacon.
51/2 lbs of bread.
10 ozs of margarine.
10 ozs of Cheese
10 ozs of Vegetables
10 ozs of Cake, Jam, and tea.

These amounts were all increased slightly just after the war finished in June 1945.

A typical daily menu for the German POW consisted of the following:

Breakfast – A quarter of bread, margarine and tea
Dinner   - Pork with potatoes
Supper   - Milk, Soup and a fifth of bread.

A very important aspect of prison camp life was the sending and receiving of letters to and from loved ones back home. Sometimes a few kind and heartfelt words written down in a letter could make all the difference to a prisoner of war some of whom had been incarcerated for years. In such cases there was always a thin line between sanity and insanity for those concerned.

Although the Red Cross provided a lot of assistance with the routing and delivery of prisoner's mail from the camps it still wasn't ever going to be a simple process. Attempting to collect mail and then send it from POW camps that were spread out all over Great Britain was a logistical nightmare.

To have the added burden of then delivering it to a war torn Germany just added to the problem.

The process of a POW writing a letter, sending it and then waiting for a reply must have been a very lengthy one indeed which I can only imagine must have run in to weeks.

It couldn't have been very nice for a prisoner seeing the mail turn up each week and watching his friends and comrades receiving and opening mail from their friends and family alike only for one individual not to receive anything themselves.

The following is an example of some of these very letters;

From: Obergefreiter Gerhard Patzdol B38199
Hutted Camp 266 G, Langdon Hills, Laindon.

To Mrs Toni Lippett
ALTENWEDDINGEN
Over Schoenebeck Elbe
New Way 20a
Deutschland
Russische Zone

England 24/04/46

My Dearest Mousie

Again it is Easter time gone for ever. I am in some days to another camp in the area of the English East Coast going. I (have) to thank you again for your letter of 18 March to me and more of (the same to you!) and again I come back. In (this) letter more. Where is our Klaus! Wait until the new address. For you have 1000 regards and kisses. Home (house).

Obergefreiter would be similar rank to a senior Corporal. Mousie appears to be a nickname and who is Klaus? One would assume it was their son.

From: Ulrich Muller (U)
B68480 (L)
Langdon Hills
W.Hutted 266 POW Camp
Laindon-Essex

To: Frau Paula Muller
Apollensdorf ub

Wittenberg (Lutherstadt)
Alte Darfstr 52
Deutschland
Russion Zone

08.08.1946

Dear Mother,

The card has a different date but I', writing it on the same day as the letter. How are you spending your birthday? Just think its 6 years since I was able to spend it with you. Thank Lotti Rolor for her greetings. I would like to write to her sometime but I have to apportion my few letter and cards and you deserve to be considered first. Were you at my little niece's birthday in Sollichau.
Lots of Love, Ulrich.

Sollichau is a village near Bad Schmiedeberg, south of Wittenberg in the former Russion Zone in the state of Sachsen-Anhalt.

These two letters show that the POW's were clearly thinking of their loved ones back home, no different to what our boys would have been doing. For those of us that have never been in the arm forces, it just makes you think what everybody all go through. The soldiers who are away doing the fighting and their loved ones who are patiently waiting for them back home.

Each German POW was allowed to send a post card to his family as soon as was practicable after they were captured and in any case not longer than seven days after they had arrived at a prisoner of war camp. It would be a natural desire for any captured combatant to want to let their loved ones know that they were alive and well. Their own authorities might not even know whether they were alive or dead. All they might be able to tell a family at the time is that their loved one is missing in action.

An uncle of mine, my mother's brother, was a Sergeant in the Canadian Amy. Whilst serving during the Vietnam War he was on a flight from Hanoi to Saigon which suddenly went missing minutes after taking off from Vientiane. That was way back in 1965 and to date not only has his body or remains never been discovered the aircraft that he was in has never been found either. It remains the only lost aircraft from that war that has never been located. He was officially listed for years as Missing in Action (MIA) but in the nineteen nineties that status was changed by the Canadian government to Killed in Action (KIA).

I know from my own experience and having spoken to other family members about it down the years the worse part of it was the not actually knowing whether he was alive or dead. Over time I have reconciled myself to the fact and belief that he is dead. I have to admit though that in the dark deep recesses at the back of my brain a part of me still thinks and hopes that he still might be alive living out his life in harmony.

Once at a camp, prisoners were only allowed to write two letters home to their loved ones each month. If you have ever seen a letter that has been written by a POW the first thing that you will probably notice about it is the size of the writing and how small it is. This wasn't because they were trying to send some kind of coded message. It was simply because they were restricted in the number of letters that they could send. Space was at a premium when it came to writing letters, so to make sure that they could say as much as they could their writing was almost minuscule.

The two letters a month ruling only applied to what was lovingly referred to as 'the other ranks,' or Privates, Corporals and Sergeants. Officers were allowed to send three or four postcards a month. The reason behind this difference was down to nothing other than rank. It was obviously a thing of the time. For security reasons and regardless of rank German POW's were not allowed to write either their names or the names of the camp they were staying at on the mail that they were sending home to their loved ones. By return all letters were simply addressed to the named POW with the camp number he was staying at.

Numerically there were 1026 POW camps located throughout Great Britain during and immediately after the war, but in truth there were most probably a lot more as some camps also had satellite camps and hostels that would hold considerable amounts of prisoners. The prisoners that stayed at Camp 266 in Langdon Hills stayed in nice wooden huts that could be kept clean, tidy, dry and warm in the winter. Prisoners held at the satellite camp in Purfleet fifteen miles away had to make do with tents. To make matters worse for them the guards who were their gaolers had their quarters in a purpose built brick built building.

The numbering of the camps doesn't appear to have any reasoning or structure behind it at all. It simply seems to be more about when they were opened rather than where they were. For example, Camp 266 is of course as we know in Langdon Hills in Essex, whilst Camp 265 was Park Farm just outside

Peterborough in Northampton and Camp 267 was Mereworth Castle near Waterinbury in Kent.

The northern most location in the UK where there was a POW camp was at Warebank, Kirkwall, Stromness in Orkney at the very top of Scotland which was number 34 and the southernmost location was at Consol's Mine camp at Twardreath Par in Cornwall, which is now The Mount holiday park. It was camp number 674.

What all camps most definitely had were interpreters who played an extremely important part of daily life within the camps. Camp 266 had two of them who both spoke fluent German. More on this later.

Most of the camps had a mixture of prisoners from different sections of the German military in them as did Camp 266. The early ones who were taken prisoner in the first couple of years of the war tended to be from U Boat crews or Luftwaffe pilots, some were even SS, but the numbers of prisoners in the UK was still comparatively low. After the allied successes in North Africa which culminated with the defeat of the Afrika Corp and the surrender of the Germans in May 1943 along with the D-Day landings a year later in 1944 all of that changed. What had once been a trickle became more like a monsoon. Camp 266 was the very proof of that when it was opened in April 1945. With an increase in German prisoners so the problems around where and how to house them became more of an issue. More prisoners meant more POW camps. More POW camps meant more men were needed to guard them and every one of the prisoners and guards needed feeding.

On top of this the British authorities also had to consider what type of prisoners they had in the camps. Were they diehard Nazis who believed in a political doctrine or just ordinary German Werhmacht Soldiers simply doing their duty for their country. How a prisoner was graded was largely determined by how much of a threat it was believed they posed.

For example;

White (A). Those who held no Nazis sympathies which were usually Werhmacht soldiers and the like.
Grey (B). Those that appeared to have no particular views either way, for or against the Nazis.
Black (C). SS and other Diehard Nazis.

Surprisingly you might think the group that was of most concern to the British authorities were the greys. The other two groups had their views and opinions but were not really going to waver too much on what they believed if at all. Those who didn't really care either way were a potential problem as they could lean one way or another. If there was any trouble in the camp it was relatively easy to separate and deal with the warring factions because the guards knew who belonged to which group and where their allegiances lie. Depending on what the issue was no one could be certain which side the greys would take in the matter.

Even though there were all different grades of prisoners held at Camp 266 there are no reports of any major disquiet amongst the different factions. Everybody seemed to stay within their own groups.

During the early stages of the war the intention was to send any and all POW's with diehard Nazi ideals to camps in either the far north of Scotland and as far afield as Canada and America. The main reason for this was that if Germany ever successfully invaded the main land of Great Britain the authorities didn't want to make their job any easier by providing them with a readymade additional Army of German POW's.

Although large numbers of German prisoners of war were sent to both Canada and America, in the end because of the sheer numbers in which they were being captured throughout Europe it was just not possible to send all of them across the Atlantic and so over 400,000 of them did end up coming to the UK along with over 150,000 Italians prisoners of war.

Although the camp didn't open until 1945 it had been there we believe since 1943. One of the remarkable facts about Camp 266 was that it was never once hit by any jettisoned bombs or other such incendiaries that were discarded by German aircraft on their way back home after having carried out bombing missions on London. Langdon Hills just managed to find itself on the main route between Germany and London.

Another factor that helped was that literally just down the road was RAF Hornchurch which is where both Spitfire and Hurricane aircraft were stationed and they liked nothing better than attacking returning German bombers. It was a like a brown bear waiting to catch a nice big juicy salmon as it fought its way back up stream whilst swimming against the tide.

No German pilot or crew wanted any munitions on board other than enough bullets to be able to return fire with their machine guns. To take their chances by being shot down and either safely crash landing or parachuting out into enemy territory was one thing but to burn to death in an exploding aircraft because they still had bombs on board, didn't bare thinking about.

Both Langdon Hills and nearby Laindon suffering a lot of damage and a few deaths by such munitions been jettisoned from escaping German aircraft in this very way.

With the end of the war in May 1945 there was a belief amongst some of the German prisoners that now that the war was at an end they were all going to be released and just allowed to stroll back home, with their rifles slung over their shoulders, as to a large extent they had done at the end of the 1st World War. Then the war ended, an announcement was made, and the defeated German armies who were still in their trenches on the Western Front, just simply packed up, marched back home back to their families and got on with their life's as they had been before it had all started back in 1914.

So it was then that in May 1945 German POW's believed that they were going home. After all they had only done what they had been ordered to do. But, for numerous reasons, they were not immediately repatriated. Germany was in a state of chaos, and with no civilian government in place, it was now under military rule by foreign powers.

There were severe shortages of food and accommodation in Germany with hugh amounts of damage having being caused by the widespread allied bombing of most of their major cities, so although Germany could have done with the men's labour, it was not possible for them to be sent back. There had to be a thought out and considered structure to their return. You couldn't just have hundreds of thousands of German POW's all returning home at the same time without any thought or planning.

Besides, until Britain's own servicemen had returned from fighting abroad and had been demobbed, the German labour was needed here, particularly in agriculture, roads and general rebuilding. Also the British Government wanted to de-Nazify and re-educate the POW's before they were returned home, which after all had been one of the main reasons for the camps in the first place, so for the time being the camps remained. For some that meant another three years of captivity. But perhaps the main cause of discontent amongst a small percentage of them was the uncertainty as to how long they were going to be in captivity for. They simply had no idea of how long they were to be held. How long is a piece of string?

As time went on though things got better for POW's officially it was an offence for there to be any social fraternization between them and the local population although this had become slack and generally ignored over time, which culminated with the British authorities allowing German POW's to go to people's homes if invited and spend Christmas with them in 1946. Although the laws around fraternization had been slackened, intimate relationships were still forbidden, officially that is.

When POW's were released from Camp 266 and all of the POW camps, each and every one of them was given what was known as an Army Group form 105. It was simply an instruction page given to released POW's who intended to work in rural occupations in Germany. The forms were printed by the allied military authorities. The original form was typed in German so that all of the POW's could fully understand its content. It read as follows.

"We do not exterminate any nation; we do not slaughter any people." Churchill, 18-1-1945.

Total defeat.

Germany is substantially defeated, militarily, politically and socially. The evidence stands before you. The German Army no longer exists. The German government is equally non- existent. German families are dispersed in all directions. Your cities lie in ruins. The rail network is torn up. Millions of your people are dead. All of this Germany and you owe to the presumption, the greed and cruelty of your leader. Millions have suffered under the German knot. To have the world attain decent living conditions, the United Nations have assembled their strengths and destroyed the German tyranny. Some of you have fanatically supported these madmen others have tolerated them and quietly complied. You are all guilty as to what happened. You all will have to take responsibility. The guilt that you have to carry now and in the future you have to attribute to yourselves.

Germany will never again wage war.

The defeat, that Germany through its own arrogance has suffered, will never again be altered by the use of arms. Regardless of how the political story of the world develops the allied military powers, that have now conquered Germany, will stand in the way of any future aggression. That the German arms industry is completely destroyed and millions of German soldiers have fallen, will give the United Nations the advantage in industry and personnel for years to come, as it already was before.

And even the losses in human lives, in the course of time, will be replenished by the birth of children: the German industries will never be allowed, to produce weapons for a German war of aggression. Germanys defeat will never be altered by the use of weapons. Only with peaceful work can Germany hope to establish itself again as a nation.

Self Help.

You are being released from imprisonment (POW), to engage in life sustaining work for the future of Germany, to produce food. Germany has plundered the occupied countries of Europe and stolen their production. Just in Holland alone thousands have died of hunger this spring. Now you Germans have your own problem. The United Nations do not have the intention of importing food into Germany for German consumption. Every usable surplus of food is destined for countries previously occupied by Germany. Your cities are destroyed but your lands and farms for the better part are undamaged. The foreign workers, who under threat of extortion were sent to Germany as forced labour from the previous occupied territories, can return to their homelands. Therefore a very serious deficiency of farm labour exists. You are being released to perform this work. If you do not completely fulfil this task, and therefore do not use your entire workforce, you and your countrymen will suffer this coming winter.

Performance of duty.

Where ever you are sent to, there you must stay and work. Offenses will be severely punished under ordinance of the military government. Whoever does not work well and diligently is negligent about Germany's future and shows himself unworthy of the trust that is allotted him as a thinking person.

Reconstruction.

The United Nations do not wish to destroy Germany as a nation. The guilty will be severely punished, and the people can through hard work and moderate expectations, make restitution for the committed offences. But with time Germany can be reconstructed and flourish through the peaceful work of German hands. The time will come, again when Germany again contribute to the progress of civilianisation but only, if you and your countrymen honourably contribute. The responsibility rests with you. On you it depends.

(1). After the registration you will receive a release (dismissal) certificate and an application form.

(2). To have the uniform that you have retained, become totally civilian in character, all insignia re to be turned in (inclusively, service rank insignia and embossed buttons, insignia of high distinction, lanyards and every national socialistic badge, medal and decoration.)

Medals and honours for long service in the Wehmacht or service in the Wermacht you are allowed to retain but not wear.

(3).You will be brought, by mechanized transport, to the capital of your registration district. There you will give the registration form to the military governors appointed officials in the labour office.

(4).You will then be taken by motor vehicle to the capital of your home district, where you will report yourself, to the district official (register again).

(5).The district official will give you instructions, as to where you should report for work.

(6). Those that are only provisionally released from the Wehrmacht will not be sent back to their hometown. They will have to work, where ever the district official sends them. Whoever leaves his work place (designated town etc) without authorisation, will be prosecuted. They must report to the district official in a timely interval.

I know it is difficult to judge people and events that happened over sixty-five years ago by today's standards and morals but in effect that is all we can reasonably do. We can avail ourselves with as much fact and information about those times and individuals as is possible but we see through today's eyes what makes up yesterday's history.

When I first read the Army group form 105, I tried hard to put myself in the mind of a German soldier who had just been handed it. I tried to think about how I would have felt after having been held as a POW for maybe four years. In a foreign country separated from my friends and family.

On the one hand I would be feeling extremely happy and excited because at long last I would be going back to my home, to my country that I loved and cared for. My feelings of elation on being freed from my years of captivity would have very quickly been dashed by realising that I was still in fact going to be a prisoner of sorts but now it would be back home in Germany.

I believe the form 105 is quite a hard hitting no punch pulling document which on its first read really grabs the reader by the throat and makes them sit up and realise the enormity of where they are in life, what they have been partly responsible for and what is expected of them to pay back their part of the debt owed. You have to realise that for the previous four years these German POW's didn't really have to individually or collectively address any of these issues or give them any kind of thought at all, because to a certain degree they were living in a kind of protected bubble.

As the saying goes, Rome wasn't built in a day, so I suppose on reflection getting to go home would have been good enough to start, anything else at that time would have been a bonus. Only time would tell how they managed and dealt with their emotions and their re-adjustment back in to the normal civilian life which they had been plucked from before the outbreak of war.

The first German POWs to arrive Great Britain, in November 1939, were housed at Camp No. 1 at Grizedale, which was a large country estate house in the Lake District and was for German officers. Later most POW's lived more modestly where space was available, ranging from disused factories to tented accommodation on race courses.

Growing numbers of Italian and later German POW's necessitated the erection of over 100 'standard' camps, settlements of prefabricated wooden or brick huts, each generally capable of housing about 1,000 men. The facilities accorded with regulations on sanitation, heating, bedding, space per person, and so on agreed under the Geneva Convention.

Although these camps were initially surrounded by barbed wire for obvious security reasons, after 1945 watchtowers were rare and virtually all camps removed the surrounding barbed wire by Christmas of 1946. Nonetheless, 'barbed wire disease' or 'stalag syndrome' as it was known to British, Commonwealth and American POW's, the feeling of homesickness, isolation, and loss of freedom, and more serious symptoms such as intense irritability, moodiness, depression, and even paranoia persisted and exacerbated the risk for some, particularly the older men, of psychotic and psychological illnesses.

The day-to-day management of the camps followed rules prescribed by the British military authorities. Both provision at, and the running of, the camps were periodically checked by the Red Cross (ICRC) inspectors. The overall responsibility for camps, satellites, and billeted-out men rested with the British Commandant of the main camp, reconciling in this capacity the various, at times conflicting, policies of the War Office, PW Division of the Foreign Office, the Treasury, Public Works Department, and so on.

It seems that the POWD had underestimated the psychological traumas that a lot of the POW's were experiencing. It had, it would appear, been forgotten or missed totally that the German POW's saw themselves as the forgotten prisoners of a defeated and vanquished nation. They were despondent, some even feeling stigmatized by the defeat of an enemy who they had considered inferior and thought of as beatable. The vast majority of them were fit, young men. Initially they either had their spirit, beliefs or ideals but over time these all dissipated from the majority of them.

Man becomes a very dangerous animal when he feels that he has no value; no purpose and nothing to live for. Add to that incarceration in a foreign land with no light at the end of the tunnel in relation to your release and that becomes a powder keg just waiting to explode.

However, far-reaching systemic changes were a foot. From early 1946 what many POW's saw as the oppressive rules and restrictions of camp life were progressively relaxed. An official programme of Repatriation had been agreed at Westminster in July 1946, and the programme was begun on 26 September the same year and was finally completed in latter part of 1948.

Postal services were already more or less 'normal' by the end of 1945 and from 26 October 1946, POW's could send parcels and remit money to Germany. From December 1946 fraternization with the general population and movement outside of the camps were allowed and even encouraged, although in reality this had been going on for a considerable time. This did vary from area to area, although there are frequent newspaper reports about miscreants being taken to court and fined or even imprisoned.

Under such changed circumstances the second series of Wochenpost did eventually attract more favourable comment, not least in camp reports sent in by the training advisers.

The official German history records show that a total of 994 German POWs died in Britain from all causes between 1944 and 1948, 219 of whom were suicides. British records list 1,254 POW deaths between 1939 and December 1947, but they rarely featured in the newspapers unless they involved accidents.

There were also quite a few romances that took place between local British women and some of the German POW's. Some of these are recorded in the pages of this book which stand as a living testimony of that same era.

Marriage between German POW's and British women was officially allowed from July 1947. Prior to this Werner Vetter had been sentenced to a twelve month custodial sentence simply for having had a sexual relationship with a British woman who subsequently became pregnant by him and bore him a child. Initially by marrying a German POW a British woman lost her British Nationality, this was only changed in 1948 when the Nationality Act came into being. If the German soldier in question was still being held in a POW camp the couple had no right to live together. Such a marriage also did not prevent a German POW from being repatriated back to Germany. There was a belief at the time that this was one of the reasons behind such marriages.

In total there were 796 recorded marriages that took place in Great Britain between July 1947 and December 1948, between German POW's and British women. How many ex German POW's subsequently married British women after 1948 is not recorded because by then they were of course no longer POW's.

The first ever wedding which took place between a German POW and an English girl made the news all around the world, as it was at the time quite a monumental event.

The wedding took place on the 14th August 1947 at the Civic Centre in Southampton between June Tull who was only nineteen years of age at the time and Heinz Fellbrich who was twenty-six. June was also three months pregnant at the time which added to the interest.

Heinz had been a German Paratrooper who had been captured in Alsace in France in 1945 by American troops. He ended up at POW Camp 402 which was located in Southampton. Their relationship had begun in January 1947 after June had finished with her boyfriend who was a Royal Marines Commando.

The funny part to the story was that on their wedding night Heinz was returned to his POW camp and June had to go back home to her parents. No romance was going to take place between them that night.

Heinz was finally released and given his freedom in February 1948. On 14th August 2007 Heinz and June celebrated their Diamond wedding anniversary (60 years). They went on to have six children, twelve grandchildren and 15 great grandchildren. What a wonderful story.

Up until June 1946 POW's could only officially work and eight hour day up to a maximum 48 hour week for which they received a maximum six shillings. They could then only spend their wages in the camp canteen. In addition they were given two cigarettes eight hour day and those who carried out heavy manual work were also given extra rations to keep up their strength. Not a bad incentive.

In September 1946 wages paid to German POW's were raised to nine shillings. Local employers were now able to pay them additional wages which they were allowed to save so that they could spend it on their eventual release or if they so chose to, they could send it back home to their loved ones in Germany.

By 1948 civilian workers were paid a weekly wage of £4.10.00d for working a 48 hour week. If they were still living in a POW Camp they had to hand over £1.10.00 to the local County War Agricultural Executive Committee towards the costs of their board and lodging and the rest was theirs to with what they wanted.

The work wasn't just about the money they could earn, to some it became a sort of therapy which allowed them to cope better with camp life. It got them out for most of the day and gave them a focus, rather than sitting round the camp thinking about the predicament that they found themselves in. Even officers, who under the terms of the Geneva Convention of 1929, did not have to work, volunteered to work for the same reason.

Quite often POW's would work for more than forty-eight hours especially over the weekend. If they did they were paid cash in hand or for extra food or meals which officially wasn't allowed. If the farmers were caught doing this by the Ministry of Agriculture they could have the German POW's stopped from working on their farm which in turn didn't help the farmer tend his fields and animals

The National Archives in London actually holds very little information of German POW's from the Second World War, as what they did have, was handed over to the German authorities back in the 1960's.

Consequently, it is extremely difficult for researchers to trace individual prisoners held by the British or even what camp they stayed at. Indeed the best sources in the United Kingdom are often local archives, libraries, newspapers or history groups.

When researching this book we both hoped that it would be possible to come up with a full comprehensive list of every single German POW who had ever stayed at Camp 266 in Langdon Hills. Although we didn't know it at the outset but that was never going to be possible. This is because the records that were held started with the POW's name and were not kept under the heading of each of the individual camps.

During the Second World War the Prisoner of War Information Bureau (PWIB) was again responsible for dealing with all enquiries concerning enemy POW's. Initially the work of the PWIB was centralised in London but the geographical spread of the conflict led to delays in the transmission of information.

The Bureau's primary functions were to provide, both to the appropriate enemy power and to the central agency organised by the International Red Cross Committee, particulars of all individuals held as a POW with an address to which correspondence could be sent, details of any movements of POW's between different camps. Notification of any casualties, whether that be from sickness, combat or other causes and the collection and transmission of any personal effects of POW's who had died whilst being held in captivity or who had been repatriated back to Germany.

The PWIB also carried out the function that was required of it by Article 4 of the 1929 Geneva Convention concerning the care of sick and wounded combatants, namely the transmission to the enemy of details and the effects of those found dead on the battlefield.

The PWIB continued to operate until the repatriation of the last remaining enemy POW's who were held in the UK up till 1948.

CHAPTER
(V.E Day Celebrations)

The chapter on Bomb Alley highlights just a few of the main incidents that took place in the Laindon and surrounding district, there were many more before peace came at last when Germany surrendered on the 7th May 1945; 8th May was declared a Public Holiday and Victory in Europe (VE Day) was celebrated. Barely a month after the Prisoner of War Camp at Langdon Hills had received its first prisoners. VE day celebrations were held all over the district. Defeat of the Japanese came in September.

Although there was great joy very little was going to change for the better over the next few years, other than there were no more bombs dropping out of the sky. Life was going to be just as hard, rationing was going to last for many years, for some items to 1954. In fact on the 27th June 1946 bread was ration for the first time. For those that had lost love ones, life must have been difficult as they experienced others celebrating. For a time things seemed the same, such as people respecting others, waiting their turn, queuing, ethics and common decency still existed and yes there were still shops around every corner, food shopping carried out every day, Red Phone and Post Boxes, coal fires, steam trains running on time, cinemas in every town etc, etc but things were changing. Crime exploded and in 1947 some £13 million worth of property had been stolen. Service men coming home from the terrors of war were not the same; the women they had left had also changed. Within two years there were 60,000 divorces compared with 12,000 in 1944.

However, for a short few weeks Laindon and District enjoyed itself with victory parties in the flag decked streets. The parties were mainly for the children. Samuel Road and Emanuel Road got together and held a party in the Hut Club in Samuel Road. Mrs Ling from the High Road, Laindon gave a parcel of gifts along with the residents of both roads who also made gifts of food and money. After the children had a bumper tea, games were played and in the evening a dance was held for the Adults. Music was provided by the St Louis Dance Band who gave their services free. A gift of £3.2s.6d was given by the organizers to the Laindon Cigarette Fund.

Neighbours and Friends in New Century Road, Laindon organized an impromptu street party. Families provided table and chairs and on a piano. Most of the families spent four days making cakes, sandwich which included four iced victory cakes all this from their precious rations. Sports were arranged for the children after their tea and money prizes were awarded, followed with more refreshments for young and old alike, the day was finished off with a jolly sing song.

The Kings Road party had so much food that the parents were try to persuade the children to have at least another tart to no avail. Community singing took place accompany by an accordionist. There were children's races with adults joining in and the day ended with a bonfire and fireworks.

One of the most successful parties was held at the Fortune of War, its large hall was kindly lent to them by the Home Guard. Between 40 to 50 children attended from the Kings Crescent and surrounding area. After a fine tea the children played games. Guest artistes were Mr Stillwell, well known ventriloquist and Betty Moss and her juveniles gave a grand display of sole and ensemble dancing.

Martindale Avenue held an open-air children's party with 42 sitting down to a lovely tea on tables under a canopy of streamers in the national colours. The usually children's games and races followed. In the evening there was a juvenile concert in aid of the Red Cross, followed by dancing to the accompaniment of radio or piano with more refreshments from a mobile canteen.

Another 25 happy children were guest of the party held in Denbigh Road. After a splendid tea including blancmange and Jellies the children gave a dancing display and took part in games and races. The children received sweets and ice cream supplied by Mr Brockwell and Christmas cracker from John Wagner of Samuel Road. The evening was finished off sitting around a bonfire eating sandwiches.

The Women's section of the Laindon British Legion organised for adults a Victory supper social at the British Restaurant (Memorial Hall). The evening was open with by Mrs Houser with a silent tribute to the fallen. This followed with refreshments and an entertaining evening of songs.

At last, after six years of fighting throughout Europe the war is over, the killing has stopped and once again people can start to get back to a new normality of life. For some the celebrations are bitter sweet as they also remember friends and family who they have lost because of the war.

VE Day celebrations at Laindon Station.

VE Day celebrations Claremont Road, Laindon.

CHAPTER
(Working POW's)

While all this was going on the POW's were settling in at the camp and it was not long before they were being sent out from the camp to work on the farms, house construction or to help the locals.

From the beginning of the war in 1939 it was recognised that there was the potential of inherent dangers involved with the long term incarceration of enemy Prisoners of War, both for them individually and for the staff tasked with looking after them. Long periods of inactivity could easily lead to both medical and mental health issues for the POW's which could then in turn cause problems for the camp staff.

In an effort to try and prevent such problems the decision was taken to put them to doing useful work. Under the terms of the Geneva Convention forcing enemy combatants to work was not allowed, but the idea was to pay them a fair wage for the work which they did, hence not being in breach of the Geneva Convention.

In 1946 there were just over 400,000 German Prisoners of War being held in POW camps all over Great Britain. Most of them were employed either in the construction industry, the building of roads or working on Britain's many farms.

The terms of the Geneva Convention (Established rules for the treatment of prisoners of war, the sick, and the wounded.) stipulated that prisoners of war should not be forced to work while they were being held in captivity. However, given the choice, many German prisoners of war chose to work rather than sit around the camp doing nothing. There were those that chose to work on the farms harvesting crops, digging ditches or repairing fences and there were those that opted to work in the construction industry where they were used to rebuild homes that had been damaged by the Luftwaffe's bombing raids, or clearing bomb damage. Some also worked on the building of new roads.

The Geneva Convention of 1929 was a bill of rights for every prisoner of war taken by an opposing side and should have been displayed openly in every POW camp. The protecting power which was a neutral government appointed by a belligerent to look after its interests in enemy territory until the normal restoration of diplomatic relations was restored. Delegates from these countries were permitted to visit the camps and to investigate complaints. As well as these appointed delegates the International Red Cross were permitted to visit the camps and this soon became standard practice.

Article 79 of the Geneva Convention entitled the International Committee to enforce the opposing powers to set up a Central Information Agency for the reception, recording and forwarding of information and replies to enquiries about prisoners of war and this agency was set up in 1939. There were two main powers who were not bound by these terms and did not apply these regulations to their prisoner of war procedures. These powers were Japan and the Soviet Union.

The International Red Cross condemned the on-going use of the enforced labour of German POW's by the British Government after the end of hostilities. The British government knew that there was a drastic shortage of its own manpower after the war. Over one million British troops were still posted overseas, mainly throughout Europe and it was not known when they would return to the UK and be demobbed. They were badly needed to help rebuild the nation and ensure that crops did not rot in the fields which could result in large numbers of civilian deaths due to starvation.

According to the conditions of the Geneva Convention it was not allowed to force officers to work but it was possible to expect the lower ranks to work. The problem was that there was not a clear long term plan in place as to how long German POW's were expected to remain in this country working before they were to be repatriated. This led to frustration and animosity amongst them.

The following letter in a National Daily dated 26th August 1947 will help explain how some of the German POW's were feeling about how they were being treated;

'I am a Slave'

We German prisoners fell very bitter because, when we send part of our wages to Germany, the rate of exchange is 15 marks to the £ instead of the usual 40 marks to the £. It seems to be not enough that we cannot go to our families. We must be robbed, too. Our families at home are suffering because the breadwinner and father is working here in your country as an underpaid slave.

Desperation, resentment and hatred have taken possession of thousands of us. It is better not to mention the words "humanity" and "democracy" among POW's in connection with the name of your country.

I have become acquainted with many Englishmen of the most different circles during the last 15 months. I feel deeply touched by the kindness and even heartiness I have found in many cases. I am the more sorry that the inhumane and very often silly policy of your authorities must create considerable bitterness in us and in our suffering families. Goebbels did not succeed in making the German people hate your country; your authorities understand this task much better.

Some weeks ago Mr Bevin said that the German POW's live much better here than they would in German. We got into a rage when we heard it. We know that behind these beautiful and cheap words of care there is the will to hold the good and cheap German slave workers as long as possible. If he would really take care of us he would secure to us a decent payment for our work and help everybody of us who wants to do so to go home.

- German POW (name and address supplied)

As we have already mentioned in 1946 there were still some 400,000 German POW's in camps up and down the country and the British government saw their use as the quickest solution to the crisis that faced the country. Before long, German POW's made up a quarter of the nation's agricultural workforce. They were put to work on building new and much needed roads as well as construction. It seemed like an ideal solution to the problem.

The war had been extremely costly to Britain, not only from a financial point of view but also in terms of manpower.

German POW's had their uniforms dyed either maroon or dark brown and had coloured patches which clearly identified them as such. Whatever work they were employed to carry out was done under strict supervision. There was still a Fraternisation ban in place which forbade German POW's from having any kind of contact with local people. There were notices erected in towns and villages warning that the Germans were forbidden to fraternise with members of the public and vice versa. The POW's were also forbidden to accept any food, money or cigarettes from members of the public." It was actually an imprisonable offence for a member of the public to be caught fraternising with a German POW, and although it was a rare occurrence, people were still punished in this way.

The government's justification for using the German POW's for labour purposes was quite pragmatic and simple. Germany had started the war therefore it was Germany's fault that Great Britain was in the state that it was in so it was only right and proper that Germans should help put it right. Although some British people felt uneasy about these events, there had after all been a war going on for six years and if in the aftermath of it some of those same people had died due to starvation the remainder of those still alive would have been asking the bigger question of the government as to why they hadn't done anything to prevent such a catastrophe from happening.

A petition signed by 875 of Britain's most influential people pleaded with the government of the day to have German POW's released at the earliest possible opportunity. Here we were in the aftermath of a war that had seen millions upon millions of people, civilians as well as combatants lose their lives and certain elements of British society still wanted to play by Queensberry rules. Some appeared so concerned about preserving the moral high ground for themselves that they appeared to be losing sight of the bigger picture which was making sure that no more of our people suffered and died and without the help of those German Prisoners of War there is every chance that large numbers would have. However distasteful to some it was a policy that undoubtedly helped save the lives of many more. Some used the terms of the Geneva Convention to bombard the government to add strength to their argument. The response that they received would not have been what most would have been expecting. The British government argued that the Geneva Convention didn't apply in this case. They argued that the Geneva Convention stated:

"The repatriation of prisoners shall be effected as soon as possible after the conclusion of peace." The British government argued that, "the conclusion of peace," required a peace treaty and as Germany had surrendered, there was no such treaty in effect. That legal technicality was to lead to a change in the convention's wording in 1949 from "conclusion of peace," to "cessation of active hostilities."

While the official position became increasingly difficult to defend, both morally and legally, the Fraternisation ban was lifted in late 1946. By1947 only those who came in to category of Black, ie Nazis, were not allowed the right to leave their POW camp and attend dances and drink in pubs.

Many German POW's found the reaction of the vast majority of British people towards them surprisingly friendly taking into account that some had lost brothers, fathers and husbands in the war themselves. Christmas 1946 was the beginning of the softening of official attitudes as for the first time German POW's were openly invited into the homes of British families for the first time as a direct result of the removal of the fraternization laws.

CHAPTER
(Local Memories)

The following witness stories are either told by the individuals themselves or by their descendants who had contact directly or indirectly with the German prisoners.

It would appear that the vast majority of people actually accepted the Germans, realising they were only doing what they had been instructed to do by the German High Command and were powerless to do anything about it. In many cases strong friendly relationships were formed that went on to endure for many years. We must however keep in the back of our minds that these recollections are memories of at least sixty years ago.

However, it would not have been a surprise if the local population had been hostile towards the Germany POW's but I have only come across two recollections of people being frosty towards the Germans and the people that gave them work.

My mother remembers that when one family in Pound Lane, Laindon allowed a prisoner to do some gardening work for them, her father took a very dim view of the situation but as he had been injured in the First World War at one of the battles of the Somme, it was to a certain degree understandable why he still held a grudge against the Germans, but this was soon forgotten.

Andrew Ince also tells us that his mother June Root told him that when his grandmother Edith, who was living in Kennilworth Gardens, Hornchurch took tea out to the German POW's from the Langdon Hills camp, her neighbours shunned her for a time.

Emma Thomas

Emma Thomas Great Grandparents Albert and Eva May Perry lived in a plot land bungalow called 'The Nest' in The Chase, Langdon Hills (towards the Lee Chapel Lane end). Albert died in 1956 but Eva May continued to live there until 1974 when 'The Nest' was finally compulsory purchased after a long battle against it.

Living next door to the Perry Family in 'Lyndhurst' were her great, great grandparents, Raphael and Eva May Ellis. Raphael died in 1952. Lyndhurst was also compulsory purchased so Eva May Ellis moved to Nevendon Road, Wickford with her daughter Eva May Perry but she died a few months later at the age of 84 brought on by the drama of having to move late in life or as the family put it, 'after being forced out of her home.'

The Nest had a small holding attached to it where the Perry family mainly grew fruit trees. For a short time after the war two POW's from the Langdon Hills camp would come and help them out. One of them would not eat fish, due to the fact that he had spent sometime in the sea before being picked up.

Emma remembers being told that they were well fed and looked after by her great grandparents. There wasn't much work for them to do, the family just let them come and stay and mix in with the family. The reason for this seems to be that May appreciated that the POW's had family back in Germany worrying about them, also she had an elder brother in the army serving in Germany and she only hoped that he was being cared for.

Pat, Emma's grandmother, remembers that they often stayed overnight and understood from conversations with her parents (Albert and May) that they were always very polite.

The Perry family with Hans and Henry. The Baby on the left is Pat.
Picture by kind permission of the Perry family.

Their names were Hans Baumuller and Henry (surname not known) both spoke and wrote good English, it was obviously a very friendly relationship from the looks of the contents of the letters written by Hans and Henry thanking them for food parcels and money the family sent them. One letter talks about Henry coming over for Christmas. Albert had to write to the camp commandant, requesting that he be allowed to visit over Christmas. He also had to send the train fare. Pat remembers very clearly how much he enjoyed the Christmas with the family.

Christmas letter from Henry – 6th December 1947

(We have left the letter as it was written and not altered any of the spelling.)

Dear Family Perry,

Now I will write you from my new camp. I hope you all are keeping well, I am alright. I am sorry I didn't write for a long time. I am working with sand now, this work is better than the work I have had before. Now I have to thank you, for the letter and for the parcel. Did you hear about Christmas, so if you like that I come over to you at Christmas, you have to write to our camp commandant for a invitation before 15 Dezeber and you have to send the money with for the train. When I get the invitation from our camp, I will write to you then. So I still will sai many thanks for the parcel. Now I will end my letter with many greetings and kindes regards from your

cencerely

friend Henry.

The following is an early letter from Henry that I found very amusing;

Laindon 15.08.1947

My dear family,

Herewith I inform you that I have got the parcel and I am very thankfully about it. Unfortunately it is impossible for me to come down on sarteday because I make myself punishable and so I have to work every evening in the camp, for thics week.
Well, I promise you definitely, that I come down at Monday. Then I will tell you further particulars abou my punishment. At present that is all what I can tell you.

Now I will close my letter and hope that thics letter will find you in the best of health.

So cherrio till to Monday.

Yours sincereally

Henry.

On repatriation of Hans and Henry the Family kept in touch for many years at least until Albert died in 1956. Below is one of the letters from Hans, it would appear that the family was still sending food parcel to him and even some money.

Hans Baumuller
Greuth No 13
Post Zentbechhofen bei Bamberg ObFr
U.S.A Zone Bayern Germany

Dear Mr & Mrs Perry!

Now I will send you a few sign of my home. Bevor F write this letter many thanks for your parcel and the ten bobs. I'm in the best of my health as my familie and I hope the same of you too. I'm so sorry I kan not write to you in England. I have not the time. In Germany it es verry bad. I'm going to my onkle of the farm xxxx foot and all. I'm sorry I hav not to be enough time. I'm going to my xxxx I'm verry verry happy xxxxx many thanks for all.

I will now close my letter
With best regards Yours ever so thankfully,
Henry.

Hans and Henry with Maureen
(Pat's sister)
Photograph by kind permission of the Perry family.

From the letters we can see that Henry and Hans were very appreciative of the help and occasional home comforts they received and even wrote when they were moved to other camps. From the letters we can see they were moved around quite frequently. Camp 129 'Ashford Camp' was in Halstead, Essex area, and then there was Camp 268 at Norduck Farm, Aston Abbotts, Buckinghamshire and Luton Airport Camp, Bedfordshire.

I wonder why they kept moving them around so much, I can only imagined that it was because the authorities did not want them to get too acquainted with the area or the camp reducing the chance of them escaping but in many of the cases many of them were very young did not want to fight and were quite happy to be POWs, realising that if they behaved themselves it would increase their chances of earlier repatriation. It is also possible they were moved around where there was an urgent call for labour. I can also fully understand why some POW's were happy to go and visit those families that had taken them in as it helped break the boredom of camp life.

Francis Turnage (nee Wright)

Francis was born in Timberlog Lane, Vange and was about 2 years old when the camp took in its first German Prisoners. Although the camp was about two miles away she remembers her mother taking her there but is not sure whether it was during the time when it held prisoners or afterwards when it had been taken over by Shell to house their Irish workers. However, her Aunt Dorothy (Dot) West actually worked at the camp as a house keeper. It was her job to ensure that the prisoners had clean bedding, clean clothing and sufficient toiletries. It is possible that she got this job because she had spent many years in South Africa and got to understand the Afrikaans language which is a mixture of Dutch and Flemish which has similarities to German, so she was able to converse with them. Dorothy stayed on in the role with shell when the camp was closed down.

Francis does remember her Aunt Dot on occasions bringing one of the prisoners home to her grandmothers who lived close by in a wooden plot land bungalow and was struck how neatly dressed he was. Her mother purchased from the Germans a small child size wicket basket with a handle for her and a couple of wooded boxes which her mother kept her jewellery in.

One of the jewellery boxes unfortunately the lid is now missing.
Photograph by Ken Porter.

Francis also remembers that her Uncle Jack Laver who worked for the Ministry of Agriculture as an Agricultural driver would pick up POW's from the camp and take them to the various farms around the area.

Francis's husband Gerald, a Laindon Lad, initially lived in Elizabeth Drive and then in Northumberland Avenue, both addresses were wooden bungalows which had the same name, the 'Haven'. He remembers very well going up to the field opposite the Crown Hotel with his mates on Sunday afternoon and watching the Germans play football against each other. He also remembers that many of them spoke very good English and were able to tell him when they were playing next.

Gerald only talks about football matches played amongst themselves, I wonder if he actual saw the following two matches that were reported in the SDT&LR. The first on the 30th April 1947 when the POW's took on the Royal Ordnance Corp Sports Association Royal Arsenal, Woolwich (RAOCSA) the previous Sunday at the Crown Meadow ground opposite the Crown Hotel.

The Match had been organised by the Chairman of the ROFSA Football section with permission from the Camp Commandant.

The POW's soon took the lead and added another before RAOC could settle down. 20 minutes later the ROF managed to reduce the arrears and soon afterwards were on level terms and just before half time George Doherty completed his hat trick to put the RAOC 3 goals to 2 up. In the second half the POW's scored again but ROF put two more past the POW's goalkeeper running out winners by 5 goals to 3. The ROF were then entertained for tea by the POW's.

German POW's football team   from Camp 266 in Langdon Hills.
Picture by kind permission of Eberhard Fischer.

During the Second World War my late father, David Wynn, served with the Royal Army Ordnance Corp and was a keen sportsman and he especially loved his football. In April 1947 he would have just turned twenty-one years of age and been a very fit young man. I wonder if he played in that game. How spooky would that be if he had?

Two weeks later the POW's took on Lee Chapel Rangers and this was a very evenly fought game, with Rangers taking the lead after 10 minutes through Leslie Hymas (Leslie was Ivy Powells nephew. See her story). The POW's fought back and equalised 10 minutes later, the score was unchanged at half time.

The game ebbed and flowed from end to end until 15 minutes from the end when the POW's centre forward through a misunderstanding between a

Rangers defender and goal keeper managed to find the back of the net; resulting in a 2 goals to 1 victory for the POW's.

David Simmonds

David Simmonds was born in Queen Mary's Hospital, Stratford in 1938 and lived with his parents in East Ham until war broke out when his parents evacuated him to live with his grandparents and two aunts in Benfleet. Later his parents moved to a plotland type bungalow in Berry Lane, Langdon Hills. The bungalow 'Rubinda' is still there next door to the Triangle shops, although it has been completely renovated from when David eventually moved back with his parents in 1947.

When David moved back in with his parents the building was in a very poor condition with internal asbestos walls. Externally it was a wooden building that had been shingled dashed. It had gas and mains water laid on but no main drainage, only an outside 'bucket and chucket' toilet. The front door was always chained up with the main way in and out of the property via the back door. It was a very damp building with the wall paper peeling off most of the time. It seemed a never ending chore of sticking it back down before it once gain came back off. He remembers very clearly washing in the big tin bath.

While living in Benfleet with his grandparents he was never sent to school, so his education only really started when he moved to Langdon Hills and went to the Langdon Hills Primary school at the tender age of 9. He later went to Laindon High Road Secondary school.

Although David does not have that many memories of the POW's from the Langdon Hills camp, the ones that he does have are very vivid. He remembers the troops from the Army Camp at the bottom of Old Church Hill escorting the German prisoners either on foot or in the army lorries to the various nearby farms in the area.

His sister Hazel affectionately known as Avis became very friendly with one of the German POW's and because Avis had a very good voice, she was invited to attend one of their concerts and sang with one of their bands. The whole family were invited and David remembers sitting in the front row as Avis sang a number of her Cole Porter favourite songs. One in particular David remembers was, 'begin the beguine'. The audience included not only the German POW's but also the local inhabitants as well as British Soldiers from the Army Camp. From what he remembers the camp was always very clean with well-kept gardens.

Avis became very friendly with one of the German POW's (Gerhard?) and initially the family were quite happy with the liaison, although whenever he called to take her out for walks around the Country Park David would have to go as a chaperon. He used to get bored having to walk several yards behind them. When it was time for Gerhard to be released and return home he wanted Avis to go with him but their parents would not allow it. Avis to this day has a wooded Jewry box made by German prisons from the camp.

David is also aware that many of the Germans attended services at St Mary's Church and this is where Avis, with her beautiful voice, was to sing in the choir. Audrey Clark (see her memories) had a beautiful voice as well and she was also in the choir with her as well as both being members of the Laindon and District Amateur Operatic Society.

Audrey Clark

Audrey recalls that her parents had two German POW's who came to their home in Butlers Grove 'Hillview' to work in the garden, after the war. As Audrey puts it one was an old Man probable someone who was called up in the last few days of the war. He would work at the bottom of the Garden, whilst the other one was more an officer type, a little reserved/standoffish /arrogant even but he was a brilliant pianist and would spend most of the day playing the piano.

She also remembered going to the camp for the concerts and that the Padre from the Army camp used to go to the POW Camp.

Picture by Kind permission of Eberhard Fischer

Another one of the churches the Germans often went to was the Methodist Church in Langdon Hills and Doris Hands (nee Carter) a lifelong member of the church tells us that her father Charles Carter would repeat part of the service in German.

The SDT&LR reported on the 16th April that many soldiers and prisoners of war were included in the congregation of the Langdon Hills Methodist church the previous Sunday, when an address was given by Paster W Smith on "Bethel re-visited".

Ivy Powell (nee Hymas)

Ted, Ivy and daughter Joan Powell established a very close friendship with a couple of German prisoners from the camp.

It all started with husband Ted who was with the ARP and the St John's ambulance during the Second World War. After the war Ted joined J Toomey Motors in the High Road, Laindon. It was one of his jobs to pick up several prisoners from the camp in one of Toomey's Trucks and drive them to various sites in Aveley, Chadwell and Brentwood, where they were put to work erecting prefabs for the locals who had lost their homes in the horrendous bombing of the Tilbury dock area.

Laindon ARP's on the steps of Laindon Cinema

Although there is no date for the above photograph we can tell by the name of the two films that were showing at the cinema at the time that the earliest it could have been was the 6th February 1942 as that was the release date for the film, "Valley of the Sun," a western, which starred Lucille Ball and James Craig. The film was directed by George Marshall.

The other film, "Three Girls About Town," a comedy, was released on the 23rd October 1941 and starred Joan Blondell, Binnie Barnes, John Howard and Janet Blair. The film was directed by Leigh Jason.

It was interesting to note that both films were shown as being, "Your Sunday Programme," the assumption being that different films were shown throughout the rest of the week.

The Radion cinema, to give it its proper title, sat on the corner of the High Road and New Century Road. Today a library sits in the same place. The Radion, began life in 1929 as the Laindon Picture Theatre. It finally closed its doors for the last time on the evening of Monday 3rd February 1969 with the showing of the thriller, "Wait until Dark," starring Audrey Hepburn.

Back to Toomey's truck's. It was custom for one of the prisoners to sit up front with the driver. This was usually someone who spoke good English and over a period of time friendships developed. One such man was Willi Diemar. Ivy tells us that he was a charming, well-educated man who spoke excellent

England. It is understood that Willi was far a time Deputy Mayor of Cologne and had close connections with Cologne Cathedral, either as Choir master or Organist or both. After the war Ted and Ivy met Willi (Pictured below) and his family in Cologne and they made a real fuss of them.

Another was Fritz Garbode, who became one of the Powell family's closest friends and over the years the families spent time together both in England and Germany. Ivy believes that Fritz was stationed in the Channel Islands. On one of his early visits as a POW to the Powell home he found Ted wallpapering the bedroom and asked if he could help. Ted said he felt he could manage only to be told by Fritz that back home he was a master Painter and Decorator. The job was perfectly done in half the time it would have taken Ted who always reckoned that his own skill at paper hanging was down to the Master Class he received in the early 1940s.

Many of the prisoners were sent to help out on the farms and Ivy remembers "George" who she described as a "poor little devil" tying his horse to the school railings in Archer Road (Laindon High Road School) and coming in for a cup of tea and bread and jam.

She also remembers that in the terrible winter of 1947 when there were snowdrifts 6 foot high, many of the prisoners were put to work clearing the roads in the Langdon Hills area.

After a while with restrictions being relaxed the prisoners were allowed out on Sundays and many local people invited them into their homes for Sunday lunch. Ivy remembers one young chap, overcome by homesickness, crying and saying he didn't want to be at war; he simply wanted to be at home with his family. Many of the prisoners had only been conscripted for military service towards the end of the war and their average age was probably in the region of about 20.

Joan often went with her father on the trips to Aveley, sitting in the middle up front. The prisoners made a great fuss of her and they made several wooden toys for her birthdays or Christmas. She was particular overjoyed when for one of her birthdays they made a wooden scooter painted red and in white. A prisoner named 'Otto' made a cigarette box for Ted (Ivy has given me the box). It is made from various pieces of wood that were obtained locally. It is beautifully inlaid bearing in mind the absence of any tools.

Cigarette case given to Ted Powell.-
Now in the possession of Ken Porter

The prisoners also organised many concerts at the Camp and often invited the locals. Ivy remembers them well, the hall was always packed and they played wonderful German and Viennese music. One of Joan's earliest memories was one man playing a violin.

One of the prisoners who stayed behind and married a local girl was a good tailor and he made Ted some trousers and Ivy a skirt. (Was Ernest Stryczek – See his story)

Ted in a paper interview in 1972 told the reporter that one of the Colonels in charge of the camp was a kind hearted individual. Even the prisoners said he was too soft to be a camp Commandant. The colonel tried an experiment letting the prisoners out for two hours provided they returned. That worked well so he extended it to four hours. The gates were often left open, none ever run away or did anything silly. By all accounts the camp resembled a holiday camp without the trimmings. The inmates slowly won everybody's sympathy and with the freedom of the streets they became just part of the local community.

Although a report in the Basildon Recorder and Times in May 1961 about Mrs Elisabeth Thurston who lived in Langdon Hills and who stated that one day when she was making the beds she looked up to see a face staring at her through the window.

She opened the door to find a man standing there who could not speak English. When he managed to get her to understand that he was trying to find Laindon Station she realised he must be a German who had escaped from the local Camp.

She reported the incidents to the police and later picked him out at an identification parade. We have not been able to verify this story.

Ted in another interview commented that it must have been quite a shock for our returning warriors, arriving home for good or on leave to see all the smiling, relaxed German's enjoying a meal and mending a shattered window or other repair work on their home that had been damaged over the previous five years.

Ivy as a child lived with her mother and father in the Old Railway cottages near Laindon Station remembers her mother telling her that the first German Prisoner of War Camp was established in Langdon Hills during the First World War. She was told not to talk to the men with the patches on their back. These were apparently prisoners who had been sent to clear woodland on the East side of the High Road, Langdon Hills, this however is another story.

This story of German POW's working in the are during the First World War has been verified but not where their camp was located

Mary Hawkins

Mary's parents had a German POW called Hans who came twice a week to help out with their large garden and animals. He spoke a little English when he first came to their home, by the time he left he was speaking fairy good English, he often spoke to her parents about his wife Barbara and his little girl who was only 3 years old. They were living in a cellar hiding away from the Nazi soldiers. He was forced into the army at a young age and towards the end of the war.

He would bring a pair of old boots and any old jumpers and Mary's mum would parcel them up with homemade jumpers made out of old wool and second hand clothes, a few treats and old toys because anything new would be confiscated at check points in Germany.

At Christmas time after a letter from Mary's father to the camp commandant he was allowed to come to Mary's home on Boxing Day. He made Mary a clown on two sticks which you pushed together and it would jump and dance over a bar. The Germans appeared to be very clever with wood. He was very nice and was liked by all the family. After he was repatriated the family received two letters from him and at the time he was still trying to reach his wife. The family never learnt if his wife and child were alright.

Val Boniface

Val's grand parents moved down to the Primrose Estate, Lee Chapel from Seven Kings in 1926 and bought two plots of land and a bungalow 'Fairview' in Haywick Drive.

Her parents then later bought a house next door 'Haywick Lodge' also living nearby was Val's Aunt and Uncle Pegram in another bungalow called 'Avonlea'. The bungalows were wooden, stone dashed, the only utility they had were gas lamps. Water was from the well and it was a typical plotland bucket and chuck-it toilet. Needless to say the roads were unmade. What is difficult to understand today is that they left Seven Kings where they had all the modern day utilities to move to a rural area with only gas. In-fact they were lucky to have gas.

Val's parent's bungalow was initially only a kitchen, living room and one bedroom, at a later date an extension was added to make two extra bedrooms for herself and her brother but there was no door between the two rooms just an opening.

Although very young, Val can still remember that two German POW's from the Langdon Hills Camp came and helped her grandparent look after their vegetable plots.

One was called Wilhelm, she remembers his distinctive blue uniform (two piece boiler suit) and the fact that on one hand he only had half an index finger. She understood the other half had been shot off. She believes that his home town was on the German border with Holland.

Val's grandparents being fairly old could not look after their garden so when the Wilhelm and his colleague left to go back home the garden became somewhat of a wreck.

Peter O'Rorke and Joan Wilkins

Peter who lived with his parents in a prefab number 57 Worthing Road was very friendly with Sonny and Joan Finch the son and daughter of Walter and Elizabeth Finch who had a Greengrocers store in the High Road, Laindon. He tells me that William supplied the POW camp with its vegetables and that Gibson's Greengrocers supplied the camp with fruit.

The Finch's at the time lived in the last house on the left hand side in Manor Road; Nearby in Victoria road Sonny and Joan's grandparents had a small holding where they grew vegetables etc. To help with the heavy work of digging William had a Rotovator unfortunately it broke down. He mentioned it to the camp Commandant who suggested that he bought the broken bits up to the camp and he would see if one of the German prisoners, known as Johnny real name Werner Heimans, could fix it as, he was an engineer. (Refer to Eberhard Fischers story)

Finch's Greengrocers store in the centre (1947).
By kind permission of Eberhard Fischer.

This he did and William struck up a friendship with him and two other prisoners, Eberhard Fischer and Rudi. They would visit William and his family at weekends for lunch and tea.

Peter remembers that he and Sonny taught them the game of darts. The amusing thing here was that although they could speak a little English they struggled to add up in English and though Peter and Sonny tried to teach them, more often than not, they added up in German and Peter and Sonny in English. They always came up with the same answers. In response the Germans showed Sonny who had an air rifle and Peter how to fire it properly and how important it was to control their breathing. The family, like so many other residents, went to the various concerts and dances that the POW's organised. We see from the following invitation that Eberhard and Miss Else Finch were invited to a dance at the Langdon Hills Parish Hall on the 4th December 1947.

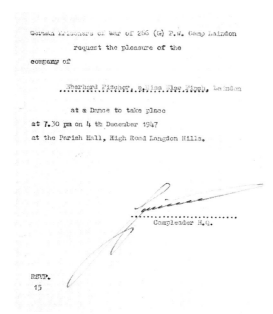

German Prisoners of War of 266 (G) P.W. Camp Laindon

request the pleasure of the

company of

.....Eberhard Fischer, 9, Tina Rise Finch, Laindon

at a Dance to take place

at 7.30 pm on 4 th December 1947

at the Parish Hall, High Road Langdon Hills.

Campleader H.Q.

RSVP.
15

Eberhard, Johnny and Rudi were guest at Joan' sister's (Winifred) wedding at St Nicholas on 4th December 1947. The reception was held at the British Legion Hall and among the other guests were Dr and Mrs Chowdhary.

On repatriation, Rudi went back home and was not heard of again. Johnny stayed behind and married a local Laindon girl Louise Holmquist who worked at Cottis the bakers on the Langdon Hills side of the railway in the High Road.

Johnny for a time worked at a garage on the old A13 opposite the Five Bells pub, later he moved to Ramsden Heath and opened a Car Garage. Eberhard returned home but keeps in touch with the family to this day through Walters's daughter Joan.

It was either Johnny or Louise who was god parent to Hans Baldes (see his story) and Edna daughter, Maria. It was also one of his POWs friends who lent Hans a suit to get married in.

Finch's bungalow in Manor Road – By kind permission of Eberhard Fischer

Harry Horton

Harry as a young child moved several times with his parents Henry and Florence before settling down in Laindon. The first move was from Southend to Laindon in 1937 then to Hornsey in London in 1940 because his father thought London would be well protected from any German invasion. Obviously very little thought at the time was given to the possibility of London being bombed. They moved back to Laindon in 1945 just before the end of the war to Bush Cottage in Essex Road.

During Harry's first stay in Laindon he went to Mr King's private school in Sandringham Road, the cost being 1 shilling and 6 pence a week. He had attended both Langdon Hills Junior and Markham Chase Junior schools but had been expelled from both as he says 'I must have been a little devil but Mr King always gave me a good reference'.

Bush cottage had a very large garden and it was too much for his parents so when the opportunity arose they had two POW's from the camp come two nights a week after they had done a shift working on the local farms. They would help with the digging and planting of vegetables etc. He remembers that they both spoke fairly good English. His parents were not allowed to pay them, other than the odd cup of tea they gave them packs of 20 player's cigarettes.

One of them he knew as Richard, a big man who stood about six feet tall. He told them that he had been captured somewhere in a town in France. He had turned this corner and facing him on one side of the road was Russian Soldiers and on the other English soldiers. He decided to be taken prisoner by the English. His biggest worry years later when he was repatriated was that his home was in the Russian Zone but he had not heard from his family so he had no choice but to go back.

Harry provided us with the photograph of the VE day celebrations at the junction of Sandringham Road and Essex Road. Harry is in the foreground in the centre looking over his left shoulder wearing a party hat. All he really remembers is that all the children had a great time.

VE Celebrations, Sandringham Road. By kind permission of Harry Horton.

He also remembers that there was a corn field off of St Nicholas Lane near the junction with Pound Lane were haystacks he played on were made by POW's who worked in the field for the local farmer.

Gordon Swift

Gordon Swift a second cousin of mine who was living in Bracken Mount, Laindon, at the time with his parents used to after the war drive a 3 ton Bedford Truck for Mr Birch a neighbour who had a haulage business. One of Gordon's tasks was to collect from the Purfleet Camp (Satellite Camp of Camp 266) 12 POW's and take them to South Ockendon to work on building prefabs.

One amusing story is that on occasions when he was driving around the prefab site one of the Germans who could speak reasonable English would ask him that whenever they banged on the cab once would he stop and for him to go again they would bang on the cab twice. Being only young he was quite happy to carry out their request but obviously he wanted to know what they were up to. He found out that when they stop they were jumping off and stealing bags of cement to take back to the camp which they used to make a water fall at the entrance to the camp.

Although not connected to Gordon's story the Chelmsford Chronicle reported on the 27th July 1945 that the Chelmsford Town Council intended to get German prisoners to help relieve the housing shortage in the area. It was their intention to get them to dig out and lay sewers and mains for temporary houses to be erected on the Springfield Park Estate. They would be paid the Trade Union rate wage, plus travelling expenses. It was also made clear that when British Labour became available it would take over from the German's in actually building the homes and leaving the Germans to do the digging.

Another report, this time in the SDT&LR in December 1945, reported that the Council Housing Committee Surveyor subject to the approval of the Committee, was going to transfer the work to be carried out on the Billericay temporary housing site to direct labour by using German prisoners who were currently working on another site in Wickford. The change was approved by the council.

It was on the farms that a great deal went to work and their skills were greatly appreciated. Many of them having been farmers themselves back home in Germany. Nearly all the farms in the Laindon and surrounding district had them working for them either directly or indirectly.

John Bathurst

John Bathurst had been a school teacher before his retirement, has a vast amount of knowledge on the history of Laindon and the surrounding district although he admits that it is very limited in regards to the POW camp. He does recall that two of them called at his parent's home in Basil Drive offering to tidy up their garden. He only remembers one by name 'Willi' and he was a Heidelburger. Neither of them spoke much in the way of English and his parents did not speak any German at all. Consequently they all found it difficult to communicate with each other.

He remembers going to the camp concerts and was impressed by the good classical instrumentalists that the German POW's had in their midst. On one occasion when it came to the comedian's turn the only recognisable words were 'Winston Churchill' and as the accompanying laughter only came from those who could speak German, the jokes were possible on us.

His family were given a carved wooden box as a gift by the two POW's.

In an early interview in 1997 with the Evening Echo newspaper, John Bathurst said that the German prisoners were a familiar sight in the area with their distinctive brown uniforms with yellow diamonds on their backs and that they were even allowed to go to the pictures in Laindon. Some of them even ended up marrying local girls after they were released from the camp.

"We used to walk down to the camp and see them. We weren't scared of them at all. There was no need to be as far as we could see. They were all pretty decent chaps, not the fanatical Nazis you read about and see in films. They weren't interested in the war that much, all they really wanted to do was to be back home with their families."

Geoff Williams

Toni Hänfling was one of a number of German prisoners of war who worked at Dry Street Farm in the immediate post-war years. He hailed from the village of Theuern, some five miles from the city of Amberg in eastern Germany's Oberpfalz (Upper Palatinate) region. His parents at the time had a small farm in the centre of the village with fields, in the small farmer fashion, at various locations around the village

Toni was captured in Ostende, Belgium in 1944 and transported to the UK. It is not clear where he spent his first months as a POW but he ultimately arrived at Camp 266, or more exactly one of its satellite camps at Purfleet or Orsett. He certainly worked on farms in both places and does not seem to have been a prisoner of the main camp at Langdon Hills.

Toni was a likeable and popular character and at one stage was planning to marry and settle down in England, but the family farm back home in Germany was in dire straits, his parents needed him and when the time of his release came he returned to Germany. Although he worked, as mentioned, on farms in Orsett and Purfleet, his fondest memories were of Dry Street Farm. There he developed a close relationship with the then tenants, Mr and Mrs Arthur Partridge, their son Roland and his wife Mary. Toni was and remained a devout Catholic and it may be that the Partridges, who were staunch non-conformists of the Methodist tradition, recognised this amongst his many attributes. Whatever the reason for the good relationship that had developed between them, it was such that several years after he had returned to Germany, Mrs Partridge senior made it possible for him to return to England in the early 1950's to visit the Partridge family. Mrs Mary Partridge recalls how much thinner he looked on his return than when he had been here before as a POW.

Toni kept in regular touch with the family in the ensuing years. In 1973 when Roland Partridge's eldest daughter Linda, now Linda Williams, moved with her husband Geoff to a village in Franconia some 60 miles away from Theuern in Germany, the Williams's and Hänflings met up. This was to be the start of years of close contact between the two, which lasted until Toni's death.

Toni was determined to repay his treatment by the Partridges with the same hospitality and generosity of spirit.

Although a farmer by inheritance, Toni also had remarkable skills as a wood-turner, carver and woodworker, something which he turned to good use both at home and for his village community.

As so often was the case in rural Germany the small farmer supplemented their income with additional regular employment. So it was with Toni who during the 1960's, 1970's and early 1980's worked at a bottle making factory in Amberg producing the distinctive brown ½ litre beer bottles. At the same time he managed the small farm with half-a-dozen indigenous milking cows (Oberpfälzer), chickens, cereals and beet.

Toni never talked much about his time as a POW in England, except to sing the praises of the families, particularly the Partridges, that he came in contact with. At one stage in his imprisonment he met a young woman, fell in love with her and but for the call to return home and run the family farm would have remained in the UK.

In 1976 when he revisited Langdon Hills he sought out his erstwhile sweetheart, then resident in Dagenham. Thirty years is a long time; he was he said after the reunion, quite happy with the choices he had made....

Ken and Peter Gray.

Ken and Peter's parents by the end of the war had been farming in the area for over fifty years. They farmed out of Northlands and Haslett's farms in Dry Street, Langdon Hills, neither of which were further than half a mile away from the camp.

Both farms used the services of the POW's and Peter remembers that their mother who lived at Haslett's often cooked them meals.

Sister Jean recalls going to variety show put on by the prisoners at the camp, some of whom dressed as women. She also remembers that at the rear of the camp where it joined the woods, the prisoners had worked hard to make a garden with paths made of stones.

The family were also given a jewellery box which appears to have been a normal way for the prisoners to say thank you to the families that they became close with.

Geoff Buckenham

Geoff is now a retired Laindon farmer who for a time was also leader of the Basildon Council. His father Reginald and later Geoff farmed out of Mundles Farm which was situated in Wash Road, Laindon.

After the war his father would receive two or three POW's from the Langdon Hills Camp each day. Their work involved potato picking, hedge clearance and at harvest time, stacking straw. Geoff's recollection of the POW's is that they were very polite and all seemed to speak very good English. On one occasion when they were stacking the straw one of them said to his father, "you are doing it wrong, this is the way we stack it in Germany," which was in round bales, his father responded, "thank you, but do you mind doing it my way," to which the German replied, "no sir, not a problem."

If you look in the fields to day most of the stacking is now done in round bales.

It was quite normal for his father to feed them but Geoff thinks his father was recompensed by the military for feeding them.

Geoff said the Germans liked talking about the war and often expressed their disappointment that Germany and England had not joined forces. Also if ever the question of the Jew's came up their response was, "Yew's, no good to England, no good to Germany."

I feel that if these comments and conversations had ever got back to the Camp and the ears of the Commandant, they might well have found themselves in deep trouble and a trip up to one of the POW camps in Scotland on the basis that they still had strong Nazi tendencies.

Jack Doodes

The Doode's family ran what was known at the time as Hunts Farm. The main farm house and out buildings were in the vicinity of where the Basildon Sporting Village is today. Thrashing of the corn back in the 1940's was normally carried out by contractors who went from farm to farm. The main contractor in the area at the time was 'Keeling's'. Jack Doodes remembers that although his family did not have any POW's helping them the contractor 'Keelings certainly did'.

With over a hundred shops stretching along the High Road from the New Fortune of War to over the Bridge up to where Stanway is now, it is not surprising that many of the shop keepers took the opportunity to use the services of the Germany Prisoners.

Jimmy Gibson

Jimmy Gibson tells me that his family who had a Green Grocers shop in Laindon got dispensation to allow them to take one of them up to the early market in London, presumably Covent Garden, to help them load and unload their vehicle.

Jim Townsend

Jim Townsend whose father also had a Green Grocers shop in Laindon near the Station and a three acre site in Hot Water Lane, Lee Chapel had at least six prisoners helping to cultivate out on the Hot Water Lane site where they grew runner beans and tomatoes plus a small orchard. Jim remembers clearly that after he left the army in 1947 that he helped his father out by collect them and returning them to the camp. They were not allowed to pay them so they used to give them food and cigarettes.

Peter Hayden, Jennifer Lindsay (nee Burr) and Geoffrey Burr

Peter can remember that his father, Sydney who was the manager of AMA Building Firm, Laindon Depot one of the main contractors that built Laindon Cinema, used to pick up prisoners from the Purfleet camp and take them, he believes to Aveley where they used to erect pre-fabs. Many other local business men used their Lorries for this same purpose and I think it made a little bit of extra cash for them on the side.

My father had a flat-back lorry which he put a canvas canopy over the back for the POW's to travel in. I can remember sitting in the middle of the cab with my father driving with one of the German NCOs in the passenger seat. The Germans were very kind to Peter and they used to make him toys. He remembers two of the toys, which were quite sophisticated. One was a dog sitting on a base and when you pressed the bottom of the base it would stand up. The other was a propeller that was on a piece of wood and you pulled the string and the propeller flew off.

Jennifer Burr a friend of Peter's lived in number 2 Water Tower Cottages that was situated about a 100 yards along Dry Street from the camp and though only five at the time can remember clearly walking pass the Guard House on her way to school with friends and the German guards always acknowledge them. Geoff her brother who was a few years older remembers that a bugle was played every evening. Also that his father had two POW's often come and help out in the garden and they were usually given cigarettes.

Michael Toomey

A number of our recipients have mention that Toomey's one of the few business still operating in the Laindon area since before the war used to ferry German POW's from the camp to their place of work. Joseph Toomey was the young energetic entrepreneur who started up the business in Laindon in 1929 selling motor cycles.

It seemed then only sensible to contact his son Michael who is still heavily involved in the business which now trades under the name of Laindon Holdings Ltd but to the locals it is still 'Toomey's'.

Michael kindly replied by letter, explaining that although he was only a young boy at the time he remembers the camp well. With regards to transporting the Prisoners he tells us that they did not work for his father but he had a contract to transport them to places of work. At the time his father had three lorries delivering sand and ballast and in the mornings they used to put benches in the lorries and a tarpaulin cover on a frame over the top and then take the German POW's to building sites, mostly to Shell at Coryton. Michael often travelled in the lorries with the drivers.

He also remembers that the Priest, Father Harold Cahill of the local Catholic Church in the Langdon Hills High Road, was over the moon because the German POW's doubled the size of his congregation overnight.

Although his father was in the First World War and fought in the trenches in France he didn't have any problem with four Germans coming to their house every Sunday for lunch and as Michael rightly says, "as I get older, the more I feel that this was a real Christian outlook".

Michael also kindly sent me a small book on the history of The Catholic Church, Laindon (St Teresa) and in it I came across the following snippet : During the war Laindon had two POW camps (This as we know is incorrect, there was only one POW camp the other one was an Army Barracks for British soldeirs).

The men held Mass, celebrated by their own padres, on Sunday in St. Teresa's Church. I have been told by a parishioner that to sit through an over-long sermon in German was, "Could be quite a penance!"

Ted Crudgington

Ted remembers as a young boy going to the Langdon Hills Camp and others during his school holidays with his father Harry who worked for the

Ministry of Works as an electrician. The camps he remembers visiting are Langdon Hills, his father's main base, Rawrath, High Garrett and Purfleet.

Joachim Kaiser, one of the POW's from Langdon Hills used to help Ted's father regularly and as was often the case in these circumstances a friendship was formed. On at least one occasion Joachim got a pass to spend Christmas with the Crudgington Family (1947).

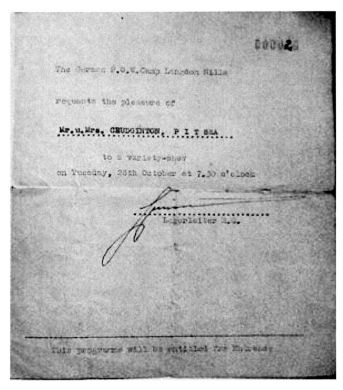

Ted believes that Joachim had been a sub-mariner during the war. He kept in touch with the Crudginton's when he returned to Germany after the war.

Unfortunately for him he found himself and his family in Berlin's Russian Zone. A letter Joachim wrote to the family in February 1952 gives an idea of what it was like for him to live under Russian control.

"My wife and I are living now in Berlin in the Russian District. I have my job but you know that perhaps from the wireless."

The letter also goes on to say

"What about Nobby, Ted's elder brother, he is perhaps in Korea? And Teddy is he naughty?"

Although Ted was only very young he does remember also going with his family to one of the concerts at the POW camp at Langdon Hills, where the Indian rope trick was performed on stage and one of the German POW's climbed up it, right to the top and out of view of the audience and a friend of his father's shouted out,

"It must be bloody cold up there,"

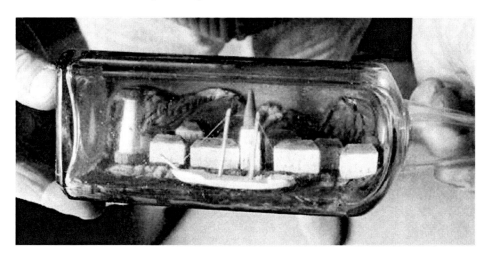

Photograph taken by Ken Porter with kind permission of Ted Crudgington.

The family were given a bottle with a model of a sea side harbour inside it by one of the camp's POW's. The bottle originally held Camp Coffee. Camp Coffee is a glutinous brown substance which consists of water, sugar, 4% coffee essence and 26% chicory essence. It was generally used as a coffee substitute and it was the closest the camp could ever get to having actual real coffee, but there was a war going on after all.

Another of the POW's made Ted a wooden toy bus for Christmas. It was a replica of one of Pitsea's Campbell Coaches and was at least two feet long. The POW's sold many of the wooden models and items which they made. Ted knows his father bought what he refers to as a box which he describes as having secret compartments in it and a beautiful inner tray with inlaid designs.

Joachim Kaiser with his wife on their wedding day, the message on the back says: 'With very kind regards to my Dear 'English Friends' for everlasting remembrance always yours Joachim Kaiser.'

Jill Barnes

Jill remembers as a very young child a German Prisoner of War from the camp called Wilhelm and a Polish man presumably also a POW called Jacob would come to the family home in Victoria Avenue, Langdon Hills to do the gardening and other odd jobs. Her parents, Grandparents and cousins all lived in large houses or bungalows in Victoria Avenue. Jill's parent's house had a frontage of 90 feet and the back garden was at least 150 feet deep so there was plenty of work for them to do. Neither could speak any English and Jill's parents could not speak any German but somehow they managed to get by and become very close friends. Wilhelm returned to England in 1952 around the time Princess Elizabeth became Queen. He bought Jill's mum a compact and a German doll for Jill.

Jacob holding Jill, Jill's mum and Wilhelm. By kind permission of Jill Barnes.

Wilhelm and his family back home in Germany. By kind permission of Jill Barnes.

CHAPTER
(Camp Interpreters and Pay Master)

There were two interpreters who worked at Camp 266. One was Peter Sinclair and the other one was Mr Noble.

We know a little of Peter Sinclair experiences at the camp due to an interview he gave to one of the local newspapers. He was a German-born Jew who at the tender age of twelve had managed to flee Germany with his mother in 1939 just before the outbreak of the war. Whether the German POW's knew of his Jewish background and if they did know how they reacted to Sinclair, is not known.

With his obvious command and fluency of both English and German, not surprisingly when he grew up he became an interpreter which resulted in him becoming a front-line liaison officer between the German prisoners and the British authorities. We make the assumption here that he had joined the British Army as he was in uniform. What rank he held is not known either.

Shortly after VE day on the 8th May 1945 and at the young and tender age of only 18, Sinclair found himself being posted to the Langdon Hills Camp. It was a camp with a difference, as there was no barbed wire or any other heavy security attached to it.

The first group of German POW's, arrived at the camp in April 1945. It was not long before their numbers swelled to nearly 800, swelling the camp almost to its limit as it was only designed to take a maximum of 750.

Peter Sinclair's first job was to help settle the POW's in to the camp and then interrogate them to try and establish if there were any Nazis or war criminals amongst them. The next stage would then be for him to arrange some of them to be posted to other satellite camps, such as Purfleet or Tillingham.

Sinclair, despite his comparatively young age, was a very well organised individual. He had very quickly amassed a huge card index with the names, ranks and backgrounds of every single prisoner and what their political leanings and ideologies were.

Many of the German prisoners, who were returning from their incarceration in POW camps in Canada, were still wearing their uniforms and badges of rank. It was Sinclair who was tasked with the delicate job to see they were, as it was called in the camp jargon of the day, demilitarised. This meant him, a raw and relatively inexperienced young man having to tell battle hardened German POW's that they had to get rid of their badges of rank, formal parades and military attitudes.

In the main these were U-Boat and Luftwaffe air crews who had been POW's since the early days of the war and who were used to doing pretty much exactly as they wanted to. Many of them were now not so happy with the stricter regime that they suddenly discovered was being imposed upon them on their arrival back in the UK. Not all of them were compliant with these new restrictions. Those who weren't were quickly dispatched to special camps in the North of Scotland.

Sinclair soon found himself responsible for the welfare of between 3500 and 4000 POW's who were either in camps or billeted on farms all around South East Essex, which was a massive responsibility, especially for someone so young.

There were POW camps at Chelmer Village and Hylands Park in Chelmsford, Steeple, St Lawrence Bay, Orsett, Purfleet, Rawreth, Southcurch, Great Wakering and two at Tillingham. Many of these POW's would have passed through the Langdon Hills camp as it was not only a working camp but also a central transit camp for the area.

Naturally after the war the majority of the German POW's wanted to return home to their love ones as quickly as possible but it was only those who were fit enough to return that were initially sent back to the new Germany. The reason for this was because they were not just being released and that was the end of the matter. Once back in Germany they had to register with the local authorities for their area and be put to work, physically helping to rebuild their country.

Before they could be repatriated back to Germany they first had to stay here and help in clearing up and rebuilding the bombed sites in our cities or helping out on the farms replacing the men who were in the British armed forces, still overseas serving their country.

Nazis and war criminals would be held for longer periods but there were not too many who were brave enough to admit being either. Sinclair, through a combination of investigation, interrogation and observation was aware that there were members of the SS in the camp, along with others who had served the Third Reich as concentration camp guards. There were even those who had once been proud members of Hitler's personal body guard. They would all try to hide their identity but for the SS it was not so easy. They had tattoos on their arms which recorded their individual blood groups.

Overall, Sinclair believed that the majority of the camps POW's were a fine bunch and that it was a happy and contented place to be. It was like a small town with its own bakery, hospital, theatre and dance band. It also had its own German Lutheran priest.

With regards to the band it was not unusual for them to play to the local Langdon Hills and Laindon population. On one occasion in September 1947 they joined the Laindon Festival Orchestra for a concert at the Memorial Hall which was located in the High Road, Laindon. It is interesting to note that their attendance at the concert was with the kind permission of the camp Commandant, Lt. Col. H.S Hobby.

On the reverse of the programme for the occasion there was an insight in to the austere, everyday conditions of those post-war days. The Laindon Festival Orchestra's next concert was advertised so. "Cars and petrol permitting".

In the camp at the end of most of the huts the prisoners had built their own little gardens to make the place more homely, a number of them had models of churches and other buildings erected on the gardens. There was magazine's produced by the POW's that circulated across the camps in Essex.

Peter Sinclair Photograph by kind permission of Erwin Hannermann.

Mr Noble Photograph by kind permission of Erwin Hannermann.

The camp also had an extensive re-education programme for the German POW's with lecturers coming from Switzerland and the Red Cross. The prisoners were also shown films of the concentration camps on liberations, it created a tremendous impression, although many did not believe it at first or thought it was because of the bombing and the disruption of food supplies.

The German's at the Langdon Hills camp had elected their own leaders, although were in turn then carefully vetted by the British. It was a very interesting period in Sinclair's young life with all these German's having to report to him and although there does not appear to have been many real problems at the camp it did on occasions make the headlines of the local or national newspapers.

For example a few of the prisoners, on Hitler's birthday, 20th April 1946, somehow managed to raise the swastika flag, however the majority of the camp were not amused and it was just as quickly taken down again.

The biggest scandal to hit the camp was created when a group of local residents with Fascist inclinations invited the POW's from the camp to a garden party at one of the group's homes. After everybody had settled down and were eating, drinking tea and homemade lemonade the group started playing recorded speeches by Hitler, Goering and Goebbels. To their credit a large number of the Germans walked out in shock and disgust but there was a tremendous hue and cry about it in the national press.

Sinclair was away from the camp on leave at the time but was soon recalled by his Commanding Officer to help defuse an uncomfortable and potentially dangerous situation.

On another occasion a local husband and wife tried to break into the camp to give vitamins to the Germans who they believed were starving. They were arrested and charged at Billericay Court. It turned out that they were also both British Fascists. More on this later.

There were however some other more humorous events that took place at the camp.

The Daily Mail newspaper reported that the guards at the Langdon Hills camp had to borrow footballs from the POW's. The heading read 'Fuhrer, may we borrow your football?" "The Army, being very stingy at the time, hadn't allocated any footballs to the guards. They had quite a happy and friendly relationship with the POW's and they used to use the Germans' ball."

It was not long before the camp was swamped with footballs. It seemed that everybody was sending them in from all over the country.

The one occasion that amused everybody including the Germans was when a high powered Allied Military Intelligence team suddenly turned up at the camp. The team was made up of a small America naval commander with a large cigar, a high powered British intelligence officer, a Guards officer and a beautiful Marilyn Monroe look alike driver who not surprisingly turned every body's head.

Some of the camps prisoners were part of a U-Boat crew that had been captured towards the end of the war. It is possible that Eberhard Fischer is one of those who were interviewed by the intelligence team. (See his story). They were questioned about their submarines log books as it was suspected that they may have helped senior Nazis to escape to South America. Despite the seriousness of their visit they had not thought to ensure that at least one of their team could speak German, so once again Sinclair had to be called back from his leave to help out.

Whether any relevant intelligence was obtained is unknown, but it certainly broke up the monotony of the camp to have a beautiful car and an even more beautiful woman to stare at, both the guards and the prisoners alike.

Captain Bob Beanie (The same one who is mentioned in the Chapter on ICRC Reports) served at the camp for approximately 18 months towards the end of the war and afterwards as an Army paymaster. He was an Italian born Londoner and because of this he was not conscripted into the armed services at the outbreak of war in 1939. However in 1941 he volunteered for the Army, but before they would accept him, the British Authorities insisted on him anglicising his name, so Bob Benney came into being.

He was fortunate to be allowed to join up so early because of Italy's involvement in the war at the time on the side of the Germans.

The 20,000 or so Italians who were then living in England suffered restrictions and internments; many were even sent to Canada. In spite of this many Italians were willing to contribute to the military efforts of Great Britain. Benney, was one of the early ones to do so.

With the large influx of POW's he responded to the Army's request for fluent German and Italian speakers, so Captain Bob Benney became an interpreter travelling around the country from camp to camp before taking up the Camp Commandants offer of training as a paymaster and settling down at the Langdon Hills camp. His job involved looking after the camps money and financial matters, which included paying the POW's a shilling a day for work that they carried out, which was part of the requirements of the Geneva Convention.

Like Staff Sgt Peter Sinclair, Benney describes the camp as being like a real community, a little village with its own bakery, barbershop, chefs and many other facilities such as two musical bands. One played classical type music and the other one played more popular and up to date music.

The German bands, after the war were allowed to entertain the local inhabitants either in the camp or in one of the nearby halls in Laindon.

Photograph by kind permission of Erwin Hannermann

On one such occasion they were allowed to play at a wedding in the Nissen hut that had been erected at the back of the Crown Public House, which was litererally a stone's throw away from the camp.

One of Benney's other functions was to take work parties of POW's from the camp out to various nearby locations. One such group he use to take to Southend Hospital, which was about 15 miles away, to help out with fetes and other similar activities. It was slowly through activities like this that the local populations became to accept the presence of POW's in their communities.

As far as we have established no prisoner escaped from the camp and we doubt if any tried being an Island it would have being very difficult if not impossible to escape back to Germany. This is the belief of many but in fact the German's were just as inventive in their escape plans as the British POW's were. There were numerous attempts from camps in Britain, the most famous being from Island Camp 198 in Bridgend. On the night of 11th March 1945, seventy tunnelled to a short lived freedom, the majority were captured within the week; some managed to get as far afield as Southampton and Castle Bromwich, 110 miles away. You need to read the account, it is very amusing and would I believe make a great story and film. The following is an extract from the following web site www.islandfarm.fsnet.co.uk –

'As Ludwig and Herzler made their way, they encountered a drunken man returning home. Ludwig and Herzler decided to hide in a nearby garden but unfortunately the garden they chose to hide in belonged to the drunken man. As the man entered through the garden gate he decided that his call of nature was too great and decided to urinate into one of his garden bushes. Unfortunately, this was the hedge Karl Ludwig happened to be hiding! Having to relieved himself the drunken man went into his house unaware that he had done something to an SS Officer that many people in Britain at the time would have given up 10 years of their lives to do.'

One or two German POW's did manage to escape and get back home. Two managed to escape from Glen Mill camp 168 to Hamburg and then had the cheek to send a letter to the camp Commandant:

"Would not be coming back to enjoy any more of your kind hospitality."

One of the most colourful attempts was reported in the Daily Mail on the 16th July 1946.

People waiting on Stowmarket station for the 10.30am train were surprised when a beautiful blonde girl and her escort were arrested.

Although the blonde girl spoke excellent English this did not fool the Victor Noller a shunter who immediately notified the police. Fortunately they offered no resistance. The blonde in fact was 20 year old Richard Siegfried. He was wearing a smart blouse, blue trousers and padded out to show a fine womanly figure and make up. His escort Norbert Wedel was wearing his prison suit and is probably way Victor was suspicious. They had both escaped Botesdale, Suffolk.

Italy signed an armistice on the 3rd September 1943 which came into force on the 8th September 1943. 50,000 Italian troops transferred over to the Allied side. Mussolini who had been arrested on the orders of King Victor Emmanuel III was dramatically rescued by the Germans and on the orders of Hitler set up a puppet state in Northern Italy. He was eventually shot by Italian partisans on the 28th April 1945. This meant from 1943 the situation in Great Britain improved for the Italians and many more joined the British war effort.

CHAPTER
(International Commission Red Cross Reports)

On Saturday 26th March 2011 a large brown envelope dropped through my letter box. It was from the International Commission of the Red Cross (ICRC) in Geneva. Thankfully it was still in one piece and hadn't been seen as a play thing by my four German shepherds and literarily ripped to pieces, which was their want if the mood took them with such invasions of their home when we were out.

My wife and I had been out shopping in Basildon Town centre on what had started out as a slightly misty and over cast morning. The onset of spring hadn't quite managed to break through yet even though we were fast approaching the month of April. Once we had managed to fight our way into the house through the throng of 'glad to see you dogs' I panicked momentarily when I saw the envelope on the floor. My worst fears were quickly relieved when I picked it up and realised that it was still intact although slightly wet from some inquisitive slobbering from one of the dogs.

I knew exactly what the contents of the envelope were going to be as I had previously e-mailed the ICRC requesting copies of official reports for visits to Camp 266 by ICRC personnel during and immediately after the end of the Second World War. Even though I knew what was in the envelope I was suddenly overcome with excitement. I was just like a little kid who had just received a long awaited birthday card that he knew had a fifty pound note tucked away inside it. I calmly walked in to the kitchen placed the envelope down on the granite work surface, switched on the kettle and made myself a much needed couple of tea.

These reports recorded visits that had taken place at the camp over sixty years earlier so I guessed that a few more minutes wouldn't really make that much difference in the greater scheme of things.

Once up in my study I switched on the computer, placed the still unopened brown envelope on my desk and took a sip of my tea. As soon as I had opened it I was almost transported back in time to a bygone era.

Looking at them and holding them in my hands, even though they were only copies was truly an amazing feeling.

Each was written in that old fashioned and easily recognisable type set that recorded everything and anything that was typed back in those days was universal the world over, well certainly any country where English or European languages were spoken.

What I had in front of me were four official reports from the ICRC of visits that they had carried out at the German prisoner of war camp, number 266, in Langdon Hills in Essex. At first glance I noticed that the reports really did give an insight into what life was actually like inside the camp for those who were incarcerated in it. It was as if the camp was being reborn and brought back to life all these years later by ordinary sheets of paper and black ink from a type writer, a piece of equipment that is rarely used these days.

Here I want to pick out some of the points that are contained within them which I feel highlight camp life and what it was truly like for those incarcerated there.

The first report that we are going to take a look at is actually a record of the last of the four visits which ICRC staff paid to the Camp on the 22nd March 1948 which was almost three years after the end of the war. The visit was carried out by a Mr E. Aeberhand.

It struck me whilst looking at the date of the visit how difficult an experience it must have been for those prisoners who were still being held there that long after the war had finished.

I take in to account of course that these men had been soldiers of an enemy army who had chosen to fight against us for whatever reason. I then tried to imagine what it must have been like fighting in a war for my country, out of what I saw as being no more than a sense of moral duty, only to then be taken prisoner and incarcerated as an enemy combatant. Most of us would understand that chronology of events however much of a negative experience it might prove to be.

It must have been a further trauma to subsequently find out that their nation had in fact lost the war in which they had fought in and that they now had no idea what had happened to their loved one's back home, nor their loved ones about what had become of them.

My own sons had each been to war on two occasions whilst fighting in Afghanistan during 2008, 2009, 2010 and 2011and as a parent one of the things that helped keep me sane through those difficult times was knowing that each tour of duty that they were sent on would only last for six months and not years. During those deployments they came home for a two week period of recreation and recuperation (R&R) and whilst out in Afghanistan they could speak to me on the phone quite often, with duty commitments allowing of course.

For soldiers who had fought during the Second World War those times scales would have been totally different with some not returning home or seeing their loved ones for years.

The report started off by recording that the officer in overall charge was the camp Commandant, a Lieutenant-Colonel F. Cronin. It struck me that for a position that was not the most prestigious of jobs by any stretch of the imagination, he was a very high ranking officer indeed. The position did have its advantages, the most obvious one being that it came with a lovely big house that was situated just opposite the main gates of the camp, although as far as we have been able to establish the only officer to actually have lived in it was Captain Messenger. It still stands there today as a private residence.

Having stood outside the house and looked across the road to where the prisoner of war camp had once stood it struck me that not only was it as close as it was possible to be without being inside the camp itself but the Commandant could have actually stayed at home each day, opened his upstairs bedroom window, barked out his orders and instructions, closed the window and gone back to bed.

The report then moved on to the number of prisoners that were being held at the camp. I was absolutely staggered when I read that there were a total of one thousand seven hundred and ninety one. I immediately knew that number could not possibly be correct. It would not have been possible to have held that many prisoners in the camp knowing the size that it once was. This was now 1948, nearly three years since the end of the war, but when I looked at it more closely I noticed that although the report was about a visit to the Langdon Hills camp when it came to the overall numbers of prisoners it also included those who were billeted at nearby satellite camps and hostels at such places as Tillingham, Purfleet, Harold Wood and Great Wakering to name but a few.

There were only two hundred and fifty German prisoners still being held in the main camp at Langdon Hills, which was designed to hold some seven hundred and fifty men. These were waiting to be released and repatriated back to Germany. Some had even taken what I can only imagine for them as being the extremely difficult decision to stay behind in England and start a new life for themselves. For some this was a decision based on emotion having met and fallen in love with a local girl. For others it was based on practicalities rather than a burning desire to stay in England.

After the war Germany was split up with different areas coming under the control of the allied nations of France, America and Great Britain in what became West Germany and other areas that were to remain under the control of the Russian authorities in what became East Germany. The thought of returning to their homeland that was now in the control of the Russians was more than some could contemplate. In total there were approximately 25,000 German prisoners of war who remained here rather than return to their own country to become as they saw it, a prisoner all over again.

For some reason (I am not sure why) I had always believed that Camp 266 had housed Italian Prisoners of war as well as Germans. This report showed that this was in fact not the case, as all of the camps prisoners were clearly recorded as being German.

The report also listed the senior German officer at the camp and therefore the person who was in charge of all of the German prisoners present as being Feldw. Rolf Zimmerman. Feldw. was the shortening of the German rank of Feldwebel, which would be the equivalent rank of Colour Sergeant in the British Army.

In February 2011, we managed to purchase the following letter on e-bay that had been sent from camp 266 in Langdon Hills to a Herr. Zimmerman who was at the time was living at an address in Germany.

Chelmer Road 25 Nov. 1946

To Franz Zimmermann

"I was so grateful to receive your lovely letter. I hope you're in good health. I'm now exchanging letters with Anneliese and Gerd. Werner has also written from Mainz and I received it within 10 days. I think you can just try to write direct now. I was shocked at Anneliese's circumstances. I've often written that you should write the truth to me. I'm interested in anything to do with her, with Mainz or anything else that's happening. I would also ask you to write more often than once a month.

Don't think that in England we've got heaven on earth. Even if we've got it better than you, it is what's happening to you in your mind that is crucial. I can assure you that with time 75% of all prisoners are affected mentally, and you'll be amazed at what strange figures will come home one day. I also think that we'll bring our own particular view of life back with us, quite different from the current one. I hope and wish that this letter will reach you in the best of health. Chin up! Love and kisses. Ralf. Georg

The script the letter was written in was a form of old German that was taught throughout the 19th Century until the end of the Nazi period. So it was difficult to translate some of the words. For example 'a' and 'o' was difficult to distinguish. One of the signatures at the end of the letter translated as 'Ralf' could and is more likely to have been 'Rolf'. This being it was possible that of Rolf Zimmermann the senior German Officer at the camp.

The addressee was Franz Zimmermann, so was there a family connection, possibly brothers. The tone of the first paragraphs' – *"I've often written that you should write the truth to me"* strengthens the possibility of a close family connection.

The tone of the letter also indicates that the POW's in England were fully aware of the state that Germany was in following their defeat. The second paragraph also strengthens our belief that it was written by a senior officer *" I can assure you that with time 75% of all prisoners are affected mentally and you'll be amazed at what strange figures will come home one day etc, etc, "*

This does not appear to be the writing of a private within the Germany Army but of an Officer who could see the change in those beneath him. Either through the education program that they were obviously subjected to or their increasing involvement with the local population that was changing their views on life.

The next question is who was Franz Zimmermann, well it appears that he was a well-known entrepreneur from Mainz in South West Germany and whose main claim to fame seems to have been the invention of a pressure lamp (like a Tilley Lamp).

The German rank structure was such that somebody with the rank of Feldwebel could either be in the regular German Army or the Luftwaffe. The report doesn't go as far as informing us which branch of the German armed forces Rolf Zimmerman was part of.

The report also recorded that Zimmerman's deputy was Uffz. Heinz Froebel. Uffz. was the shortening of the German rank of Unteroffizier which again meant that he could have been in either the regular German Army or the Luftwaffe and was the equivalent rank to that of a Corporal. The report also recorded the details by name and rank of the Germans Priest, medical officer and dental mechanic.

The day after the visit by the ICRC the report records that a group of twenty-three of the prisoners were being released from the camp and being repatriated back to Germany as was their choice. That must have been a very surreal moment for them all. On the one hand they would have had a feeling of happiness at being free again after having been held in captivity for so long, only to be quickly followed by mixed emotions of the uncertainty of not knowing what they were going back home to. Were their homes still there intact? Were their loved ones still there waiting for them? How were they going to feel about each other after being apart for so long?

Even down to not knowing whether they were they alive or dead?

One has to remember some of these prisoners had not been home to Germany or seen their families for up to nine years. They had gone off to fight a war one day, kissed their loved ones good bye and that was the last they had seen of each other.

I couldn't begin to imagine how I would feel emotionally and mentally if I had been separated from my family for such a long period of time. It doesn't bare thinking about.

Each prisoner lived in a wooden hut which gave the place its nick name amongst locals of the Hutted Camp. They had their own bed and were allocated four blankets, one pillow and a straw mattress which rested on a number of wooden slats that ran across the bed. Imagine how uncomfortable that must have been. I bet it was a very slow process when it came to getting out of bed in the morning. Just getting the aches and pains of a nights slumber out of their bodies must have been a major achievement in its self.

The camp had its own small infirmary which had 12 beds in it. The report records that on the day of the visit by the ICRC inspector only two of the beds were being used by patients but there is no record of why they were there. The infirmary was also well staffed. Besides the senior German medical officer there were also three junior medical officers all of whom were German and not provided by the British. Also surprising the medical supplies were described as being sufficient during a time when everything was in short supply. There had been no deaths at the camp since the previous ICRC visit the previous year.

For some reason which isn't explained in the report some other prisoners were moved into the camp and at the time of their arrival they were badly dressed. What was actually meant is not recorded, but the fact that they came from Camp 116 which was the Mill Lane camp in Hatfield Heath also in Essex and Camp 286 which was from just down the road in Purfleet, is a slightly strange comment to make without any additional explanation attached to it.

That got me thinking about why they were transferred in to the camp in the first place. I could come up with only two possible conclusions, one that these other camps were in the process of closing down or that Langdon Hills was been used as a sort of transit camp for soon to be released prisoners. Hans Baldes, (More on him later in the book) we know had been a prisoner at Camp 286 in Purfleet and although they were closer to the docks at Tilbury, he was transferred to Langdon Hills when it came time for him to be released and repatriated.

Under point twenty-four of the report and under the heading of 'any other remarks,' the following was written.

"Some difficulties have arisen lately with the accounts officer, Captain Benney who was formerly of the Berkhampton Court camp, about the welfare fund and the disposal of money and musical instruments. When our delegate was about to leave the camp, no officers could be found to speak with them."

There was no explanation in the report explaining why or when Captain Benney had moved from his previous camp to the one at Langdon Hills or what he had actually done, only innuendo. One has to assume that the musical instruments had gone missing somewhere along the line as later in the report the senior German medical officer in the camp asks for '3 Isoplast, both sizes,' and a set of musical instruments.

Three prisoners were also in 'detention' when the ICRC member visited the camp, but what they had done to deserve their punishment or how long it was to last for were not recorded.

It intrigued me somewhat that there were no British officers present at all when the visit took place, a point that was commented on by the ICRC representative Mr E. A. Aeberhard in his report. I would have thought that this was a most unusual situation for him to have found himself confronted with. Was it because the financial irregularities with the accounts were known of within the camp and no officer wanted to put themselves in the potentially embarrassing and difficult position of having to be questioned on the matter by Mr Aeberhard?

What would also have been embarrassing for the British officers was the knowledge that the German POW Camp leader would have also been given a copy of the ICRC's report covering his visit. The next meeting between the camp Commandant and the German camp leader would I assume have been an extremely awkward one indeed, for the British.

The next report that I want to look at is of the previous ICRC visit which had taken place only four months earlier on bonfire night, 5th November 1947. It was carried out by a Dr G. Hoffman. The camp Commandant was shown as being Lt. Colonel. J.C. Cronin. The German camp leader and his assistant were both the same as they were for the next visit. When I compared this report with the other three that I had it somehow didn't seem as complete as they were. I don't mean there was anything missing from the report it just seemed that there were more detail in the other reports than this one.

Besides the camp at Langdon Hills, Dr Hoffman also went on to visit German POW's at accommodation hostels at Chelmer Road in Chelmsford, another two at Tillingham, one at Great Wakering and another at Hylands Hall in Chelmsford.

A very brief history of Hylands Hall is worth a mention here seeing as it is included in the report as one of the satellite camps to Langdon Hills. During the First World War it was requisitioned for use as a military hospital and over one thousand five hundred wounded British soldiers were treated there. The owner of it during the Second World War was Christine Hanbury whose late husband had been John Hanbury who was the Chairman of the brewers Truman's. The Hanbury's son, John who was affectionately known as Jock, was a member of the RAF and became one of the first pilots to die during the war as a result of a flying accident.

Ironically at the same time as a part of the grounds were used as a German POW camp other parts of it were being used as the wireless command post for the 6th Anti-Aircraft Division.

In 1944 the house itself became the headquarters for the newly formed SAS. Mrs Hanbury cheerfully accepted their presence and was regularly invited to dine in the Officers Mess. On one memorable occasion, Captain Paddy Blair Maine (who went on to become this country's most decorated soldier) attempted to drive a Jeep up the Grand Staircase for a bet. The incident caused much commotion and Christine Hanbury dispatched the men to bed with instructions to remove the Jeep in the morning when they had clearer heads. The Jeep had to be dismantled before it could be removed.

The first thing that struck me about the report of November 1947 was the number of German POW's that were being held in the camp, 206 in total, yet at all of the satellite camps the numbers were always higher, maybe not excessively so, but higher all the same. I found this slightly odd as I naturally assumed that what after all was the main camp would hold the most prisoners especially as it had a capacity to hold up to 750 men.

One of the items on the report was so strange that I had to read it again to make sure that I had not misread it. Point 15 covered the heading of clothing. I read on, and I quote; "Winter underwear has been supplied. No complaints." I never knew that there was a difference. A thicker pair of socks. A heavier jacket or a wooly jumper I can fully comprehend and at different times in my life I have had owned all three items. Even a pair of gloves a scarf and a bobble hat for when it really gets cold and the snows come, I would even stretch to a vest if I really had to, but what are winter pants? Not only have I never seen a pair I didnt know they even existed. It really must have been a very cold winter back in 1947 thats all I can say. Mind you in the same report the prisoners were also provided with short sleeved shirts as part of their winter clothing which in some ways seems just as strange a thing to do as the issuing of these winter pants.

It also noted that 75% of the prisoners were working in agriculture. Seeing as the entire area near to the camp was a combination of farms, green fields, wooded areas and cows that was something I didn't find too surprising. The rest worked for the Ministry of works which was a combination of roads and contruction projects. This wasnt slave labour either, with all of the prisoners being paid a fair wage for their endeavours.

Another thing that surprised me reading through the report was the amount of books there were for the prisoners to read. There were a selection of fiction and non-fictional titles both in English and German. In total it is recorded in the report that there were 2780 books and still more were being requested. That was an astonishing amount of books for just over two hundred prisoners.

Dr. Hoffman commented on the fact that he thought Langdon Hills was a "Fairly good camp."

Eight months earlier Camp 266 had been visited again. This time the date was 18th March 1947. The visiting ICRC member was once again Dr. G. Hoffman. The German Camp Leader was different on this occasion. This time it was Uffz. Horst Berg and his deputy and the Assistant Camp Leader was the rather unfortunately named Obergefr. Hans Nobbe. Although in saying that I am not sure if it had the same conetations all those years ago as it has today.

The camp Commondant had once again changed, this time it was Lt. Colonel. H. S. Hobby and at the time of the visit there were 382 German POW's recorded as being incarcerated there.

The report stated that each of the accomodation huts had two tierd wooden bunk beds for the prisoners to sleep in who in turn were each allocated three blankets. The camps provided for a strange environment for the prisoners depending on what time of year it was. In the winter months they could be far too cold as they had no insulation to help keep the inclement weather at bay and in the summer they could be far too hot and almost sauna like inside.

During the miners strike of 1983/1984 I was a young Police officer starting out on my policing career. I stayed at an old Army camp named Proteus, as I recall it was actually part of Sherwood Forest somewhere in the Nottongham area. During the winter months of the strike I stayed there twice and during the night it could be very cold indeed, so I thought I was being very clever by getting myself one of the bunks that was closest to the coal fuelled heaters that were set out in the middle of each hut. There were three in the hut if I remember correctly.

My bed space was so warm when I went to sleep that I had to lie on top of the bed just in my underpants. The problem was that at about two oclock in the morning when the coal fuelled heater ran out of coal and the heater turned itself off, it would then start to get cold very quickly indeed. I can remember waking up in the early hours one morning feeling so cold that I quickly darted under the bed sheets and blankets in an effort to warm myself up again.

After a week of living like this I was exhausted. I would wake up the following morning feeling like I hadnt been to sleep but as I was only there for a short period of time it was doable, but how I would have felt after a month, a year or longer, I really couldnt say. That aspect of camp life alone must have been relatively draining.

I always thought that the name Proteus was a strange one for an Army camp so I looked into the origins of the name. In Greek mythology, Proteus was a sea god and according to the Greek Poet, Homer, he lived on the sandy island of Pharo which was situated just off of the Nile Delta. There you go, I bet you didnt think you would be finding out about Greek Mythology when you picked up this book to read. When I stayed there back in 1983/1984 it was an Army training camp and had been since the early 1940's when it was used by both British and American troops. The MOD eventually sold it off in October 2004 when it was then turned into holiday lodges.

Anyway, back to Langdon Hills again. The camps infirmary was quite an affair with thirty-eight beds available for sick prisoners at anyone time. On the day of the visit nine of the beds were occupied. Three of them were prisoners who were suspected of having T.B. To administer all of this was just one Doctor and two medical orderlies.

Since the previous ICRC visit there had sadly been two deaths at the camp. On the 10th November 1946, 39 year old Obergefr. (266669) Richard Shulze died of T.B. and on the 23rd May 1947, Gerf. (733530) Guenther Meise died from a combination of T.B. and Menningitus. In Meise's case he had only just 'celebrated' his 21st birthday a matter of days before he died. I found it really sad reading about their deaths. Here were two men, two soldiers who had both survived the horrors of war but who ultimately were still to be claimed as its casualties two years after the war had ended without having had the opportunity of returning home to see their loved ones.

It was even more poignant for Ken and I in the case of Meise. Before I had received the ICRC reports we had managed to discover Geunther Meise and the story of his death and subsequent burial from local church records. We were even more fortunate when Ken discovered two photographs of Meise's funeral which allowed us to pinpoint exactly where he was buried.

On a really nice spring afternoon in March 2011, Ken and I visited the cemetery where Meise had been buried. We had the number of his actual grave and from the photographs we had we were able to accurately pin point where Meise's grave should have been. Although search as we might we could find no trace of Guenther Meise's grave. We are left with the only possible conclusion that his remains were eventually sent back to his family in Germany. If that was the case it was most definately not the repatriation that they would have been hoping for.

It was a very moving moment for both of us to have been stood by the grave of a brave young man whose life had sadly been expunged at such a young age, not by injuries sustained in war but by an unrelated illness.

My feelings were heightened even more so, because in March 2011 both of my sons, who were 23 and 24 years of age at the time, were serving their country in Afghanistan. Thankfully both of my sons came back to me safe and well.

When you hear of young men dying of such ailments whilst living in such a tightly confined environment with so many of their colleagues you naturally assume that there must have been an epidemic taking place, but thankfully there wasnt as the general health of the prisoners was recorded as being, "Gut."

The report recorded the fact that when German POW's were repatriated they were only allowed to take with them one set of clothing from the camp. I have no idea what happened to the rest of what was left behind.

Returning to Gunther Meise for a moment, Ken found an article from the Southend District Times and Laindon Recorder, dated Wednesday 4th June 1947, which was a report of Gunther Meise's funeral. I have copied it word for word below.

POW's Funeral At Landon Hills

Impressive Service

The first German POW funeral in Laindon & District took place at St Mary's Church Langdon Hills when more than 40 prisoners of war from Tillingham Hostel and the Headquarters camp at Langdon Hills (266 German POW Working Camp) paid tribute to POW Gunther Meise aged 21 (Tillingham Hostel) who died twelve days ago after he had been admitted to Southend Hospital. The Church was beautifully decorated with wreaths and bunches of wild flowers which were later laid at the grave by the deceaseds comrades.

Particularly impressive in its sincerity was the singing at the grave which followed the removal of the coffin from the church.

Lieut-Colonel J.H.Constable, officer Commanding 266 POW Camp and the Adjutant Capt. J.E.Messenger, represented the British armed Forces at the service conducted by a German Catholic padre, POW Jacobs. The grave is in the east side of the churchyard, beneath two large elms just inside the Church gates.

After the service had been completed, a close friend of the deceased stepped forward to place a large and magnificent wreath on the grave and at the same time paid respect to his dead comrade in a lengthy speech of tribute."

I was interested to note that there was no mention of what Meise died of, whether that was a simple oversight or for other reasons, I don't know.

The funeral of Gunther Meise. 4th June 1947
Photograph by kind permission of Erwin Hannerman

Just 14 days after Meise's funeral, Camp 266 was visited by the Red Cross. In the subsequent report of the visit the death of Meise was recorded. Reading through the report it reads as if he was a prisoner at the Langdon Hills camp, where as the above newspaper article shows him as being from the Tillingham camp, which also makes no sense or otherwise he would most probably have been buried at a Church nearer to Tillingham rather than bring him all the way to Langdon Hills to bury him.

The report also showed that there were 382 prisoners staying at the Langdon Hills camp and 92 staying at Tillingham, a total of 474 POW's, yet only 40 attended Meise's funeral.

It was also interesting that in the two weeks between the funeral of Meise and the visit to Langdon Hills camp by the Red Cross the Camp Commandant had changed from Lieut-Colonel J.H.Constable to Lieut-Colonel H.S.Hobby.

An interesting fact about Lieut-Colonel J.H.Constable is that he was the great-grandson of the artist John Constable (1776 – 1837).

For the first time in any of the reports this one mentioned prisoners who had managed to escape. There was nothing recorded about the names of the prisoners. How they escaped. How long they were at large for. How far they managed to get or how they came to be recaptured. It did record that all three of them were recaptured and that one was punished with fourteen days, but fourteen days of what it doesnt say. I am assuming that refers to loss of privileges or days locked up in a cell. Another was court marshalled for a combination of the escape and additional charges (No clarification about what these were). The third man was transferred to Camp 186 which was at Berechurch Hall near Colchester which was also a screening and interrogation centre. He also had his repatriation deferred for three months

On the one hand you might think it strange German POW's trying to escape two years after the war had finished. It didnt make sense especially as travelling anywhere without the correct papers would certainly have made life extremely difficult especially for a German. Not having papers on you that proved who you were and where you had been for the past couple of years would raise suspicions that would most certainly get you arrested and locked up yet again. Only when it came time to being designated for repatriation were you provided with the relevant documentation. It was possible to purchase similar forged documents on the black market, but at great expense and much, much more than an escaping German POW could ever possibly expect to be able to afford.

I think this simply hi-lights the extreme stress that most POW's found themselves experiencing, knowing that the war was over and simply wanting to be able to get back to their families and loved ones, whilst not being able to fully understand the reasons that were preventing them from doing so.

The Daily Mirror reported on the 22nd August 1946 that almost every day reports were being received of German prisoners escaping in and around the towns of Broadstairs and Folkestone. Also at least six vessels had disappeared in the previous five days. One such yacht was the Laiun which disappeared from Dover.

The following day the Daily Mail reported that Mrs Doris Blake, 25 year old English mother and German prisoner Alexander Todt had been arrested in France trying to escape back to Germany.

Alexander Todt was the son of Hitler's Minister of Labour the man who built the West Wall and Germany's motor roads. Doris had met him before the war at a dance when he was a university student and was surprised when she met him again working as a POW on the same farm in Hoddesdon, Hertfordshire where she was working.

They decided to try and get to Germany, after a few days in London, Ramsgate and then Dover they swam out to the yacht Laiun. Actually Doris could not swim so she floated on her back and Todt towed her by her hair.

Bad weather forced them into Calais harbour and were arrested when they landed. They were both returned to England.

There were also 13 prisoners at the camp who had been placed on 'light duties' for different reasons. It was intended to send them to the POW hospital at Diss in Norfolk which was actually part of the German POW Camp number 231 that was situated there.

There were four priosners who had been identified as being the most urgent cases.

(1). (246449). Uffz. Gerhard Neumann, who had a relapse of a hernia
(2). (788482). Soldat. Heinrich Killich, who had a relapse of a hernia.
(3). (052365). Obergefr. Karl Zimmermann, who was suffering with chronic eczema.
(4). (727394). Gefr. Guenther Groth, for after effects of concussion.

There was also a request by Prisoner B254073. Soldat. Jacob Berchtold who wanted to be transferred to Camp 145 at Battle in Hastings. The reason behind this request was because his brother, B126388. George Berchtold was being held there.

Langdon Hills was described in the report by Dr. G. Hoffman as being a big, well organised Camp with good accomodation.

All of the camps throughout the UK had a real mixed bunch of prisoners in their midst to accomodate and deal with. A lot of the early prisoners taken between 1939 -1941 in particular would have been of the more die-hard Nazi symphasizers from U-Boat crews. Luftwaffe pilots or the Africa Corps. They quite often had an arrogance about them that came hand in hand with the genuine belief that they were part of a master race. As time went on this arrogance wained as normal everyday Whermacht German soldiers swelled their ranks coupled with a somewhat belated understanding that the Third Reich was not in fact going to last for a thousand years but was a defeated Germany which now lay in ruins and destruction.

The most interesting of the reports and the reason why I left it until last to talk about was because it was typed up in French and not translated into English. It was of a visit that took place on the 3rd September 1945, just four months after the 2nd World War had ended. I managed to translate it with a combination of my own knowledge of French from my school days and a French friend of mine.

This visit was conducted by Monsieur M. Chavan. The Camp Commandant at the time was a Major. F. W. Lynch. The Camp Leader was (934511). Fedlw. Oswald Fullner and his deputy was (B74028). Wachm. Erich Mueller. In total there were 660 German POW's being held in the camp.

Monsieur Chavan's report also includes information that suggests that the Camp was not in fact designed and built for a life as that of a Prisoner of War camp but in fact for the well being of the local population should there be the need to evacuate them to a central location ay in the case of a major bombing of the area by the German Luftwaffe. I feel that this was highly unlightly because other than plenty of fields and forestry in the immediate vicinity there was nothing of that importance in the local area.

The report doesnt expand on how Monsieur Chavan knew that information or where the need for such a camp ever came from. It goes on to say that prisoners live in well aired barrack style accomodation. The prisoners appreciated the absence of any barbed wire around the camp which helped influence their opinion of morale.

Each prisoner had their own bed which had a straw matress. Although that might sound strange to hear today, back then it would have been quite normal for the time. They were also given three blankets and a pillow case. Although the camp had no showers, which in fairness were still a comparitively new invention, they did have access to 15 baths to share.

The POW's from the camp worked between 48 to 56 hours a week, mainly in the local agricultural industry. Their rate of pay was one and a half pence per hour with the POW's not been allowed to earn more than six shillings per week. Once again there is no explanation as to why this is was the case.

There was a request for a full time dentist in the camp as those who performed the role at the time were only prepared to carry out extractions in the case of an emergency suggesting that they were not actually qualified dentists. The prisoners teeth were generally in a poor state of repair according to the report which would suggest an urgent need for a full time, qualified Dentist.

There appeared to be some constination concerning the amount of cigarettes that were available to the POW's with each prisoner only being provided with 15 a week. It was noted that although there is the space available in the camp for a sports pitch the POW's lack the equipment to use it to any great degree. There was also a request for a radio and a notification that the showing of films were soon to commence.

There were requests for a football and a handball. More cigarettes for each of the POW's. Medical literature for the Doctor. More books were requested along with teaching materials in both French and English. They also wanted, in no particular order, coloured crayons, a violin along with other musical instruments, playing cards and books

In closing his report Monsieur Chavan noted the positive mood in the camp mainly he said due to the excellent communication between the Camp Commandant and the camp leader.

The reports record that the camp was well run and that morale was generally very good amongst the prisoners. It doesn't strike me from having read any of the reports that there was any disquiet in the camp. In saying that I fully accept that written reports do not always record correctly and honesty how any given situation is, but whilst researching this book and listening to the accounts and memories of ex German POW's who stayed at the camp, it would appear that the ICRC reports are absolutely spot on in their diagnosis.

CHAPTER
(Tillingham Camp)

Tillingham is a large village that is situated about two miles from the sea and the estuary of the Blackwater river. It is a very peaceful and tranquil location.

During the Second World War there were two German Prisoner of War camps situated in the area. Tillingham one and Tillingham two. Tillingham was one of the satellite POW Camps that was attached to the main camp at Langdon Hills.

A report of a Red Cross visit to the Tillingham Camp on the 5th November 1947 by a Dr G. Hoffman, showed that there were125 German POW's incarcerated at Tillingham one camp and a further 293 POW's at the Tillingham two camp. The report makes no other comment about either of the Tillingham camps. The Red Cross paid another visit to Tillingham on the 22nd March 1948 this time by a Mr E. A. Aeberhard. This visit doesn't distinguish whether the visit was made to either camp one or camp two. It just records the visit as having been to the Tillingham camp, showing a total of 160 German POW's.

Photograph by kind permission of Kevin Bruce.

Local farmer Bob Hawkins with German POW's at Shinglefords Farm, Tillingham, Essex. From the look of the snow the picture was probably taken in the bad winter of 1947.

The site of the Great Wakering POW camp.
Another satellite camp attached to Langdon Hills Camp 266
Photograph by kind permission Eberhard Fischer.

Mitza Balaam was the sister of Hubert Meyer, a German soldier who had been held as a POW at the Tillingham camp. She remembers her brother talking about a place called Leggets Farm in Tillingham where German officers were kept. Maybe this is Tillingham two and the reason for the two camps was no more than one was for the ranks and one for the officers.

The location of the second Tillingham camp was believed to have been at Lower Barn Farm, but this has never been totally confirmed. It's strange to think that all these years later some other POW camps up and down the country have still not had their exact location fully identified.

In September 1943, Bow Challis saw a German Messerschmitt aircraft brought down by a Spitfire. The pilot only just managed to get his parachute open in time before he hit the ground. Challis recalls that the German pilot was a young lad with blond hair, "just some mother's lad." Challis started to approach him to make sure that he was alright but soldiers got to him first and he was taken away.

Challis had a gang of 4 Germans working, for him. They were often used for sugar beet hoeing, and thrashing on his farm.

147

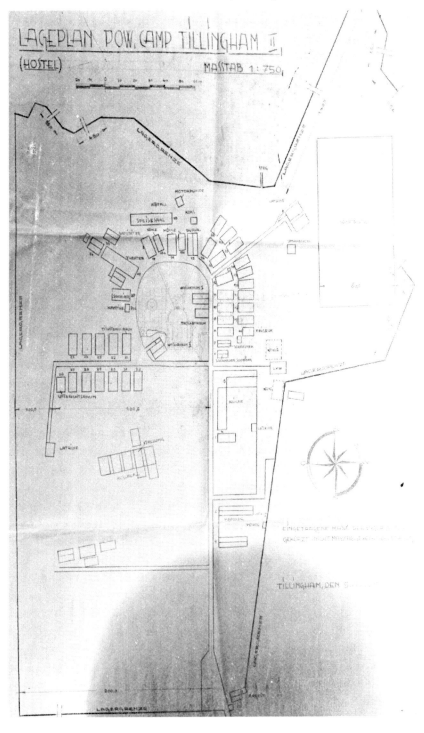

POW Camp Plan Tillingham, Translation of details from plan.

Lagergrenze	Boundary
Auslauf	Outlet
Stallung	Stabling
Kammer	Clothing room. ...store?
Trockenraum	Drying room
Waschraum	Wash room
Tischtennisraum	Table tennis
Unterichteraum	Instruction room
Kohle	Coal
Sanitater	Hospital. . . . .sick quarters
Kuche	Kitchen
Duschraum	Showers
Jauchegrube	Cess pit
Steg	Footpath. . . . bridge
Abfall	Refuse
Koks	Coke
Speisesaal	Dining room
Friseur	Hairdresser
Schuchmacher	Cobbler
Schneider	Tailor
Schreiner	Carpenter/joiner
L K W	Lorries. . . .M.T.Section [Lastwagen]
Schreibstube	Administration.... orderly room
Arrest	Gatehouse. . .entrance. . . compulsory stop

The map of the camp and the following information concerning the POW camps at Tillingham is kindly reproduced here with the permission of Kevin Bruce.

The other Tillingham POW camp we know was situated at Marsh House Farm (TM 017033) or to be precise it was actually
situated to the south of Marsh House Farm House. The field it was in is still known locally as Camp Field.

This was originally the site for anti-aircraft guns. The camp was originally set up for use British forces, and included all the expected facilities needed for social life and recreation.

It was first used as a POW Camp following the allied invasion of France in June 1944, for German Prisoners who were subsequently employed to work on local farms. Several were employed at Cage Farm in Southminster for the owner of the farm, Mr Sibley. Others were also employed on Shinglefords farm in Tillingham, for Mr Hawkins. Some were also employed on Marsh House farm by the owner Mr George Raby.

Quite a few of the prisoners made items that they could sell which were usually wooden gifts or toys. They were not supposed to have money, so they kept their little enterprise well hidden from the camp guards. It wasn't just wood they turned any available materials into goods. Sacks were unravelled to be made into slippers. The rubber from old tyres was used to make soles and heels for shoes and boots. They even made small broaches in the form of different aircraft.

The central part of the camp was transformed into a delightful garden area. There were well maintained rockeries that had running water, willow trees, crazy paving as well as bridges.

Just as they did at Langdon Hills, local villagers were invited into the Tillingham camps to watch musical concerts and the like which were arranged and put on by the POW's.

Tillinghams POW's were no different from any others around the country and after the war several of them decided to stay in this country to work and live. Others on the other hand did the same simply to start a new life, whilst some did it to marry local girls.

Hubert Meyer married Barbara Keys. He used to work as a cow man at Eastlands Farm, Bradwell, for the farmer Mr Muirhead. He later went on to work for many years with the Essex Water Company.

Frank Fisher, was a single man became a welder at Rushton's Engineers, Southminster. He later helped out by working behind the bar at the Green Man public house in Bradwell.

CHAPTER
(Camp Newspapers)

Some 268 of the POW camps throughout the UK had their own newspapers or Lagerzeitungen that were written in German for the POW's. These camp papers are reported to have started out for no other reason than the POWs' desire to want them. In doing so they helped record how life was in the camps and also helped remind them of how life was back in their homeland before the war.

Most of the prisoners welcomed the papers even though the content of them was often vetted before they were sent off to be printed. A lot of the prisoners did not speak English so having something to read in their mother tongue was literarily a sight for sore eyes.

Those same papers are just as important today as they were when they were printed all though years ago. The difference is that today they are important not for the German POW's but for today's historians and authors who not only want to know what life was like in the camps, but they want to know about these men and how they filled their days. What they were thinking? How they saw life? What they were feeling? What were their expectations of the situation that they found themselves in now and in the future?

Being incarcerated would have been difficult enough but being incarcerated in a foreign country for doing your duty during a time of war and being separated from your loved ones as a result of it, must have been extremely difficult for the hardiest of individuals.

Newspapers, their content and the subsequent reading of them by the German POW's was useful to both sides and the longer the camps were open the more of a part they played.

This was certainly the case at Camp 266, whose inmates had started a paper quite spontaneously in order to enjoy doing something together, buying the necessary paper, stencils, and ink through the camp welfare fund. When a new duplicating machine was needed, funds simply did not stretch to a replacement, until a visiting adviser informed them that the Prisoner of War Department (POWD) would provide one and set the wheels in motion, with the result that the paper flourished once again.'

The newspapers were very popular amongst the prisoners as it gave them a direction, a positive that they could focus on together which helped give them a form of unity. It was something to a large extent that they had control over.

Although collectively they were simply called Lagerzeitung (Camp Newspaper) they were also given individual names by different camps. Some of the camps put a bit of thought in to the titles of these publications with names such as Wegweiser (signpost), Gluckauf (Safe Journey), Regenbogen (Rainbow) which I assume had some kind of unintentional sublimeable message attached to them for the prisoners benefit even if it was only a means to help them stay positive in their thoughts through what must have been difficult times.

Fortunately for us Peter Sinclair lodged 66 additions of the newspaper produced at Langdon Hills with the Imperial War Museum in London. Arrangements were made with the museum and I spent a pleasant day in their reading room perusing through them before arranging to six additions copied.

Camp 266's Lagerzeitung edition number three was entitled Vormarts. Which in English translates to, In front of Arts, It was only six pages long and although I am not going to translate it in its entirety in the pages in this book I will certainly give you a flavour of the contents of it. I will also take a look at some later editions of it as well to see if there were any noticeable changes in it such as attitudes, perceptions or editorial content for that matter. I suppose to a large degree that would depend on who the editor was at any given point in time.

It was printed Strangely enough on a Sunday and even more surprisingly on Armistice Day, 11th November 1945. Just above the date it had the word Halbmonartsschrift (Half Monthly Revue). Here are some of the sub headings of the articles it covered. Die Kluft Zwischen Den Generation (The Gap Between the Generations). Nutzt Die Zeit (Use the Time). Politik und Wirtschaft (Politics and Economics). There truly was a mixture of articles on widely different topics.

Under the heading An Alle Gutgessinten (And all disposed) the following passage was part of the article;

"Do you remember the conclusion Dr Hirch left us with after his recent lecture? He described the tremendous emergency which oppresses our homeland. What terrible misery our loved ones are exposed to at home, the inconceivable difficulties with reconstruction. He spoke of the lack of materials and a lack of people and he said to us how our homeland needed us, we who are still prisoners of war.

From talking to him I could tell he had a great love for his wife back home when he asked us to work ourselves and to use the time in captivity. Working ourselves to help those back home. You young ones for your mothers and fathers and us older ones for our women and children."

Another article particularly intrigued me to know what it said in English as it conjured up all kinds of possibilities with its title of Eines Britischen Offiziers Verteidigung. (A British Officer's Defence).The article relates to the trial of Nazis war criminal Hauptsturmfuhrer Josef Kramer who was the Deputy Camp Commandant of Auschwitz from May to November 1940 and from May to December 1944. He also went on to become the Commandant of Bergen-Belsen from December 1944 until it was liberated on the 17th April 1945 when he was arrested by British troops.

What I found really interesting about this is that Kramer's trial was actually going on at the time the article was printed in the Camps newspaper. It was complimentary of Major Thomas Winwood who the report says 'carries out a valiant and chivalrous defence of Kramer' throughout the trial which lasts for exactly two months, despite some would say his obvious guilt. When Kramer is subsequently found guilty on two counts of the ill treatment and

killings of prisoners under his control at both Bergen-Belsen and Auschwitz, he is sentenced to death. Winwood even goes as far as appealing the decision to Lord Mountbatten for clemency but is turned down and Kramer is eventually hanged on 13th December 1945 in Hameln prison in Luneburg, Germany.

When I first read the article I initially thought that the story related to a POW who had been incarcerated at Langdon Hills Camp 266, hence why it had been mentioned in the newspaper but it wasn't. Once Kramer was captured at Bergen-Belsen in 1945 he never left Germany before his trial and subsequent hanging.

On the bottom of page five of the newspaper there is even a request from the Lagerfuehrer for the men to box when they get the opportunity. There is no explanation as to why he requests this. There is no mention of any forth coming camp boxing event. Maybe it's simply because he wanted his men to stay fit and active.

There are also some jokes in English and songs and a crossword in German.

A high percentage of the German prisoners could not speak, read, write or even understand the most basic of English mainly because they had no desire to learn the language. The same had to be said of the soldiers who were guarding them when it came to their inability to speak German which wasn't very useful when it came to the need to communicate with each other on a regular basis and with just two interpreters in the Camp 266, that wasn't necessarily a good position to be in.

In an attempt to change these statistics, between April 1946 and May 1948 the British authorities brought out a fortnightly publication that was sixteen pages long that was entitled, 'English for All.' For some reason its starting point was an assumption that everybody who read it had a basic knowledge and understanding of English vocabulary which was most definitely not the case amongst the German prisoners of war. Each issue had a print run of 40,000 copies which were then distributed amongst all of the camps.

Prisoners were classified as A=Advanced, B=Intermediate, C=Beginners. Some parts were in English and some were in German and difficult words were always recorded in both languages. Articles that were included in the paper were parliament, the free press, Hyde Park speakers, ballet, radio, the postal system, police, the Oxford and Cambridge boat race, coal mining, Quakers, lifeboats, historic houses, pantomimes, Christmas, stories, sayings, jokes, biographies, crosswords, crafts, humorous anecdotes, English grammar, English & American phrases, medicine, the home, railway stations, street scene, gardening, public schools, horseracing, football, cricket, art, plays and music.

The Prisoner of War Recreation Association (POWRA) was aware that the prolonged incarceration of prison life could lead to the stagnation of the mind for anybody who is detained in such a manner especially when it has the added stress of being in a foreign country.

In 1941 POWRA started a German language newspaper for German POW's being detained in Great Britain. Its title was Wochenpost (Weekly Post).

The newspaper was edited by Bernhard Reichenbach and published in London and sent out to all camps across Great Britain. There was enough for at least one copy for every six POW's. The papers content and what was allowed to be included in it was decided on by The Prisoner of War Department at the Foreign Office.

One of its editions contained the facts that between 1939 and December1947 there were 1254 deaths throughout all of the camps. 219 of these were recorded as suicides. It didn't however record the causes of the other deaths. Why someone had made the decision to include such a piece of information in a newspaper intended for German POW's was not explained. I for one couldn't see the sense in it.

However, as the national dailies were reporting such events, I suppose there was no need to keep it from the POW's. The Daily Mail on the 27th August 1946 reported the following two suicides:-

"Twenty-one year old Heinrich Holze, German prisoner of war hanged himself in a camp in Guildford Surrey. The coroner said:

"The continual confinement may have something to do with this unfortunate boy taking this extreme course. It is hoped as many of us think, that these German prisoners will be returned to their country with the greatest of speed."

Another unfortunate, 39 year old Karl Panwitz hanged himself in camp Swanwick Derbyshire. He left the following message:

"I have been very nervous and sick at heart and my spirit is broken. I am not German born, though German extraction remains German."

Papers that were produced in-camp, the Lagerzeitungen, were not censored before being internally distributed. A summary of the Prisoner Of War Departments (POWD) attitude to censorship of camp newspapers published in November 1946 states at Regulation number 4:

"Due to the lack of British interpreter-translators all camp newspapers are regarded as not subject to censorship."

It was the duty of the camps Commanding Officer to inform himself of the paper's content and tone, a task he would normally delegate to his intelligence officer (IO), and instruct him to pass on any suspicious material.

In civilian life there are different types of newspapers that cover all types of tastes. These are basically split in to two categories, those that are known as the broadsheets and those that are known as the tabloids. Each paper will have reporters who cover different topics such as sport, politics, the arts, foreign affairs and so on. Even then the papers political allegiance tends to rest with the owner not the editor. At Camp 296 at Peters Hill, Sheffield, the unusual decision was taken to issue two separate newspapers to cater for the different needs of the POW's.

Zeit (Time) which was for what would be classed as the more discerning type of reader in the camp, came out on the first day of the month, and Halbzeit (Half-time) which was for the 'tabloid' type of reader, minus the semi-nude picture of a woman of course, came out on the fifteenth of each month.

Other camps papers focused on what they saw as the real day to day problems which they all faced as long term POW's. Such as health issues both of the mind and the body, nutrition and the main thing that ate away at all of them was the issue about when were they going home and why was it taking so long?

Not only did the newspapers give some really good insights into the lives and changing attitudes of the POW's, but they were also regarded by the Prisoner of War Department (POWD) of the Foreign Office, which had taken over the responsibility for re-education of German POW's from the Psychological Warfare Education Department (PWE) in 1944, as a good barometer as far as re-education was concerned. The POWD had noted in 1946 that 'they would reflect changes in political orientation, in mood, and in political activity', and in 1947 the department had described the camp newspapers as being both 'important as a means of exchanging free opinion' and also as 'a rich source for assuring the success of re-education'.

By June 1942, when the threat of invasion of mainland Britain was real, most German POW's had been transferred to camps in either Scotland Canada or North America (their numbers in Britain having dwindled to a mere 200). Because of the extremely low numbers of POW's now being held in the UK the decision was taken to suspend publication of Wochenpost.

After the allied successes in North Africa in 1943 and the Normandy landings in June 1944 and with the threat of invasion to the UK now no more than a distant memory, the numbers of mainly German and Italian POW's that were now flooding into the UK were very quickly heading into the hundreds of thousands. Mainly because of this Wochenpost was revived in November 1944, eventually publishing a further 186 weekly issues before it finally ceased publication in September 1948 when the last of the German POW's were repatriated.

The ending of political screening of the Lagerzeitugen finally took place in mid-July 1947 which provided POW's with a new freedom to express their own thoughts in articles and letters in what had in every sense become their own papers. It had recorded their lives and very existence for the past four years. It was actual proof, a written record if you will of what they had endured during their time as POW's and how they had overcome. War is hell, there is no argument against that but being held as a prisoner in a foreign country not knowing how your loved ones are, the state of your country and when you are going home, are feelings that can defeat the strongest of minds.

There were, of course, measures in place to pre-empt the need for censorship. Though POW's volunteered to act as editors, they were appointed or dismissed by their fellow in mates. It was often believed that those prisoners who were graded A, or at least B, were likely to be the more acceptable category that the British authorities would prefer, much more so than those who were classed as C's; in fact no more than 20 per cent of the chosen editors were graded A.

Grading had not been completed when the first papers were started, and was abandoned in July 1947, while papers continued to be issued until March 1948. More important than political orientation was the ability to attract contributors and readers, in short, to be an activist. All those who fancied becoming their camps Lagerzeitungen editor were sent away on six- to eight-week courses at Wilton Park, in West Sussex. It was also known as the 'Prisoners University'. Today Wilton Park is an executive agency of the British Foreign and Commonwealth Office, but back in 1946 it was part of the allies' mechanism at establishing a post war democracy in Germany.

Between January 1946 and June 1948 some 4,500 German POW's passed through Wilton Park. It would train future editors for the Camps newspapers and on passing out, equip them with a handbook of recommended topics and their presentation in future camp papers. Roving advisers would regularly visit these new camp editors' offices, thus forming a critical link between the POWD and POW's.

A statement by the POWD circulated for training advisers in March 1947 insisted that 'Censorship within the camp of origin, i.e. the withdrawal of the right of editor and contributors to express opinions freely, would entirely undermine their value for re-education.'

Some believed that this was a slightly risky strategy, but with the papers only for the POW's in the individual camps that they were written and distributed in, there was never any real substance to this belief.

Allowing and promoted the growth of the Prisoners own papers proved a much more beneficial strategy than forcing Wochenpost on them, a paper that not only wasn't liked by most of the POW's, but was despised by them as well. Most of them saw it as a British propaganda tool and were very unlikely to believe most if anything that was contained in it. Any attempt at either informing or re-educating German POW's was greatly wasted with Wochenpost.

For those who did read it the main reason was nothing more than they had the opportunity to read something that was written in their mother tongue. It was dogged by mistrust which was not helpful to British attempts at re-education.

Initially neither the content nor the tone of the 1944 to 1948 issues of Wochenpost differed much from the earlier ones of 1941to 1942. The main content of the first couple of pages of both was centred on either political or war-related events of the day, which were taken from the German, British, and international media. Other general cultural matters filled up most of the following four pages, while the last two were reserved for specific POW interests such as crosswords, poems, jokes sport and the like.

When Wochenpost re-appeared in 1944 the revived editions had a comments page which was intended to stimulate discussion, but it was soon dropped because the responses were becoming more emotional than objective.

In April 1946 the editorial board of Wochenpost had received a perceptive letter from the A-graded editors of Lagerbrille at Camp 249 (Carburton), which set out a critique, the main points of which were as follows:

(1). Giving the impression that the readers were uneducated should be avoided.

(2). Irrespective of their upbringing under Nazi rule, young people have valuable qualities. They have shown courage, reliability, community spirit, and made sacrifices. For them to criticize their homeland, their society, condemn all that took place . . . would call forth opposition.

(3). Shorter, less academic articles might go down better.

(4). News from all four Occupation Zones and from different cities should feature.

(5). Above all, the editors were asked to be honest and not to deny that they wanted to educate or re-educate their readers.

(6). Access to authors hitherto unavailable, as well as good art etc. should be introduced.

This extremely honest and forthright feed-back was accepted and acted upon by the newspaper's editorial board.

A 1947 survey found that 55 per cent of readers now accepted Wochenpost, another 14 per cent did so whilst criticizing certain points. 11 per cent did not care and another 20 per cent were still opposed to it. Circulation had risen to 110,000 copies by September 1947.

Whilst researching this book I read this following piece concerning Wochenpost and I felt it worthy of repeating here. My apologies to the original author of the joke as I do not know who you are, but it certainly made me laugh.

"Nevertheless, muted criticism of Wochenpost continued. A manuscript play written and performed as a Christmas entertainment by Hermann Schulz of Camp 278 at Clapham near Bedford in 1947 presents a weary young POW who sees no way out but death. He knocks at heaven's gate, where St Peter, holding the traditional key, puts him through a screening. Towards the end, St Peter peers down into the camp below, where he spots more desperate inmates. He asks why one of them has such a miserable face and receives the reply: 'Oh, him! He's just read the Wochenpost!'"

Most if not all camps had their own libraries which contained both fiction and non-fiction material in both English and German. These same camp libraries also provided camps with copies of the official daily Hansard for both the Commons and the Lords along with reading material such as the Oxford Pamphlets on World Affairs, eighteen of which were even published in German from the autumn 1945.

As time went on a lot of the camps would have what was known as a Zeitungsschau, which literally translated to, 'Newspaper Show'. In reality it was a display of newspaper cuttings, usually shown in an information room or on a canteen wall, as hut space and lighting permitted. In this same chapter you will see a good example of this from a photograph taken at Camp 266 by a visiting Red Cross representative.

These displays consisted of English-language newspapers passed to POW's by work contacts, or national, regional, and local newspapers donated to or bought in by the camp, translations of specific articles from such papers, Wochenpost, and clippings from German, Austrian, and Swiss papers which individual prisoners had sent in to them by relatives back home in Germany.

In one case a complete Aachen city newspaper was regularly mailed to an inmate at Camp 31 in Warwickshire.

In mates were not only encouraged to read their camps newspaper and get involved in discussion about the topics   which they covered but also to submit articles and materials for it as well, after all it was a newspaper for them and written by them.

All of the Camp newspapers were never regarded as or intended for commercial enterprises. Technical material such as paper, ink, and stencils were provided by the PWD free of charge. The work of editing the newspapers or providing articles and stories for them was not something for which the POW's were generally ever paid for, although one camp did pay those that contributed articles or poems for it, whilst another charged one old penny per copy to help cover its running costs. To the vast majority of camps however this was something which was never really an issue. Having their own newspaper was an idea that was born out of their own needs and desires not something which was thrust upon or demanded of them.

To a greater degree it was something which they had control over that was theirs. This was an extremely important component of camp life. To have something which they had control over, something that they had ownership of in the circumstances which they found themselves in gave them hope and belief for the future. It is amazing how positively impactive and important such a relatively unimportant issue can become.

Whether it was Wochenpost, Lagerzeitungen, English for all or any other Camp publications that were produced, it has to be remembered that they all played a very important part in the life's of POW's.

For the Prisoners themselves they were a form of communication, a way of keeping their spirits up. It gave them some self-control back in to their lives and a focus and belief in a better tomorrow was just round the corner. To the authorities they saw them as useful tools to re-educating an indoctrinated enemy. They saw them as a subtle form of control. If POW's were focusing so much of their time and energy's on such past times they were then much less likely to be disgruntled or have designs on causing unrest or thinking of escape.

For today's generation these editorials are a historical record of that time. They serve as a window in to a bygone era that helps us see and understand what life was really like in those camps for POW's. It provides us with a ring side seat in to another time.

As time goes on there are fewer and fewer POW's still alive who can recount their stories of those yesterdays, some already fading from the memory with the onset of old age and with their numbers continually decreasing as time marches on the editorials that were produced in these camps or for these camps become more and more important as a record of those times.

Suddenly they are no longer just memorabilia that a few individuals have an interest in they are fast becoming important historical documents for future generations to come.

Local Newspapers.

Just like the POW's themselves the locals also wanted to know what was going on in their community, the various local papers did not let them down. My next trip was therefore to travel to the British Newspaper Library in Collingdale to see what I could find.

It's the research I find the most interesting part of being involved with writing a book, the excitement of possibly turning up some gem of a story that I hadn't previously known about.

I had been up to the library before but that had been many moons ago, whilst I was researching an article for a local history project that I was involved with. My reader's ticket had by now run out so I made sure I was weighed down with different forms of identification. It felt like I was going away on holiday. I had my passport, my driver's licence. I even had a utility bill and my previous reader's ticket, not exactly certain of what I would be asked to produce.

The last time I went down there I went by train and I remembered that it took an eternity to get to and wasn't a journey which I particularly enjoyed, maybe the reason that I haven't been back there for such a long time. This time I drove. I had a rough idea of how to get there although I had hedged my bets by printing off the AA route map from the internet and switched on my sat nav as well. The sat nav tried to send me through North East London which didn't seem to be right to me so I decided to stick with the AA route map, which did the trick and got me there in one piece and without too much hassle.

On arrival I parked up, sorted out my new reader's ticket and set about looking for what I had come down there to see. I was after copies of the now defunct Southend District Times and Laindon Recorder which was a local weekly newspaper which went out of circulation many years ago. I was specifically interested in the years that Camp 266 was open, 1945, 1946, 1947 and 1948.

Other than a short break for a cup of tea and a bite to eat I carried on looking through the papers until three-thirty in the afternoon. I then ordered copies of a few relevant articles from some of the papers that I had looked through which would take about a week to get to me in the post.

If I am honest, I was a little bit disappointed at the lack of articles in the paper about life at Camp 266. I was particularly hoping to find articles which covered the opening and closing of the camp along with maybe one or two pictures, but alas that was not to be. What I did find however gives some insight in to how the camps prisoners got on with members of the local community. One of the articles concerning the funeral of a German POW from Camp 266, Gunther Meise, appears in more detail in the chapter on ICRC Reports.

The Laindon Recorder in March 1947 reported that a POW Padre from the camp averted a serious road accident by his quick thinking.

Charles Whymark in a bakers van doing his rounds suddenly turned off the High Road, Laindon without signalling into Worthing Road and into the face of Gerd Salewski the camps Padre who was riding a motor cycle. Saleewski immediately braked and turned into Worthing Road with the van driver in order to avoid a collision.

Through an interpreter, Salewski said he was on his way from the Langdon Hills Camp to the Tillingham Hostel and was doing about 20 miles per hour. He had pre-war experience of motor-cycles in Germany and was familiar with signals of the High-way Code.

In finding the defendant Whymark guilty of careless driving the chairman of the magistrates, Mr J C Jobson said that if the motor cyclist had being going faster and not applied his brakes he could have been killed. The lack of skid marks shows he was not going fast.

Whymark who lived in Chadwell was fined five pounds.

In April 1947 the paper reported that the camp Commandant, Colonel Constable gave permission for POW's band to entertain the residents at the camp. The selection of modern and popular music to the bands own interpretation was played, under the direction of an extremely efficient conductor who also played the violin and trumpet solos.

Then in May 1947 we find that a party of prisoners visited members of the Laindon Youth Centre for an evening of table tennis. A team of eight played the Laindon Youth in a tightly contested match but the honours eventually went to the prisoners.

One of most disturbing reports that I found appeared less than a year after the camp was opened, on the 6th March 1946 when a Laindon Police Sergeant ending up fighting with a German POW at the Langdon Hills Camp.

It came about because a Doctor Robert Williams and a Jean Seager both from London had somehow managed to gain entry to the camp and then communicated with some of the German POW's and passed on parcels.

Both were eventually charged under the Emergency powers regulations, Dr Williams with unlawfully entering the POW camp and with a second charge of unlawfully acting in a manner likely to prejudice the discipline of prisoners of war. Seager was charged with aiding and abetting the same offences.

Police Sergeant 112 Sydney Thomas Harvey was on duty when he saw a Fraser Nash make off in a motor vehicle being driven in the Laindon area and having certain information on the car and its occupants, he followed it to Langdon Hills

The occupants parked the car in a nearby car park. Both got out, crossed over the road (High Road) to a footpath that run down the back of the camp. Williams was carrying two shopping bags and Seager a brown paper parcel.

Sergeant Harvey removed his tunic and left it in his car before followed them both on foot. When Dr Williams and Seager reached the South West Corner of the Camp where there was a gate, Sergeant Harvey saw them both speaking to a prisoner and Williams now only had one shopping bag.

When Williams saw Sergeant Harvey approaching he shouted something out in a foreign tongue, probably German as the prisoner immediately disappeared into the bushes. Williams continued shouting, 'Bandit, robber, damned Englishman' and accused Sergeant Harvey of being a spy. The confrontation continued for quite some time before both Dr Williams and Seager walked off in different directions.

Sergeant Harvey decided to follow Seager but when they got back to the small gate again he saw Dr Williams climbing over the fence to get out of the POW compound, the remaining bag he had had with him was now also empty.

It was now fairly late at night Dr Williams and Seager both disappeared into the woods again but Sergeant Harvey heard Williams fall and went to see what had happen. Williams continued to verbally abuse him and accusing him of trying to rob them. At the same time he was shouting to the German POW's. Two of the prisoners who knew Sergeant Harvey to be policemen came towards him and in the ensuing conversation the POW's went off to find the Camp Commandant only to return saying he was not there. They then left.

Three other POW's then suddenly appeared and spoke with Sergeant Harvey while others went and spoke with Dr Williams and Seager. He saw Williams hand over the brown parcel to one of them.

One of the POW's told Sergeant Harvey that it would be better if he went, then the three of them started to punch him.

Later when the matter went to court and although both defendants pleaded not guilty, Williams was fined £100 and Seager £50 and five guineas costs each. The alternative was three months imprisonment for both

It would appear that Dr Williams and Seager sympathized with those German POW's who were kept in captive now that the war was over and had not appreciated that Sergeant Harvey was a policeman as he had taken his tunic off.

We have not been able to establish whether any of the prisoners were either identified or punished. Fortunately this is the only unpleasant incident that we have come across.

This story encouraged me to try and find out a bit more about good old Sergeant Harvey, so I contacted the curator of the Essex Police museum which is situated at Essex Police HQ in Chelmsford, to see if I could track down exactly who Sergeant S T Harvey was. This was the only information we actually had about him at the time. I managed to acquire a copy of his Record of Service and found out the following information.

Sydney Thomas Harvey was born on the 17th February 1906 in Brighton. He was a big man for the time standing almost six feet tall. With his fair hair, blue eyes and fresh complexion he was almost Germanic in appearance.

He had joined the Army just four months after his 17th birthday on the 22nd June 1923 and finally left having served for 5 years 273 days, on the 21st March 1929. He remained on the army reserve until 21st June 1935 when he was fully discharged from his military service.

He was still only 23 years of age when he joined the then named Essex County Constabulary on the 19th April 1929 and was initially stationed at Police Headquarters, more than likely so that he could complete his initial basic training. From there he moved to Grays Police station on the 11th May1929 where he started his Police career as Police Constable 501 Sydney Thomas Harvey.

He married his wife Ethel May on the 26th December 1931. Looking back on that now it seems so strange that somebody would get married on Boxing Day, but maybe that's just how it was in those days. My own grandparents married on Christmas day in 1922 because that was the only day my grandfather had a day off.

Sydney and Ethel went on to have two children, a son and a daughter.

He passed his Sergeants exam on 15th January 1934 but for some reason which wasn't explained in his record of service, he wasn't actually promoted for another five years on the 1st March 1939. He also passed his Inspectors exam on 15th February 1943 but despite not retiring for another eleven years in 1954, he was never promoted again.

In total he served at nine different locations across Essex including Laindon Police station between 12th August 1942 and 4th January 1948.

It was interesting to look back at the wages a Police officer earnt in those days. In his last year of service in 1954 his yearly wage was only £635. The lump sum part of his pension was just over £290.

He received four Chief Constables Commendations during his twenty-five years of Police service, one of which was for his actions at the POW camp at Langdon Hills on the 6th March 1946. The citation read as follows.

"For persistence and attention to duty in detecting offences under the POW and internees (Access & Communications) Order 1940."

Even though he was potentially in a lot of danger by taking on the German POW's in a fight and was also heavily outnumbered he stuck to the task in hand in the true traditions of British policing.

During his Police service he was awarded the Defence Medal in 1945. The Police Long Service & Good Conduct Medal in 1951 which an officer can be granted only after they have served in the Police for twenty-two years and the Queen's Coronation Medal in 1953.

Sometime after he retired Sydney immigrated to Australia to see out his days in warmer climes. He married for a second time in April 1978 at the ripe old age of seventy-two. Sydney passed away on the 30th March 1985 aged seventy-nine years of age.

It has been a real pleasure for me writing about Sydney and it would have been nice to have found out even more about him so as to give a more complete picture of his life. As a fellow Police officer I salute his memory.

In 1947 five girls stood at a military court in Moreton in Lugg POW Camp while five Germans were accused of consorting with them.

The commandant of the Langdon Hills camp at the time, Lieutenant Colonel Constable, had obviously read the article that appeared in one of the national daily newspapers and commented that this must not happen at Langdon Hills. He explained, German POW's are permitted to visit civilian homes with permission of the camp Commandant, in fact it is encouraged as it is considered that it will give the Germans an insight into the English way of life and customs, thereby helping to re-educate them.

Fraternization of the amorous type however was not allowed and could result in POW's receiving punishment of between four to six months detention and a delay in their repatriation.

Lieutenant Colonel Constable probably had in mind early concerns made by the local District Council of the close proximity of the camp to the local population and he was also aware that there had been an increase in the number of young Laindon girls who had been seen walking with German POW's.

He was however, along with his Adjutant, Captain J E Messenger confident that the prisoners at the Laindon camp would continue to behave and hoped that the young girls will not encourage them and that the growing habit of going for walks with them would eventually be curbed.

Well we now know that fraternization did go on, as many Germans did in fact stay behind in England after they were released and marry our local girls.

Fraternization, well Mr Constable I wonder if you really knew what was going on behind your back. Betty Kennedy's story gives you a quick insight to what some of our young English lass's were up to.

Although Betty was only about 12 years of age at the time she can remember quite clearly the POW's being driven along Laindon High Road, she believes by the Army, on their way to South Green, Billericay to work on the prefabs that were being built at the time. It was here that she initially got to know many of the Germans, in particular Helmut or John as he was known to her. Betty and her older sister Audrey used to regularly visit their Aunt Joan who lived in one of the new prefabs. Joan used to give them cups of tea at the back door not just one or two but groups of them.

In return the Germans used to make wooden toys for Joan's children one particular toy fascinated Betty. It was shaped as a table tennis bat, on the top side little wooden chicks were placed round the outside; these were attached to a piece of string that hung in the middle underneath with a heavy weight on it. As you twirled the string around, the little chicks nod up and down as if they were feeding.

Betty and her girlfriends could run a train through the regulations around fraternisation. You will have read that in the early days amorous fraternising was not allowed between POW's the local women, well as Betty tells us this appeared to be completely ignored and it was the young teenage girls who were most to blame. Betty, Audrey and some of her other girlfriends from Laindon High Road School would walk up to the back of the Camp and climb over a low barbed wire fence that surrounded the camp, giggle and start talking to the prisoners.

On many occasions this would turn into a game of ball as a ball was thrown back and forth over the fence. Word soon got around and more and more giggly girls would join in. Then when the prisoners were allowed out they would walk in the woods with them, still giggling and talking to them.

The Camp from the woods at the back (Coombe Wood) Kind permission of Eberhard Fischer

Communication between the girls and the POW's was a little difficult at times and although none of the girls could speak any German, some of the POW's could speak fairly good English and others an acceptable form of broken English.

On more than one occasion Betty would walk up to the camp with her sister Audrey who would meet up with Helmut who had climbed over the fence, out of the camp and walked down Dry Street with her. Every now and again Audrey and Helmut would stop and have a quick kiss and cuddle. This was often in the dark so Betty always wondered why the guards at the gate never said anything as they walked past to meet Helmut further down the lane.

Helmut would have been in serious trouble if he was ever caught. As Betty puts it, we girls were little devils but it was fun.

Billy was another handsome German she also knew Johnny's twin brother who was also in the camp.

The family often went to the concerts held at the camp and Helmut was involved in a number of the acts, in one he would hold up four other men.

Helmut holding up three men in one of the concert acts.

The POW's also held dances at the memorial hall in Laindon, which were always well attended and the girls would dance with the Germans, she particular remembers that the German waltz was a lot quicker than the English version.

On a more positive note we read that in July of 1947 an unknown boy was seen to be in difficulties in Lake Meadows Park Billericay, by a POW who was working nearby, Franz Dung. He immediately dived in to the lake fully clothed, managed to get the boy out and applied artificial resuscitation. Franz was thanked by the Billericay Swimming Club and his rescue reported to the Royal Life-Saving Society.

It was first believed that Franz was from the Langdon Hills camp but it turned out he was from a Camp at Harold Hill.

A later report confirmed that the boy was 11 year old Alan Lennox Warren from Samuel Road, Langdon Hills. He remembered sinking about eight times before he was finally pulled a shore. His grateful parents and some friends of the boy were so thankful for saving young Alan, that they attempted to secure an early release and repatriation for Franz, it is not known whether they were successful or not.

We are not sure from which POW camp but around the same time and although he could not swim, another German POW jumped into a river in Chelmsford and rescued an eight year old girl who had fallen into the water while playing too close to the river bank, undoubtedly saving her life.

As the months ticked by the POW's were gradually gaining more and more freedom, a report in the Southend District & Laindon Recorder on 23rd July 1947 refers to the fact that the POW's had already visited the Radion cinema in Laindon under the new War Office Scheme. However the report goes on to say that the authorities were still unsure of the POW's reaction to the added liberty the new scheme was allowing them.

The new scheme obviously had a few draw backs as well as some additional liberties. Under the scheme they would receive half their pay in sterling and the other half in 'token money' which they can only spend in the camp. To try and encourage extra output per person any overtime money that was earnt would be paid in sterling. They were also allowed to travel on trains and buses within a limited radius of their own camps.

I have to say (Ken) after two devastating wars against Germany within the first half of the 20th Century and only two years after the end of the second war, I am a little surprised at the amount of freedom the POW's were given so quickly.

However, it does make me proud of how tolerant and forgiving the British people are.

The following statistics from the 'Wikipedia' web site indicates how fortunate those Germans captured and imprisoned by the Western powers were.

German POW's dying in captivity

German POW's held by Russia   35.8%

German POW's held by Eastern European Countries   32.9%

German POW's held by France 2.58%

German POW's held by America   0.15%

German POW's held by Britain 0.03%

By the end of 1947 250,000 of the German POW's that were being held throughout the UK had already been repatriated with the last of them eventually being repatriated in November 1948. By doing this we were in breach of the Geneva Convention by refusing to let Germans return home until well after the war was over. In Russia however it would be another eight years before the last of the German POW's were sent home, but then they would argue that as they were not a signatory to the Geneva Convention, they were free to do as they chose.

The attitude towards German POW's was becoming more and more favourable the longer they were being held. This came from all corners of our society. The Salvation Army invited around 50 POW's to their Sunday afternoon meeting on the 27th July 1947, at their hall in Northumberland Avenue, Laindon.

"The meeting was organised by Colonel and Mrs Busse, retired German born Army officers living in Ilford. For many years the Colonel was the editor of the Salvation Army publication in Germany. The POW's singing was led by the Camp's German POW Padre Salewski, from special song sheets written in German. The Sunday school children sang, 'Christ for the whole world.'

The Salvation Army then entertained the POW's to tea, they responded by singing German folk songs led by their organist Herr Reissmann.

Later in the evening, some of the Salvation service men who were themselves home on leave from service in the British armed forces, talked with the POW's about the towns and villages they had visited whilst in Germany.

The names and addresses of those POW's who were due to return home were written down so that Christmas presents could be sent to their children."

(Southend Standard & Laindon Recorder 30th July 1947)

As you will have read in the chapter on local inhabitants memories it is the entertainment performed by the POW's either in the camp or in the halls around Laindon that they remember with great affection. This also shows what an active and important part the German POW's played throughout the local community during their years of incarceration at Langdon Hills.

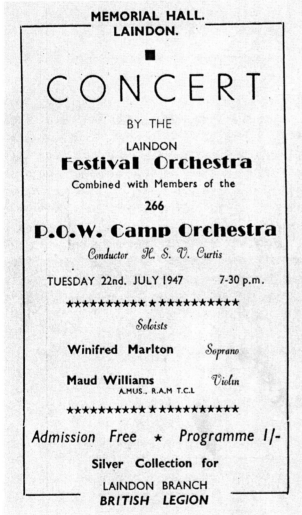

MEMORIAL HALL.
LAINDON.

■

CONCERT

BY THE

LAINDON
Festival Orchestra

Combined with Members of the

266

P.O.W. Camp Orchestra

Conductor H. S. V. Curtis

TUESDAY 22nd. JULY 1947   7-30 p.m.

★★★★★★★★★★ ★★★★★★★★★★

Soloists

Winifred Marlton   *Soprano*

Maud Williams   *Violin*
A.MUS., R.A.M T.C.L

★★★★★★★★★★ ★★★★★★★★★★

Admission Free ★ Programme 1/-

Silver Collection for

LAINDON BRANCH
BRITISH LEGION

I wonder how inmates would be treated by today's local inhabitants if say Langdon Hills was once again turned into a POW camp but this time for members of Al Qaeda captured in Afghanistan. Would they be treated in the same way by today's society? Now there's a question.

On the Tuesday before the POW outing to the Salvation Hall, the POW Camp Orchestra from the Langdon Hills Camp along with the Laindon Festival Orchestra performed at the Memorial Hall in Laindon. It was the first public appearance of the German Orchestra, although many Laindon people have attended concerts at their camp. The hall was packed and they showed their appreciation of the brilliant renditions of 'Amers (Wee Macgregor Patrol), Thomas (Overture Raymond), Rosse (Suite, Merchants of Venice) etc'.

Of the 29 first class musicians who were playing that evening, eight were POW's from the Camp. The concert was organised by Mr H Curtis who also conducted the orchestra, throughout the evening. He was ably assisted by Soloist Winifred Marlton, Soprano Maud Williams whose violin renderings of "Meditation" and "Dancing Doll" were exemplary. Accompanists to the soloists and the orchestra were Gustav Sajons, who was the POW conductor and Mrs L Baker.

A Silver Collection raised £8.13s for the Laindon branch of the British Legion. The concert was later repeated at the POW camp and again in September at the Laindon Youth Centre.

(SDT&LR – 30th July 1947)

Later in November of 1947 we have Bert Holiday who appears to have been the chief feature writer for the Southend Standard & Laindon Recorder reporting in great detail about one of the shows which was held at the Langdon Hills POW Camp. He found it to be a great experience and was impressed with the locals, Christian attitude towards the German prisoners and also the welcoming attitude of those chaps as he put it 'from across the Rhine'.

He was also amazed at the band of happy go lucky fellows that appeared to be holiday making in our neighbourhood on a mission of friendly propaganda on behalf of their nation.

What also pleased him was the programme that was given to him. It read "The German POW's request the pleasure of Mr Bert Holliday to a variety show on Monday at 7.30pm. Rolf Zimmerman".

Bert had been introduced to them as a personal friend of Mr Alwin Gleissner of Basildon one of their countrymen who had become a naturalized Englishman in 1934. When asked if he could speak German, they laughed when he told them that Herr Gleissner had been trying to teach him for years but all he could say was "nussbraun und streichhoeiger" which translated into English means "nut brown tobacco and matches".

Mrs Gleissner explained that Bert and she could not speak German because of their insufficient patience to learn. Sixty years on and nothing has changed.

The difficulty that they both found was not knowing when to applaud and laugh and on many occasions they found themselves laughing at the wrong time which obviously amused their hosts.

There were however occasions when he did get it right, for example when Gustav Sajons, played the Warsaw Concerto, he had never heard anything more beautiful and was happy to be able to applaud with his hosts.

They had an attractive young lady guest artiste, with a Cabaret personality. She was presented with a bouquet of flowers by the German POW's Commanding Officer at the camp, Rolf Zimmerman.

Music was not the only form of entertainment on show. They provided the audience with many different types of acts and daring tricks, such as fire eating, walking on broken glass, humans suspended in the air and disappearing magic acts.

In his subsequent newspaper article Bert Holiday says that 'It gave me a great deal of enjoyment to sit there among a big crowd of both sexes representing two nations which, after years of strife and bloodshed on both sides, now appear to have a common interest in making a friendly relationship and in rebuilding the world on a more permanently peaceful basis.'

Finally he said 'give credit where it is due; they know how to put on a variety show, these Germans.'

Bert Holiday was not finished he was back at the camp in January 1948, reporting on yet another concert put on by the POW's. His article opened with the following statement by a young German prisoner of war announcer on the stage at the 266 POW camp, Langdon Hills.

"I trust that the friendship which exists in this hall to-night will continue between our two nations for ever."

To think that such a statement could be made less than two and a half years after one of bloodiest wars in the history of mankind is truly amazing. To me it once again showed how forgiving the British could be, but also how hard the German POW's had worked to help forge this friendship, which thankfully has lasted to this day.

Back to the camp concert, there were two guest artists, Miss Jean Green who sang and tap danced away to the band led by Ernest Peterhaensel, who himself could play the guitar, the tenor saxophone and clarinet. Then there was Hans Engehardt who played the piano accordion, Matthaeus Eglhuber who played the alto sax and clarinet, Hans Baur the trombone and violin, Ewald Buhl played saxophone and oboe, Paul Maxcimer was on drums, Gustav Sajons on the piano and Willi and Ernst Bernhardt, twin brothers and Bernd Baumer played mouth-organs.

Guest Step Dancer

Miss Green

Guest Singer

Mr. Holiday (Tenor)

and Camp Dance Band conducted by

Ernst Peterhaensel

The German P.o.W.Camp 266
Langdon Hills

requests the pleasure of

MR. & Miss LINES, Laindon
(2 Pers.)
to a Variety-Show

on 31st Dec. 1947

at 7.30 p.m.

G Eird

Campleader H.Q.

RSVP.

POW's Band 1947. Picture by kind permission of Eberhard Fischer

What an array of talent and they were ably backed by the singing of Paul Maxcimer, Otto Hoak and the band leader.

There had been at least two previous performances all received with packed audiences, who were welcomed by the POW's camp leader, Rolf Zimmerman. The performances were also attended by the Landon Hills camp Commanding Officer, Lieutenant Colonel Cronin, Major Gill, Captain Messenger along with other officers.

Like the previous show Holiday reported on there were many individual acts of daring, clowning acrobatics, illusionists, female impersonators and of course there were even one or two jokes. One such joke Holiday felt needed repeating as it gave him the impression that the Germans had little respect for the Hitler Youth Movement.

"To the surprise of everyone on a bus in Berlin recently, a boy stood up and offered a women a seat. She was delighted. When the boy told her that he once belonged to the Hitler Youth Movement, the women said "What" You're a Nazi? Here, keep your seat." She would never say "thank you" to a Nazi, she said. Meanwhile, an American soldier intervened and after seating himself in the vacant seat, he got up and said "Here, madam, take the seat now, it is "de-nazified".

I suppose that's one of those jokes where you would have actually had to have been there to fully appreciate it. Not everything improves with age.

They also told a joke about a local country parson and the little lad who was asked how to get to Heaven. The Rector of Langdon Hills, the Rev. W. T. Hickson thoroughly enjoyed it.

There was another one where the doctor had told a young singer she should give up smoking, drinking and singing. When he next saw her she said that she had taken his advice but was giving them up in stages. She had started by given up singing.

As the end of the show approached it was time for the second guest artists, and yes it was none other than Bert Holiday. Bert was a tenor but had given up solo singing some years early and was a little apprehensive at first but after a few rehearsals in the week with Gustav Sajons who no doubt was a brilliant pianist his nerviness soon disappeared as he walked out on to the stage.

He sang in German "Walter's Prize Song' from Wagner's opera "Die Meistersingers." As he made his exit, amid the applause he became aware that these lads wanted to be back home amongst their loved ones. He therefore wished them all gods speed and a safe return to their native land.

Finally the German Commanding Officer, Rolf Zimmerman, on behalf of all the German POW's, thanked all those concerned for their kindness that had been extended to them over the years. Many had been guests of local residents and in the years to come they would remember the hospitality and happy times they had with them.

A week later the Laindon and Langdon Hills branch of the United Nations Associations (U.N.A) organised a New Year's eve Party at the Langdon Hills Primary School. It was enjoyed by over a hundred guests, which included thirty German POW's and their friends.

Mr C Shepherd the proprietor of Shepherd's Restaurant in Laindon provided a magnificent continental buffet free of charge. The European dishes were served on silver salvers which included vol-au-vent of chicken and various savouries in aspic. It was voted as the best New Year's Eve party since before the war.

A cabaret show was presented by the Mala School of Dancing from Wickford. Mr Ted Powell acted as M.C. and Ivy Hagger also sang some delightful solos. Ivy was a regular leading lady in the Laindon and District Operatic Society (now known as the Basildon Operatic Society). The dancing that followed was provided by Mr P Lucas and Mr W Silver.

This party was a prelude to an extensive programme of events being organised by the new association.

The UNA was a non-governmental organization and existed in various countries and its aims were to enhance relationships between various member states and the United Nations. The United Nations Associations of Great Britain and Northern Ireland (UNA-UK) held its first meeting on the 7th June 1945 and by 1951 it had, 191 branches worldwide.

This organisation was particularly concerned with very acute clothing shortage in Germany and the Laindon and Langdon Hills Branch following a meeting at the Laindon High Road School agreed to join the national clothing drive. It was also agreed that it would become a regular feature of the local branch activity, with their first batch of clothing parcel being sent to people in Hamburg.

Although clothing was still on ration in England the situation was nowhere as bad as in Europe and Germany in particular.

We can see from just a few newspaper articles, which were written over sixty years ago, how quickly we can establish what life was like all those years ago. I also think it helps to bring back to life a bygone era which had different moral values and standards.

CHAPTER
(German POW's)

We have read about some of the memories of the local population, read what the local newspapers have had to say, now it is time to read about the experiences of some of the POW's.

Erwin Hannemann

The first German POW's arrived at the Langdon Hills camp in April 1945, a month before the end of the Second World War. The camp was capable of housing up to 800 prisoners.

One of the prisoners who arrived at the camp on that very first day and was there until the day it closed, remained in England after he was released and went on to marry a local girl. His name is Erwin Hannemann and this is his story;

"I was born on the 10th October 1926 in the village of Scharpah now in Poland, which was originally in the district of the free State of Danzig, Germany. I was the second child to my parents, Dofferd and Lousse Hannemann. I had three sisters, Ellie who was the eldest, then Christal followed by Inge.

My father was a farmer and he farmed at Orlofferfelde farm. It was a small farm of approximately 40 acres in size. It was mainly arable but we also had about eight milking cows. I attended a local catholic school. I started there at the age of 6 through to when I was 14 years

179

old in 1940, a year into the war. During my spare time I worked on the farm, doing such jobs as ploughing with horses and milking the cows. Our farm was less than a two hour bicycle ride away from the German/Polish border and Warsaw was not much further on but life was very calm and pleasant back on the farm.

My father who had been in the German army in the First World War was called up at the beginning of September 1942, to join the border regiment on the German border with Poland. He left my mother, three sisters and I with the help of two French POW's and a Russian girl to run the farm.

At the same time my sister Ellie was working in an office in Tekernorf, whilst my other sisters, Inge and Chrisal were still both at school, but they all helped out on the farm. It was very hard work. It was my intention that when my studies had finished to find a career in farming although I realised that I would have to join the armed forces if the war continued.

I was eventually called up in 1942 when I was still only16 years of age, I was a little nervous and did not really want to go but I had no option. It was initially the Hitler Youth which you have obviously heard a lot about, but it was in fact not much different than joining the scout's movement that you have in England, other than it was compulsory from1939 onwards.

Many of my friends were called up at the same time as me. I was eventually sent to Rensburg which was then in East Prussia to be fitted up with a uniform and a rifle without any ammunition. We stayed there for just one night before catching a train the next day to Ilverston in Holland to do our basic training. We were allocated to a Panzer division. We had only one Panzer Tank to train on and though it was a joy to sit and study such a famous tank, we actually did very little training with regards to it. Instead we did a lot of infantry training.

Within a short period of time I was made a batman to a Lieutenant in the Germany army, when it was time for all my friends to go to France he suggested that I stayed behind and trained as a dispatch rider. He arranged for me to go to Wesanaur and do a despatch rider's course but within a few months following 'D' Day I was on my way to France with an infantry unit. I suppose because by then they needed every able bodied man they could get.

My attachment got as far as Lille and we got split up, we were running everywhere, we did not know where we were. We had no idea where our commanders were. The people in Lille were all waving at us and asked where we were going. We thought they were friendly and for a short time we were quite happy and we told them we wanted to go home. However, when we got into the centre of Lille, there were very few people about and those were partisans who started to shoot at us. We ran out of the town as fast as we could down a side street and tried hiding in a field. The town folk, men, women and children came after us. We got very worried and were scared that they might shoot us with our own guns. So we took the bolts out of our rifles and threw them away.

The partisans amongst them took us back to the Police Yard in the town square and stood guard over us to protect us from the local people who were not very friendly towards us. Eventually to our relief some Americans soldiers came to check what all the commotion was about. They dispersed the civilians and put us into lorries and took us to Aras. My war was thankfully over and I had not fired a single bullet in anger.

When we arrived in Arras we were put in to a prisoner of war camp in a large field, which was surrounded by local civilians and Polish troops, it was not a very pleasant experience. There was very little food, the daily ration being a packet of biscuits per person and a tin of corn beef between five of us. Surprisingly I still like corn beef to this very day. A water wagon would come round daily and I filled up every container I could find.

At night time we dug our self's a hole in the ground to sleep in, covering our self with our thick and warm over coats. In the morning when the sun was shining I would take my clothes off and just sit and count how many fleas there were running over me. It was not very nice and many people fell ill during this time. Luckily we only stayed there for about a week before being shipped off to a larger camp in Dieppe, which was a slight improvement on the one we had just left behind. The food ration there included a type of goulash soup made from water cabbage and vegetable leaves, it was totally tasteless but importantly it was warm.

Eventually we were transported across the Channel to England by landing craft. The crossing in these flat bottom boats was very uncomfortable; the water frequently came over the top. By now many of us were weak and the crossing made most of us, including myself, sick. I was at some stage but I cannot be certain when, given my own individual prisoner of war number, which was 789489.

We were sent to a transit camp, I am unsure where. Once there we had to take all of our clothes off to be deloused and showered. If there were signs of fleas on any of us we were shaved from top to bottom. I think most of us were just so relieved to be in England, at least we felt we were safe and we were able to relax and smile and have a laugh for the first time in many months.

Food was much better; we were now getting hot porridge. After a couple of days we were sent by train to Hull. This was the first camp where there were tents, before that we were sleeping in the open. The tents slept ten and the beds had straw underneath them. Other than porridge for breakfast I cannot now remember what it was that we had to eat in the evening but I know it was nice. It was like living in heaven.

I do remember that the white bread we had was so nice that we all thought it was cake. We were used to our solid German bread. Within the first week we got moved again to a very large camp at Devices made up of POW's from the Army, Navy, Air force, Merchant navy, Nazis and anti-Nazis. A more diverse mix it was not possible to have. We were now living in corrugated hangers with blankets, it was reasonably comfortable but I still felt cold at night.

Within a few weeks of having arrived at Devizes we were on the move again. It couldn't have been any further away. We were sent all the way up to Scotland, I am not certain exactly where it was but it was camp 22 somewhere in the Glasgow area. This time the camp was made of wooden Nissan huts, so things were starting to get better.

This camp was a very large one and it was guarded by Polish Troops who were not very friendly towards us. They were troops who began their careers in the Polish Army, transferring to the German Army before ending up in the English Army. I found that concept very confusing how somebody could fight for different armies. It wasn't about whether you believed in the war or whether you thought it was right or wrong. I was German and that was the end of the matter as far as I was concerned.

The food was okay and if you wanted to you could volunteer to go work. I volunteered to work on a nearby farm. It was only a small farm run by a man and his wife. That I remember they had two or three children. On my first morning I got there after the farmer had finished milking and I was set to work washing the cow shed down, and then we had breakfast together. After breakfast we went to the fields in a cart. I was a little concerned because the farmer was a continuous smoker and there was plenty of hay and dried grass about just waiting to catch fire, luckily though this never happened. I then went back with the farmer and had lunch with him. I finished around 4 o'clock, packed up my belongings that I had brought with me and simply walked back to the camp.

The one thing we always made sure that we did was to sign in and out of the camp otherwise we would have had the British army scurrying around the country side looking for us thinking that we were trying to escape.

I worked for this friendly farmer for a few days until I heard of a group that was going from farm to farm working on the thrashing machines, so I volunteered for that. This again only lasted for a few days before I joined another group going round the woods collecting dead wood for night time heating in the camp. My main concern was to keep myself busy and hopefully learn a few things as I went along. I managed to pick up English just by being in the various camps and on my work excursions; I never had any formal lessons.

While at the Glasgow camp we were shown a film on the concentrations camp at Auschwitz. We did not believe what we were watching; we came out laughing because we believed it was all just British propaganda. When we began to realise it was true, we were very sorry and could not believe that certain groups of people could treat others in such a way. It was a very bad experience for me as well as my comrades.

In April of 1945, around 25 to 40 of us found ourselves at Laindon railway station in Essex. I had never heard of the place before. We were marched to the top of Langdon Hills to the camp on the corner of Dry Street and the High Road. I remember the camp was over two kilometres away and we had to go up a very steep hill.

We were the camps first ever intake of prisoners which for some reason felt slightly strange for me, but I don't mean in a bad way. Amongst us were tradesmen, bakers, chefs, tailors, mechanics and medics. We all had different skills which could prove to be useful.

We were drafted into a big hall where we were, to our surprise, addressed in German by the camps Commandant, Lieutenant Colonel

Constable. He was a very tall officer with a typical English style moustache; he explained to us, that if we behaved ourselves, he would not put a high fence around the camp, only barbed wire to indicate the boundaries of the camp. After all, the war was still on at the time.

Lieutenant Colonel Constable. *Picture by kind permission of Erwin Hannemann*

He said that if this worked to his satisfaction he would take his guards off of guard duty and we could put our own soldiers in the guardroom. We were quite happy to go along with this, although I never did quite understand the purpose of this and how the British actually benefited from us Germans basically running our own camp. It was not long before we had our own people on guard duties.

Being the youngest soldier at the camp, I was still only 18 years of age at the time, and because of my roles in the army before being captured, I became batman to Lieutenant Colonel Constable initially and later on to Major Gill, Captain Wild and Captain Messinger. Captain Messinger lived in rooms with his family in 'Climax' a large house which was situated immediately across the road from the main gates of the camp. Today it is a private residence. The other officers resided in the camp. The house had quite a bit of history having been built around 1848. Although I slept in the camp I knew very little of what was going on there as my duties as batman was around looking after the Commandant and officers which included doing their washing, ironing and arranging their clothes, waking them up in the morning, etc. I therefore did not get involved with too many of the camps activities. There were many advantages, one being I quite often got to eat in the officer's mess.

Captain Messinger later rented rooms down in the High Road, Laindon and I would frequently go and look after his children.

One of most vivid memories though was when I went to collect his newspapers papers and other items from one of the nearby Laindon shops. On the way back I would collect up all of the empty bottles that I found and take them back to the Crown Hotel where they had come from. In those days, well before today's environmentally friendly age we now live in, people were encouraged to return glass bottles to where they had bought them from, by being paid a small amount to do so.

The proprietor not being allowed to pay me used to give me bars of chocolate instead. Also opposite the Hotel was a cricket field, occasionally if there was a game going on I would stop and watch, but I had absolutely no idea what was going on. I'm not sure that I do even today.

The camp had two interpreters, one was Mr Sinclair, who was a Staff Sergeant of Polish Jewish background, as I recall he was not a very nice man, understandable I suppose in the circumstances. The other was Mr Noble, an English Jew who was a proper gentleman. After the war Mr Noble became a Ferrier and had a shop in Regent Street, London. I called on him after I got married.

We had found out that Sinclair's Christian name was Peter but we did not know Noble's. On asking, Erwin replied 'you must remember we were still in the army and it was still 'yes sir', 'no sir', 'three bags full sir'.

Considering that we were prisoners of war, we could not complain too much, life was good and we had plenty of fun. It was known as Camp 266. It had between 15 and 20 huts, each housing 40 people. So when the camp was full there was upwards of 800 POW's. It was mainly a transit camp. Groups of prisoners would appear for a few days, be registered and then sent off to other nearby camps, Tillingham, Great Wakering and Purfleet being three of them. It was however, also a working camp as well

We were reasonably self-sufficient as a camp. We had our own Doctor, dentist, bakery and a band who played not only for the camp inmates but also for the local civilians as well. We produced our own shows and again the local inhabitants were often invited into the camp to see them. We even had sports days which were normally held on the cricket field opposite the Crown Hotel. On one occasion two pretty girls from the German Embassy in London presented the prizes which was nice for us all.

Girls from the Germany Embassy presenting Prizes. Picture by kind permission of Erwin Hannemann

We had our own football team, which played the local soldiers from the Army Camp at the bottom of Old Church Hill. Various camp competitions, normally between huts were also held. One of the displays was a Church made out of cockle shells. I am not quite sure how we managed to get so many shells. I remember quite vividly our Christmas party in 1946. Produce had been saved up by each individual hut and our chefs put on a splendid spread.

Christmas party 1946.
Picture by kind permission of Erwin Hannemann

I also remember that one Christmas I was disappointed when I entered one of the Officers Mess's and there were no decorations around. So I went outside climbed over the fence and went into the woods and cut the top off a Christmas type tree took it back to the camp and decorated it. The park warden was not too pleased and complained to the camp commandant. I was very close to being punished and being sent to the 'calaboose.' An American Wild West term we had for the internal gaol. The park at the time was still privately owned. It did not come in to the public domain until the 1950's. The British officers had smoothed the misdemeanour over for me because as they saw it, I hadn't really done too much wrong.

Sadly for me I didn't hear much from any of my family from when I was captured in 1943 until 1947. I had no idea of what had happened to them. Whether they were alive or dead, this for me was the worst part. We were allowed to send two cards and two letters and whatever we wrote could not be wiped off. They first went to the censor's office in London before being sent on to Germany. I eventually received a card from my sister with 25 words on it telling me that the three girls were okay but they did not know where mother and father were. Then a few weeks later I received another card from my sister saying we three girls are okay, all living together with neighbours but still did not know what had become of our parents. Mr Noble, kindly gave me another letter that I could write on. I was allowed to take it to the censor in London. My sister received it soon afterwards and replied that dad was.coming home. It would appear that both mum and dad were captured in Danzig by the Russians. They managed to escape but were soon rounded up again by the Russians. Because father was on border duty the family had moved to be with him. The children escaped by climbing into a cellar of a house they were staying at and covering themselves with coal bags. Mother and Father were in the street to see what was going on when they were arrested.

The next day the children were told that our parents had been put on a tank and taken to the coast to New Gotenhaven. Later they were to find out that they were put on a troopship going to Denmark. Ten minutes out to sea and it got bombed ironically by the British RAF. It returned to port. The next day on another troop ship they were transported to Denmark along with other relatives. Some of my relatives came back to Germany as displaced persons but my mother and father ended up in Siberia. They had a very rough time of it and somewhere along the way, sadly mother died or was killed, I never found out which. Dad had become very ill during his capture but somehow he managed to work and walk his way home, eventually being reunited with his three daughters. An amazing achievement but his was as thin as a rake when he arrived back home in Germany.

I was finally discharged from the German army in late 1948 but I initially decided to stay on in England as I felt I could help the family out more by working here and sending money home. By now they were living in a farm house and some of their rooms were given up to displaced persons. They had one living room and one bedroom in the loft for their own use.

I had to apply for leave to stay in England, to do this I had to get a job and accommodation. I already had a job working for Mr Partridge who owned Dry Street Farm. I had started working for him in January 1948. Mr Partridge, the Camp and I had to sign a form of employment contract. I was paid £4.10s a week. Max Ullrich a comrade of mine from the Langdon Hills camp also worked on the farm with me, he was a motor cyclist enthusiast. Like me he was to stay behind and marry a local girl. I also occasionally worked at Northlands Farm which was owned by the Grays.

If we found ourselves working on one of the fields near the A13 Peter Gray at lunch time used to take us to the café opposite the Five Bell Pub and pay for lunch.

CONTROL FORM D.2
Kontrollblatt D.2 *Urlauber*

CERTIFICATE OF DISCHARGE
Entlassungsschein

| ALL ENTRIES WILL BE MADE IN BLOCK LATIN CAPITALS AND WILL BE MADE IN INK OR TYPESCRIPT. | I
PERSONAL PARTICULARS
Personalbeschreibung | Dieses Blatt muss in folgender weise ausgefüllt werden:
1. In lateinischer Druckschrift und in grossen Buchstaben.
2. Mit Tinte oder mit Schreibmaschine. |

SURNAME OF HOLDER *HÖNNEMANN*
Familienname des Inhabers

CHRISTIAN NAMES *ERWIN*
Vornamen des Inhabers

CIVIL OCCUPATION *PRIMWIRT*
Beruf oder Beschäftigung

HOME ADDRESS Strasse .....
Heimatanschrift   Ort *OSTENFELD*
Kreis *RENDSBURG*
Regierungsbezirk/Land
SCHLESW. HOLST.

DATE OF BIRTH *11. 10. 26*
Geburtsdatum (DAY/MONTH/YEAR) (Tag/Monat/Jahr)

PLACE OF BIRTH *SPARTPAU*
Geburtsort

FAMILY STATUS—SINGLE ✗   † Ledig ✗
Familienstand   MARRIED   Verheiratet
WIDOW(ER)   Verwitwet
DIVORCED   Geschieden

NUMBER OF CHILDREN WHO ARE MINORS
Zahl der minderjährigen Kinder

I HEREBY CERTIFY THAT TO THE BEST OF MY KNOWLEDGE AND BELIEF THE PARTICULARS GIVEN ABOVE ARE TRUE.
I ALSO CERTIFY THAT I HAVE READ AND UNDERSTOOD THE "INSTRUCTIONS TO PERSONNEL ON DISCHARGE" (CONTROL FORM D.1).
SIGNATURE OF HOLDER ✗
Unterschrift des Inhabers

Ich erkläre hiermit, nach bestem Wissen und Gewissen, dass die obigen Angaben wahr sind.
Ich bestätige ausserdem dass ich die "Anweisung für Soldaten und Angehörige Militär-ähnlicher Organisationen" u.s.w. (Kontrollblatt D.1) gelesen und verstanden habe.

II
MEDICAL CERTIFICATE
Ärztlicher Befund

DISTINGUISHING MARKS
Besondere Kennzeichen

DISABILITY, WITH DESCRIPTION
Dienstunfähigkeit, mit Beschreibung

MEDICAL CATEGORY
Tauglichkeitsgrad

-FIT-

I CERTIFY THAT TO THE BEST OF MY KNOWLEDGE AND BELIEF THE ABOVE PARTICULARS RELATING TO THE HOLDER ARE TRUE AND THAT HE IS NOT VERMINOUS OR SUFFERING FROM ANY INFECTIOUS OR CONTAGIOUS DISEASE.
SIGNATURE OF MEDICAL OFFICER
Unterschrift des Sanitätsoffiziers
NAME AND RANK OF MEDICAL OFFICER IN BLOCK LATIN CAPITALS
Zuname/Vorname/Dienstgrad des Sanitätsoffiziers
(In lateinischer Druckschrift und in grossen Buchstaen)

Ich erkläre hiermit, nach bestem Wissen und Gewissen, dass die obigen Angaben wahr sind, dass der Inhaber ungezieferfrei ist und dass er keinerlei ansteckende oder übertragbare Krankheit hat.

Dr. med. H. BUTTKEWITZ

P.T.O.
Bitte wenden

† DELETE THAT WHICH IS INAPPLICABLE
Nichtzutreffendes durchstreichen

PSS 2324 6.46 500m

189

III
PARTICULARS OF DISCHARGE
Entlassungsvermerk

THE PERSON TO WHOM THE ABOVE PARTICULARS REFER
Die Person auf die sich obige Angaben beziehen,

WAS DISCHARGED ON (Date) _____ FROM THE* _____
wurde am (Datum der Entlassung)   vom/von der*   entlassen

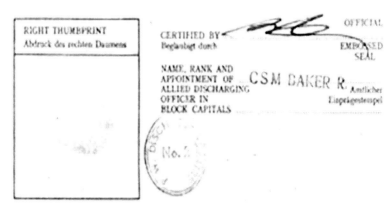

RIGHT THUMBPRINT
Abdruck des rechten Daumens

CERTIFIED BY _____ OFFICIAL
Beglaubigt durch   EMBOSSED
SEAL

NAME, RANK AND
APPOINTMENT OF   CSM BAKER R.
ALLIED DISCHARGING   Amtlicher
OFFICER IN   Einprägestempel
BLOCK CAPITALS

No.

* INSERT "ARMY", "NAVY", "AIR FORCE", "VOLKSSTURM", OR PARA-MILITARY
  ORGANIZATION, e.g. "R.A.D.", "N.S.F.K.", ETC.
  Wehrmachtteil oder Gliederung der die Einheit angehört, z.B. "Heer", "Kriegsmarine",
  "Luftwaffe", "Volkssturm", "Waffen SS", oder "R.A.D.", "N.S.F.K.", u.s.w.

40.9M. PAID ON DISCHARGE

SIGNED

PAYMASTER

German POW Camp 266 – Langdon Hills

I found accommodation with Mr and Mrs Ruffler's and their daughters who lived in Thames View, Langdon Hills, who lived just off of Dry Street.

Mr and Mrs Ruffer - Picture by kind permission of Erwin Hannemann

I received at least three reference letters from the various camp Commandants that I had looked after, which helped me continue in the role with future commandants or when applying for a job outside the camp. The first was from Lieutenant Colonel Constable dated the 13th May 1947.

"Prisoner 798489 Erwin Hannemann has been my Batman for the past 14 months. I am now retiring from the Army but I wish to record my opinion of him.

He is a perfect batman, cheerful willing, hardworking, always clean and smart. He looks for work and I never have to tell him anything twice. He has delightful manners and is more interested in a clean country life than he is in politics. I leave everything lying about, including a very valuable stamp collection but have the most complete faith in his honesty. He is the type of young man who is an asset to any country."

The second reference is from Lieutenant Colonel Hobby of the East Yorkshire Regiment dated 8th November 1947.

"Prisoner 798489, Erwin Hannemann has been my Batman for the last six months. He is an excellent man, well above the average intelligence, very cheerful, willing and hardworking.

He is scrupulously clean himself and he keeps everything he is responsible for equally clean.

He has a quiet and charming personality, speaks good English and he has considerable initiative and enterprise.

He is a man who I can recommend with confidence to any potential employer and I feel sure he would always do all in his power to give every satisfaction."

The third reference was from Major Gill, who was the Assistant Commandant, dated 6th January 1948:

"Prisoner 798489, Erwin Hannemann has been my Batman for the past two and half years and before he leaves me to become civilianised I would like to place on record my estimation of him.

During those two and half years he has been with me I have never once had occasion to be angry or raise my voice to him. He has always worked hard and at times has even looked for extra work with exceedingly cheerful countenance. He was never required to be told twice or even shown twice how to do something he had been tasked with and was exceedingly clean in everything he did. Furthermore he is absolutely honest, I am exceedingly sorry to have to part with him as I can honestly say he is the finest Batman I've ever had. My loss, will I'm sure prove to be somebody else's gain. Good bye and good luck to him."

I was officially discharged as a POW and became a free man again on the 20th December 1948 and the medical officer Dr H. Buttkewitz, certified that I was fit and not verminous or suffering from any infectious or contagious disease, which was nice to know.

I first met my future wife, Julie in Lake Meadows Park, Billericay in 1949. I was there motor biking with a colleague. We were rowing a boat on the lake, having a rest from the bike. We were splashing about all over the place, which resulted in us having a conversation with some girls on the bank. One of them being Julie I arranged to meet her the following day at Laindon Station and we went dancing at the West Ham Town Hall. We were married in Bulphan Church near Brentwood in 1950. Captain Wild and his wife came to the wedding and on another occasion we went to his house.

Erwin and Julie's wedding at Bulphan Church.
By kind permission of Erwin Hanneman.

Captain Wild and his wife.
Picture by kind permission of Erwin Hannemann.

Julie's maiden name was Robinson and she was living in Bulphan with her parents, after we married we moved in with her parents and I got a job working on the local farm Garlasters, which was opposite the Plough Motel, earning £4.10s a week with every third week off, which I didn't think was too bad.

When I was first released from the camp I was supposed to stay and work for five years on the land and be checked by the local Police every week. This arrangement only lasted two weeks and the five years was soon reduced to two years, which meant we could start moving around the country.

Somebody suggested that I should try and get a job at Ilford Ltd in Brentwood. I applied and got the job, I stayed there for ten years but shift work finally caught up with me and I was not sleeping that well, so I left and got myself a job working at the Plough Hotel in Bulphan, where I stayed for the next 23 years.

I started out as a handy-man; I then became a barman, wine waiter, waiter and eventually the restaurant manager finishing up with seventy staff working for me. Though I enjoyed every minute of it, I worked myself to a standstill, resulting in a nervous breakdown.

After hospitalisation and a year off of work, Dr Ruby advised me not to go back to the Plough Hotel. He offered me a job at the Laindon Clinic, where I stayed for the next 10 years before retiring. Then for a time I occasionally did work for a Dr Bass, who ironically lived at the time at the old camp Commandants' house in Dry Street, 'Climax' which I knew so well from the three years I spent as a POW at the camp. I also carried out work for the other Doctors as well.

Following retirement I became more involved with village life and helping keep the village in spick and span. It all started by me looking after the gardens and flower pots etc, outside the village hall. Then organising flowering arrangements on the corner of the A128 and Church Road just before you enter Bulphan village.

The village has won the East Anglia 'Best Kept Village' 2001/2010 and in 2006 I attended a civic ceremony and was awarded 'Thurrock Outstanding Citizen of the Year' award.

This is what the notes in the programme for that ceremony had to say about Erwin:

"Erwin has lived in the village of Bulphan for many years. He was a Prisoner of War at the Langdon Hills camp where he met and married his wife, Julie.

After his release from the POW Camp he became an integral part of the local community, helping out anyone in need.

Today he looks after the village of Bulphan with care and dedication and is universally known for his friendliness whether you are a newcomer to Bulphan or a long-time resident.

Erwin has "beautified" Bulphan village, transforming the gardens in front of the Village Hall into an oasis of shrubs and plants. He clears all the litter from the village and the lay-by on the A128 and plants the flowerbeds by the village hall and the pots at the entrance to the village, persuading garden centres to donate plants.

Erwin is an inspiration to us all, a real unsung hero and an asset to the community."

My daughter Linda was born in 1951 and it was soon afterwards that my father came over from Germany to visit for her christening. I now also have a lovely granddaughter Joanne. They both live in Wickford.

I have never regretted staying on in England. I had a good life in the camp and nobody did me any harm while I was there. I was however told, to steer clear of arguments over politics and religion. This I have done so and have never had any problems what so ever. I have had a good life, a lovely wife, daughter and granddaughter.

Erwin readily admits to coming to England "in 1944 free of charge" but has never regretted staying here.

My wife Julie sadly passed away in 2011. At her funeral the Church in Bulphan was overflowing with mourners. Although a sad moment for me it was nice to see so many people there paying their last respects.

Erwin Hannemann

Max Ullrich

This story is one that I have been looking forward to writing for a long time now because although I never knew or met Max Ullrich or his wife Sally, the person who told me the story knew them very well indeed over many years and I knew that person very well indeed. So I am more than happy about the authenticity of the story.

It turns out that Erwin Hannemann and Max Ulrich knew each other from their time in the camp at Langdon Hills and also spent their days working together in the nearby farmer's fields.

The person who told me this remarkable story was one of my brother-in-laws and came about by sheer chance when he heard that someone was writing a book about a nearby prisoner of war camp from a request for help that had been put out in a local newspaper. At the time he didn't realise that one of the people who was writing the book was in fact his own brother-in-law.

On Easter Monday 2011 he came round to my house and together we drove up to the old site of the camp which is now just a very large field and not surprisingly on a hot, sunny bank holiday weekend the field was a hive of activity with families having picnics, teenagers playing games of football, whilst keen dog walkers were strolling slowly across the field with their animals in tow.

I took a look at the people who were there and thought that most of them wouldn't have had a clue about what had once stood there and the part that it had played in our local history.

My brother-in-law and I walked to the only obvious sign in the field that revealed there had ever been any kind of building there at all. In the top right hand corner of the field there was a large concrete hard standing which must have been about twelve feet in width and about twenty-five feet in length.

Years earlier back in the early nineteen nineties my brother-in-law had made the same journey with Max who had walked with him through the field and showed him where all of the huts had once stood and how they had been laid out. Even down to telling him who had been in each of the hut's. Although I had walked through the field myself many times before I had never noticed any of the slight indentations that my brother-in-law was about to point out to me.

On one occasion I had gone there with my daughter Aimee to try and measure out the field and try to get some real perspective of just how big or small the camp would have actually been.

She was as keen as mustard helping me out by pacing out the distances between each corner of the camp along with the width and length of the place.

It was an interesting way for a father and his daughter to spend some quality time together, if not slightly unusual.

If you looked carefully on the ground you could clearly see slightly lighter patches of grass which were about a foot square in size and that were approximately 15 feet apart width wise and about twenty-five feet apart length. I was amazed that I had never actually noticed them before but as soon as my brother-in-law pointed them out they were in fact so obvious.

I then suddenly stepped on a patch of grass that was rock solid underneath and when I bent down and gently pulled at the grass I could clearly see one of these one feet square concrete blocks which is what the prisoner's huts rested on.

My brother-in-law told me his story about how he had met and become such good friends with Max and his wife Sally.

"I first met Max and Sally Ullrich in 1979. How I came to meet them is not really that important, rather the fact that I did meet them. They immediately struck me as both being very nice, kind and genuine people. It would be fair to say that over time because of the relationship that formed between us they became like second parents to me and I like a sibling to them, the sibling that they had never managed to have as man and wife. Our relationship became that entwined and interwoven with each other.

Although it didn't take a rocket scientist to work out that Max was in fact German, at first I had no idea of his past as a German Prisoner of War who had been held at Camp 266 in nearby Langdon Hills. I was amazed when he first started telling me about his experiences as a POW in the camp. I wasn't shocked, no not shocked because there was nothing to be shocked about. As time went on he began telling me more and more about his war time experiences. How he had come to be in the Army. How he had come to be captured, why he decided to remain here in England after the war and not return to Germany and how he and Sally met each other.

Listening to him was like reading a history book with his words bringing it all to life and making it all so real. He would rather not have been incarcerated in a POW camp for so many years, but he knew once he had been captured that his war was over and this was his fate for an unknown period of time

He never had any real desire to escape, after all where would he go. By now his own colleagues were in full retreat back to the very heart of the Nazi empire and seat of power in Berlin.

If he had escaped he would have had to have found a way of getting across the English Channel undetected. Land in France and then without any documentation in his possession make his way to Germany travelling through at least three countries en route, all the time trying to bypass advancing American and British troops who would be trying their hardest to get to Berlin first. When you look at it like that, even today, what was the point?

Before the war Max had worked on a farm and was in fact a master cow milker, a skill that would not only come in very handy but make him a much sort after individual. You have to remember that in those days the milking of a cow was done by hand, so the more cows you had the more milking that you had to do. There were no milking machines to make life easy for the beleaguered farmer.

Although he wasn't a particularly tall man, Max was very strong and powerful built and had massive hands just like shovels. He really loved working on the farms and the freedom that it gave him."

Maximillian Ullrich was born on the 24th February 1911 in Bladen, Upper Silesia, Germany. He had a younger brother who died sometime after the end of the Second World War. His father had died whilst serving his country during the First World War.

Before looking at Max's time in the German Army and his time as a POW, I first want to look at his childhood and younger years as I believe this will provide the reader with a fuller understanding of just what type of person Max actually was.

Post First World War Germany was a difficult place to live and exist, with very little in the way of work and even less when it came to food for the masses. It was not unusual for the poorer people to have to resort to eating animal feed.

Max's mother re-married when he and his brother were still quiet young. He described his step-father as a violent, lazy alcoholic, who not surprisingly, he did not like, but as he was so young at the time, there was nothing that he could do.

Any money that came in to the home was not spent on the needs of the family but on the alcoholic requirements of Max's step-father. They were so poor that his mother often had to pawn or sell his and his brothers shoes to get money to help feed the family. The pair of them would often walk to school wearing sacking and straw tied to their feet in place of their shoes. They would have to do this whatever time of the year it was, summer or winter, no matter what the weather was like.

Their clothes were, for long periods of time, no more than just rags which were very rarely replaced. This led to years of teasing from some of the better off children who lived in their village, which in turn led to Max getting in to lots of fights through standing up for himself and his brother.

Max remembered one Christmas when he and his brother were each given a wooden toy as a present. They argued over them and in a drunken rage their step-father grabbed hold of the toys and threw them both on the fire. That was the end of their Christmas.

Max didn't have too many good memories of his childhood, but on the other hand he didn't know any better. He just assumed that what he was going through was the same for all children of a similar age. His step father regularly beat both him and his mother. The family never owned any property or animals and it was not unusual for them to be behind with their rent. Any valuables had long since been sold off. It was a very limited existence.

In the early 1920's in the post war years, Germany was on her knees. She had lost the war, the cost of which had crippled the country and it continued to after the war was over due to fines and compensation she had to pay to the victorious nations in remunerations.

The next bit of his story I found absolutely breath taking. Max wasn't certain about how old he was at the time but it is something which he remembers and recalls vividly. He remembers coming home from school one day and being met by his mother at the front door. She had in her arms a bundle of his clothes, which remember wouldn't have been anything that fancy at all. He wasn't allowed to go back inside the house and she wouldn't tell him what was actually going on.

She grabbed hold of him by the arm and took him to a nearby land owner's farm. During the journey he wasn't allowed to talk and his mother didn't talk to him, she just hurried him along. He lost all track of time or distance, but when they got to the farm it transpired that his mother was actually selling him to the landowner. She handed Max over to the farmer who in return handed his mother a sum of money in payment. His mother kissed him, turned around and simply walked away.

What hurt Max the most was the fact that he wasn't even allowed to return home to see his younger brother. Although Max didn't know it at the time, but he was safely back home in doors and thankfully was never sold. This experience caused him to resent his step father even more than he already did believing that this was all of his doing, although he never found out if that was actually the case.

Ironically, even though he was sad about what had happened, his life changed for the better from that moment. He was given as much food as he could eat. He was provided with brand new boots and work clothing. He recalls that it was the first time in his young and traumatic life to date that he had never had to worry about when or where his next meal was going to be coming from.

His first night living at the land owner's farm was spent in a nice warm cosy barn where he fell asleep straight away with a stomach full of food, something which he had never done before.

He soon realised that this was to be his new life. The work was hard but he was used to that. He lived with other young adult males who he assumed had been sold off by their parents as well. They all grew up very quickly. Because the land owner fed Max so well and he worked so hard, he very quickly became an incredibly strong young man.

He was aware that his mother visited the farm regularly, but not to see and speak with him, but to collect money from the land owner. It was apparent that he was paying Max's mother for all of the hard work that he did.

Whilst working at the farm Max learnt all about what was called "animal husbandry." He was taught how to handle large animals, oxen, cattle and horses.

After he had been working at the farm for what he remembers to have been several years, he was allowed to go into town to attend local dances. He didn't have too much luck with the ladies mainly because they saw him as being an uneducated farm hand and because of the reputation of his stepfather.

As time went on he was even allowed to return home to see his mother and younger brother. Max recalls that on one such visit his step father was there and he saw him hit his mother. Max intervened and with one punch knocked him down on the ground. He told him if that he ever heard of him laying a finger on his mother again he would come back and kill him. His step father never did hit Max's mother ever again.

By now Max was as strong as an ox, fit, muscular and toned. The fittest he had ever been in his entire life.

When Max turned twenty-one he was given his full wages for the first time. His mother would still come to the farm to collect her money, but now it was from him and not the land owner.

On the farm they were self-sufficient and often had young men calling at there looking for work. Some of them he recognised from fights he had been in at school. He sent them on their way before they got to speak with the landowner. As far as Max was concerned his life was absolutely fine exactly the way it was so the last thing that he needed or wanted was anybody coming along and changing things.

Max was so strong it was not unusual for him to harness himself to the plough and plough the fields himself, if there were no animals available to do it for him.

Max recalls the first time he saw his boss strutting around the farm in a Nazi uniform. Between them, all of the farm hands had to clean and polish his boots, belt and straps. Max was spared doing this as he was so busy rearing, raising and milking the cattle. He learnt from the older "milk meister" how to deal with all kinds of animal ailments and how to give treatments to the milk cows. In all his years of working on the farm, Max never recalls ever seeing a vet visiting the place.

Max enjoyed working on the farm so much that he decided that he wanted to become a "milk meister" but to do this he would have to sit and pass some exams. Initially this caused him some problems because although Max could read his writing was not all that good. Over time he improved his writing, took and passed his exams, he was given a pay rise in line with his new qualifications and he now taught others the same skills that he had now acquired.

As there were no mechanised milking machines in those days it all had to be done by hand. Max milked the cows every day, morning and evening. There were 126 cows that needed milking each and every day. Even though Hitler and the Nazis were now in power he never concerned himself with politics or "joined the party." He was happy in his world of working on the farm and milking the cows, it was nice and uncomplicated.

Max had a very interesting war. He joined up at the outbreak of the war in 1939 when he was already 28 years of age. Because he had flat feet he was deemed unfit to serve in an infantry regiment but instead was attached to an ordnance regiment that used to ferry munitions by horse and cart to soldiers who were engaged in the fighting.

Two years into the war he was released from his military service and sent back home to Germany to return to working on the farms. There was a hungry civilian population that still needed feeding as well as all of those serving in the military. The crops wouldn't sort themselves out. Max stayed working on the farms until either late 1943 or early 1944 when he was called back in to the army again. This time, despite his flat feet, he was allocated to an infantry regiment, because by now the Germans were starting to get desperate for soldiers

During the time back at the farm he married a Polish woman, Martha, who also had a young daughter. Not out of love but to help her out. By being married to a German citizen life would be a lot easier for her. Max said that although she was a nice enough woman, there certainly wasn't ever any love between them. This was a period of his life that he didn't really like to talk about that much.

Max had already had a slice of good fortune from his first stint in the war. In early 1941 Max had been sent to Yugoslavia to undergo ski training. At the end of the course Max was taken to one side by his instructors who thought his surname was Ulbrich. Although Max pointed out to the instructors that his surname was in fact Ullrich it made no difference and he was sent back to Europe to fight. Max was extremely thankful that decision was made as everybody else who was on the course was sent to the Western Front in Russia after it had finished. They all subsequently perished a positive twist of fate (For Max) if ever there was one.

He was captured a week or so after the D-Day landings in June 1944 not far from the Normandy beaches by advancing British troops. By now Max and colleagues realised that theirs was a hopeless plight. Their own political officer had already been shot and killed by one of the German soldiers and their unit commander, the equivalent of a Captain, totally lost his nerve. As far as Max was concerned enough was enough. He removed the bolt from his rifle threw it away and with his hands in the air walked towards the advancing British troops. The rest of his colleagues followed suit.

All he remembered was that it was by a Scottish Regiment which captured him. He was then shipped back to the United Kingdom. Max couldn't remember where the first camp was that he arrived at, but along with all other prisoners he was interviewed by the allies. This was where he made his first mistake. He had been bossed about his entire life in one form or another and he had had enough of it. He had seen officers and Nazi's being separated from the ordinary German soldiers. Thinking that they were going to receive better treatment he decided to pretend he was one of them.

When it came his turn to be interviewed he clicked his heels together, raised his arm and shouted "Heil Hitler". This certainly had the desired affect because he was quickly man handled by the guards and thrown in to a separate compound with the Nazi's and officers.

He ended up in a POW camp somewhere up in Scotland. He soon realised the gravity of his mistake. Nearly everybody else who he was there with was a Nazi officer and they treated him like a slave. He had to do whatever they told him to and if he refused or didn't do it quick enough he was beaten. Fighting back wasn't an option or there could have been severe consequences for him.

When he was interviewed at the camp he saw his chance to get out of there. He explained via an interpreter that he wasn't a Nazi and the he was just an ordinary German soldier. At first his inquisitors were sceptical as they had heard numerous similar stories, but when he started talking about farming and what he had done before the war they had someone question him about his skills as a "milk meister" and the exams which he had passed. Thankfully for Max they were happy with his story and he never went back in to the camp.

He was transferred down to Essex where he spent the first few weeks in Camp 286 just down the road from Langdon Hills at Purfleet, before being moved to Camp 266 where he stayed until he was eventually released in September 1948.

Soon after his arrival at Langdon Hills he managed to wangle himself a job working in the camps kitchen. This was good for two reasons, one he was never short of food and in the winter he was always working in a nice warm place.

The camps chefs. Picture by kind permission of
Erwin Hannemann.

When knowledge of his farming prowess became known coupled with the fact that there was a shortage of men locally, especially ones to carry out much needed work in the fields he started working at one of the local farms where the milk yield quickly improved. Some nights he would not return to the camp but stay on the farm if some of the cows were ill or about to give birth.

What surprised Max was the lack of any animosity shown towards him and his colleagues by the local population, which he half expected, when he was out and about in Laindon.

By now he had already met his future wife Sally, told her all about his wife back in Germany and the circumstances of why they had married. Sally and her family lived in a bungalow that had been built by her father, at the bottom of Lee Chapel Lane near the bridle way.

Max recalled one time when he was working in the camps kitchen and made 3 extra loaves of bread. He placed them over the camp fence so that he could collect them later on and take them to Sally and her family. When he finished his work and went for a walk stopping to pick up the bread, but unfortunately for him he was spotted by the local Policeman who took him and the bread back to the camp. Max was charged with the theft of the bread and transferred to the POW camp at Purfleet but was back at Langdon Hills within a few days.

After the war Max had nowhere to go back to. His home town was now part of Poland and renamed Wlodzienin and all of the German people who had been living there had been forced out.

Max decided to stay in England and initially carried on working on local farms before utilising his strength and becoming a hod carrier for 5 bricklayers working on Basildon New Towns housing in Whitmore Way.

Max and Sally were married on the 20th March 1954 at Brentwood registry office after his divorce from Martha had come through just over a month earlier. Max ended up working as a cleaner at the Nevendon Sewage works until his retirement.

His younger brother served in the German army during the war, survived and when he was demobbed after the war he went to live in Hamburg which is where his mother ended up as well after the death of his stepfather. His first wife Martha stayed in Poland and remarried. Although Max returned to Germany over the years to visit his mother and brother, he never returned to his home town. My brother-in-law offered to take him back there once but he didn't want to go and instead just cried.

Max passed away on the 30th September 1999 at Southend General Hospital aged 88. His beloved wife Sally passed away on the 20th January 2002 at a residential home in Leigh-on-Sea. Both Max and Sally were cremated and interred in the pleasant and tranquil surroundings of Pitsea Crematorium.

Josef Kox

Above is a picture of a very young and youthful looking Josef Kox proudly posing in his German Army uniform.

One of the things which I have really enjoyed whilst researching this book is the individual stories that we have come across. Some of the individuals whose stories we have included are unfortunately no longer with us but thankfully some of them are. Each and every one of them is just as important as the next and collectively they paint a true record of what life was like in the camps and how they were emotionally affected by these experiences.

For some reason this is a part of our history that not too much has ever been written about either locally or nationally. Most of the POW camps are long since gone with often no or very little reference to them ever having existed. The first German POW's arrived in Great Britain in 1939 and by the time the last one had left and been repatriated back to their fatherland in 1948 over four hundred thousand of them had been incarcerated and become our 'guests', add to this another one hundred and fifty thousand Italian POW's and we have over half a million foreign combatants' that were held throughout Great Britain. A truly staggering figure, yet there is hardly any record, acknowledgement or discussion around them ever having been here and the part that they played in helping to keep Great Britain going especially with their work in the fields of farms up and down the country. By their efforts they ensured that the crops were collected on time, that they didn't rot in the fields and allowed our own population to be fed because the majority of our own men were fighting in wars across Europe and the Far East which meant they couldn't do it.

Let's try and put that into some kind of context. In the UK Census of 2001, some fifty three years later the entire male population for the whole of Essex was only eight hundred & fourty nine thousand and two.

Back to Josef's story written in his own words:

"I was born on the 11th of February 1926 in Osterath, Germany. I was called up in 1943 and served in the First Paratroop's Army. On the 14 of November 1944 I was captured in the Venlo pocket in the Netherlands by the 2nd Battalion of the Seaforth Highlanders.

Being taken prisoner is quite traumatic. Before they attacked, the artillery shelled us to keep our heads down. I was in a reasonably safe little shelter near Hulsen Lock on the Noordervaart. But we had high explosive stuff in there, tank mines, land mines... Anyway, they fetched us out of there, calling 'come out with your hands up'. So that was the end. But it's traumatic. You don't know what's going to happen. There are a thousand thoughts going through your mind, all in a split second.

One thing that I said to myself was that if they asked me my profession, I would say farmer. I come from a rural area, outside Dusseldorf, with lots of small holders and farmers. When the Polish campaign was finished, we had Polish prisoners there and they worked on the farms. They were looked after very well by the farmers because if you wanted any work out of them, you had to give them some food. And food was rationed and short. So I thought 'I'll say that I'm a farmer'. But it didn't work like that here! In Yorkshire were large farms, you never saw the farmer there so that didn't help!

They took us from camp Beverlo, near Leopoldsburg, to Edingen near Brussels, to Zedelgem near Brugge. One week before the war finished they brought me over here. They took me from Ostende to Tilbury, Tilbury by train to Fenchurch Street, on the lorry across to Waterloo, from Waterloo by train into Kempton Park race course. That was the big transit camp for all the prisoners coming from the continent. We were interviewed, frisked and interrogated and so forth for three or four days and then sent up to Butterwick, Yorkshire. From there we were sent to Lowestoft. They were building a big housing estate there and we worked on site, digging, drainage, building the roads. I spent the winter of 1945 there. I was moved to an ex American airbase in Seething, Norfolk for a while and then to Purfleet, Essex (No 286).

German POW Camp 266 – Langdon Hills

Purfleet was a large camp with quite a few thousand prisoners. I arrived in March 1946. We slept 8 in a tent with just wooden flooring. It was very primitive, like in the Army. It wasn't very nice with thousands of people and nothing much to do really. We were taken out to work every day by lorry, but at night time what could we do... play football, as much as poss, play table tennis. We did have quite a bit of help from the YMCA; they supplied musical instruments, proper footballs, football boots and books. They made quite an impact, it was quite something what they did for us and it was very much appreciated.

Every day some people were taken to work on farms, others to Romford to work on a building site. One day I was called to stay behind and report to the office. They told me I would go into billet and live on a farm. That evening a Captain McGregor took me in his jeep and I thought 'where the hell are we going?' We kept going and going and going...we finished up in Theydon Bois. It was a pig farm.

I was shown my quarters, which I had to share with another prisoner, Arthur. There was electric light, a stove, a radio, there were two single beds, white sheets... I didn't know what had hit me! And in the evening we were given a tray each: Welsh rarebit, bread and butter and jam, pot of tea, cup of cocoa, ten cigarettes... I said to my friend, 'how long does that have to last?' He said, 'oh that's for now, tomorrow we get more'. I wasn't used to that, you know, prisoner of war camp...

I remember Christmas '46. Christmas in Germany is very much a quiet and sober affair. Mr Morgan asked me and my friend to have Christmas dinner with him. I said 'Mr Morgan, thank you very much, that's very kind of you, very kind, but Christmas is a day for the family. Don't worry about us, we're all right'. He said 'you're going to have Christmas dinner with us you are two of the family.' So we accepted. Not only were there Mr and Mrs Morgan but their daughter Pam, their son Roger and then two American GI's, Tom and Jerry, who were friends of the family. It was a very nice and moving affair. I shall never forget it.

From Oakhill Farm I was sent back to the camp for a while and then sent to Hayes Hill Farm in Waltham Abbey. This is where I met my wife. She was an art student and during the school holidays she would go and work on the farm. That's how we met and we never looked back. We have just celebrated our Golden Wedding.

After a short while I was sent to Rochford's nursery, Waltham Abbey. I was billeted there and lived on the nursery in a hut. A lorry load of POW's came every day from Epping camp (No. 116 Hill Hall). We worked hard: picking tomatoes, stringing tomatoes, digging, washing down, washing the pots, carrying, packing, spraying... everything. The relationship between the prisoners and the local people was very good apart from the odd one who was not so friendly.

I had some difficulty with my father in law. He had been wounded by the Germans in the First World War. He was very opposed... My wife was only 19 when I met her and I was 21, in a prisoner of war camp... what future could I offer her! I could understand her father not being impressed! He was a good man, an honest man and eventually we got on very well, as I did with all the family.

I was demobbed and decided to stay here. I picked the language up as I went along. I had a dictionary and once I looked up a word, I never forgot it. That's how I built up my vocabulary. When I listen to myself talk I think I'm speaking perfect English. But in reality, when I talk to people it doesn't take long for people to say 'where do you come from!' This is after 60 years. I always say 'have a guess'. And they say 'Poland? Holland? Sweden?' Nobody wants to say 'are you German?'

Being a prisoner was the worst time of my life. To be in a Prisoner of War camp, deprived of your freedom... At the time in particular because I didn't know if my people were still alive, what was going to happen, it was an awful time. Escape? Where to? I thought of escape soon after I was captured. There were three of us, the fourth was wounded: Heinz Mirus, Karl Bente, Werner Schnabbel and myself. We were in this little compound, with barbed wire. It was very cold that night, I'll never forget. And this soldier standing there with his rifle... and I thought to myself 'I don't know. It wouldn't take very long to take that rifle off you and make you the prisoner and we'll go...' And then I thought 'go where?' We were already near the German border. We knew, it was not long before the game was up. It was only a matter of time. We had nothing to fight with. So there was no point. We knew the game was up. It was the end.

At this late stage I would like to pay a tribute to the people of Waltham Abbey. Considering the war, six years of it... and people here suffered and everyone suffered. Everybody suffered in that war, didn't matter where you were, or who you were, you suffered to some degree. So I was really surprised to find that people took to us, they were very tolerant and friendly and I will never forget that."

I always find such accounts not only very moving but so incredibly amazing as well. It is because individuals such as Josef Cox have recorded their stories for posterity that future generations can gain a greater understanding of what life was really like for these men and the conditions that they had to endure. In just a few pages Josef Kox has preceded to tell us his life story. From where he was born, to when he joined the army, to how he was captured to his life as a Prisoner of war, to meeting his wife and celebrating their Golden Wedding anniversary."

This article appeared on the BBC's website, ww2peopleswar on the 6th December 2005 having being submitted by the Epping Forest District Museum.

I would like to take this opportunity to thank the Epping Forest District Museum for their kind permission to use Josef Kox's story in this book.

Whilst browsing the internet to check my information on Josef I came across the following article which appeared in the Mercury Newspaper on the 23rd February 2007. I felt that it was relevant to his story as it helped show what type of person he was. The interview he gave to the newspaper is repeated below with the kind permission of the Herts and Essex Newspapers Ltd.

Former Waltham Abbey defender Josef Kox took a trip down memory lane this month when he re-visited Capershotts 60 years after he first turned out for the club as a player.

The 81-year-old was a member of the very first Abbey team and made an emotional return to the club to see if current first team goalkeeper John Hickman was a relative of Wally Hickman, the man who managed the side in the late 1940s.

Kox told the Mercury: *"I went to Capershotts and made myself known and asked if he was a relation - apparently he wasn't - but I met Dave Hodges the club historian and was talking to him about old times."*

The team, Abbey Sports, played at Capershotts and would later become Waltham Abbey after merging with Beechfield Sports FC.

Capershotts has changed beyond recognition since Kox left the club in 1950 and he was hugely impressed with the improvements that have been made over the years, including a seated stand, terraces and clubhouse.

"When we played there was just a football field and goalposts," he continued. *"There was no dressing room so we used to get changed at The Compass pub and walk to the pitch. It would take between five and 10 minutes to get there. It's changed a lot and I'm impressed. They've got a great set up there now. It was great to go back. They were very welcoming."*

Kox was a German Prisoner of War, captured in Holland during the Second World War, and was held at the Galley Hill camp in Waltham Abbey at the time Abbey Sports were formed.

He and fellow POW's passed the time with Sunday morning kick about's and after their official release in 1948 manager Wally Hickman approached them about playing for the team.

"We had a German team but we were not allowed to play in any leagues so we played mostly friendlies on a Sunday and in the junior cups," added Cox. *"We were invited to join the team so we did. There were no incentives in those days we just played because we had a love of football. Occasionally the manager would buy us a pint but that was it."*

Kox and friend Ernst Berkemeier, also a POW, were among those who joined Hickman's team and Abbey Sports were born.

Made up of local lads in their late teens and early 20s, the team went on to win the Waltham Challenge Cup and were runners-up in the Waltham League premier division in their very first season. The following year they did the double, winning both competitions. Spectators were few and far between in those days but one person who did come to watch was Kox's girlfriend Pamela who would later become his wife.

They met at Hayes Hill Farm where Kox worked during his time as a POW. She would regularly attend Capershotts and it was he who took one of the club's first ever team photos. Kox left the club in 1950 to concentrate on work and raising a family, moving with Pamela to. Though he never played football again Kox was a regular spectator at White Hart Lane, as well as watching matches at Arsenal, West Ham, and Leyton Orient and saw 11 World Cup matches, including all of England's games, in 1966.

"I saw all these matches for just £4 and four shillings. How times have changed!"

Kox rarely travels *to* White Hart Lane now, but said he was keen to return to Capershotts again this season.

"I thoroughly enjoyed playing there with those young men," he added. *"They made me feel very welcome then, as they did when I returned a few weeks ago."*

I know from subsequent research which I have carried out on the internet that Josef Kox was unfortunately killed in a car crash on the evening of in January 2010, close to his 84th birthday. He sounded a truly remarkable individual.

Waldemar Duemke

I was amazed to discover that some of the prisoners at Camp 266 had been very religious individuals indeed, which in the circumstances I found quite amazing taking into account what most of them had been through and experienced. Two of those prisoners in particular, Waldermar Duemke and another man with the surname Quessel were exactly that.

How people managed to balance the two mediums of war and religion, I will never know. After having fought in a war when they had seen friends and colleagues die and maybe have had to kill others themselves, simply to stay alive, it must have been extremely difficult to believe in anything, but remarkably they did.

Both Duemke and Quessel became members of the Apostolic Church and although we have not been able to find out too much about either man, we do know a few things. Whether they were deeply religious people before the war or simply found religion whilst contemplating life during their time as POW's, we do not know.

Their first religious contact between the two POW's as ordained ministers of the Apostolic Church and an English family took place on the 18th May 1947, when the two of them were invited into the homes of two local families, the Batt's and the Hopper's.

Ken Porter and Stephen Wynn

An interesting entry appears in Duemke's diary on the 22nd June 1947. He records receipt of a letter in which the Bishop Hennrich of Duesseldorf Germany, calls upon him to "give testimony to the English people". This would have been no mean task for Duemke who was still a prisoner of war in the land of the people to whom he was now being asked to testify of the re-establishment of the Apostolic ministry.

Following his transfer from the Langdon Hills POW camp to the one in Harwich, which was a Transit Camp, Duemke was given the task of monitoring the movement of German prisoners of war. He was given the permission of the British Authorities to add to the list of questions which were required to be answered by the German POW's, a request that they indicate their religion. By this means the Duemke was able to identify and make contact with any New Apostolic brothers passing through the camp. Some of these POW's would go on to become active workers and ministers in the Apostolic church in the UK after the war.

In an effort, it would seem, to clear up some misunderstanding that may have arisen at the time, Chief Apostle Bischoff wrote to the Apostles in 1949, informing them that all enquiries regarding church venues in the UK and for that matter any other enquiries relevant to their work, should be directed to Waldemar Duemke, who by now was an Evangelist in the Apostolic church

During the latter part of the war and soon after its ending, Englishmen serving in the Forces in Germany came into contact with New Apostolic families there. Among them were two English soldiers who accepted the faith and became sealed members of the Church in Herford, Germany. On the return of these soldiers to their homeland they started to arrange regular gatherings to take place. Waldermar Duemke, who was still being held as a prisoner of war, became more and more involved in the New Apostolic faith in England.

The Church's Office, in Frankfurt Germany, provided the new Apostolic's in the United Kingdom with names and addresses of members living in the UK who could then be contacted. At this time services were being held by the Waldermar Duemke in Laindon, Essex and in Camberwell Green, London, also as far afield as Great Somerford, Wiltshire.

In a relatively short space of time the Apostolic church had spread itself all over the UK with many of those ordained to deliver their message being ex-POW's who had stayed on after the war and their release from the camps.

I found the story about the Apostolic Church an extremely interesting one as it showed good can come from bad. Here we were in the aftermath of the 2nd World War, with Waldermar Duemke and Quessel both still being held as Prisoners of War and remarkably they still found the time and desire in their hearts for Christianity and God. If they had been god fearing men before the war they could have been forgiven for having lost their faith. War brings with it terrible sights, horrendous experiences and ever lasting memories, the type of which are not very pleasant. They are the memories of having lost friends and comrades and witnessed things that you would not wish on your worst enemy.

To have such humility after having lived through the traumas of the Second World War requires a very special kind of person.

The New Apostolic Church.

In early January (2012), I (Ken) bumped into an old cricketing friend of mine, Tony Williams, outside the triangle shops in Langdon Hills. We got talking about what we were up to these days and I explained that I was researching the Germany POW camp at the top of the hill. His immediate reply was that he had known one of the German POW's from the camp, Waldemar Duemke, who was involved with founding a non-conformist church in Langdon Hills. He explained that the house where Duemke and the other converts used to meet is still there on the corner of Alexander Road and the High Road, called 'Cornerstone'. From what Tony was able to tell me Waldemar's wife and family came over to England after the war once he had been released from the camp and they set up home in 'Cornerstone'.

A couple of days later I called on the house and met the current occupier, a lovely old man called Eric who had moved into the property in 1955. Eric confirmed that the previous occupier held church services in the house. He showed me what is now his bedroom and explained that when he moved in there was a picture of a sunrise at the end of the room and a small platform.

My assumption is that the platform was where the alter would have been when Duemke used the premises as a church. The bungalow was built in the mid 1920's and had very high ceilings compared with how today's houses are built. The room was initially two rooms but a joining wall had been removed and double doors had been put in its place.

It is obvious this was the room where church services and meetings took place. The double doors being there to partition the room depending upon what activity was taking place and how many people were in attendance.

On the outside on the north facing wall is the following plaque:

THE KISS OF THE SUN FOR PARDON
THE SONG OF THE BIRDS FOR MIRTH
ONE IS NEARER GOD'S HEART
IN A GARDEN
THAN ANYWHERE ELSE
ON EARTH

Tony first met Waldemar Duemke sometime in late 1947 when Tony was at Sunday school service in the local Baptist Church and the latter was still a German prisoner of war at the Langdon Hills camp.

The doors of the church were open when Duemke walked past and heard the singing coming from inside. Tony came out and asked Duemke if he would like to sing in his choir. Tony was only 14 years of age at the time and a member of the Laindon Boys Brigade which met at the Baptist Church and sang in their choir but he readily agreed that most of all he loved singing Soprano.

Services were held in the front room of the property and it was not long before he was joined by his mother, father and four sisters. Duemke would stand on the platform and conduct the choir. The choir of about 12 were also the congregation. Tony remembers going with the choir by coach to an Apostolic Church convention where exactly he can't recall. The Hymn they sung was "God be with you till we meet again".

Duemke had three children, Annilise, John and Frederick. Frederick went to Laindon High Road School. Sometime around 1949 Waldemar decided to merge the choir with another church. It was too far away and too expensive to get there so Tony left and lost touch with the church as well as Duemke and his family.

I would just like to add that during the compilation of this book every effort was made to confirm the details and information which appear in this particular chapter with reference to the Apostolic Church, as we wished to ensure that our information was factual.

Hans Albert Baldes

Hans served and fought during the Second World War as a soldier in the German army. He was captured in 1944 soon after the D Day landings and then spent the next four years as a Prisoner of War before being released in 1948.

Hans lived in the Laindon area after he was released from the German Prisoner of War Camp 266 back in 1948. Unfortunately Hans passed away in July 2010 and is survived by his wife, Edna who still lives in the local area.

He was born on the 1st August 1925 in a large coal mining town, Oberhausen in the Rhineland, Germany. His father was a shoemaker and his grandfather was a farmer in Peterswald, Hunsruck, which was some 200 hundred miles away. Oberhausen was a small, predominantly catholic village and the most important people who lived there and to whom the local residents had to take notice of were the Priest and the Schoolteacher.

From the right, Hans, his Mum and Dad, Aunt and Cousin. By kind permission of Edna Baldes.

His Grandfather died when he was only a few months old and so his grandmother took over the running of the farm, which wasn't easy by any stretch of the imagination. When Hitler came to power he decreed, one man for one job. Although the system was criticised it did more or less give the country full employment. However, it meant that Hans's father had to take over running the farm for his grandmother or else she would have lost it.

In 1932 Hans and his family moved from Oberhausen to Peterswald to run the farm. Being an only child coupled with the fact that his father was disabled, Hans had to help out on the farm whenever he could.

Farm House, Peterswald. Picture by kind permission of Edna Baldes

He started at the local village school on the 1st April 1932 when he was only 6 years old. The school had

218

only one teacher who catered for all of the children who were between 6 and 14 years. This meant he only had a very basic education with the main subject being the Catholic religion. He was also in the choir of the local Catholic Church.

Hans and his family never had the luxury of being able to own a wireless set, which meant that they had very little communication with the outside world. This in turn meant that they knew very little of what was going on in the rest of Germany let alone the rest of the world. That was until soldiers turned up one day and built a large concrete shelter in their back garden. Being fairly close to the French and Luxemburg borders the whole village was ringed with observation and defence shelters, similar to what in English we would know as pillboxes, although they were much more substantial. After the war they unsuccessfully tried to blow up the one in Hans's garden.

In 1938, a year before war broke out, when Hans was only 13 years old, he had to join the Hitler Youth Movement and attend meetings. Hans described it as like being in the Scouts, other than if you did not attend the meetings, then your parents were punished by the local authorities.

He was 14 years old when he eventually left school on the 31st March 1940. He was fortunate to get an apprenticeship in a nearby village (Kastlaun) as a Ferrier Blacksmith for Edward Bower. Hans lived in and his father had to pay for his keep but he was not allowed to sit with the family at meal times. He had to eat his meals in the kitchen on his own. Back in those days it was apparently quite normal. In saying that though, Hans was not very happy with the way he was treated by the Bower family, so he jumped at the opportunity in March 1942 to transfer to another similar position in a neighbouring village (Hazelbach) when a friend of his from school was called up into the army. The new family of Fredrich Hilz were a lot friendlier and he enjoyed his time there.

Because his father was disabled Hans was not initially required to join any of the German armed forces. As the war was drawing to an end, the authorities were calling up every man and boy they could find in a last ditch attempt to defend Germany. By now it didn't matter if individuals were young or old, abled bodied or not, every adult male was being called up to defend the nation.

Hans's father along with other villagers fled up into the surrounding hills and woods and hid out there for several months. By now the authorities were so desperate for men Hans's mother was threatened with death if she did not tell them where Hans's father was. However, like the rest of the village's womenfolk, she did not know where her husband was hiding.

Hans was conscripted into the army in June 1943, when he was 17 years of age. It was something which he had no choice in. He was enlisted into the Heavy Infantry which in effect was driving horse drawn wagons. Hans did a few months training at Koblenze before being sent with his regiment to the Russian front, although he did not realise at the time were he was actually going.

Hans at Seventeen and a half. Photograph by kind permission of Edna Baldes.

Luckily for Hans fate took over his destiny. Why? He doesn't know, but whilst on route to Russia his regiment was turned around and sent to France and saved from almost certain death.

Hans did not give much thought to the rights and wrongs of the war. At only 17, he wasn't even sure if he understood why his country was at war, or why they were fighting against so many countries. It had been instilled in all young German men from a very early age that it was their duty to fight and defend the Fatherland.

Hans was stationed near Lille and his role was that of a dispatch rider. The Germans had confiscated all the horses from the French farmers. Hans said he actually got on fairly well with the French, although he understood the partisans would have happily seen his demise regardless of his age. There was one small farmer whose daughter had an illegitimate child. The farmer had no way of supporting his family, so Hans spoke with his commanding officer who gave him permission to loan the farmer a couple of horses to help him plough his land.

The role of dispatch rider sounds a reasonably safe job, not in France though, the partisan had the habit of stretching cheese wire across the road, which meant whenever Hans was out riding he would have to lean over the horse's neck, otherwise he would have had his head taken off.

A task that really upset him was that just after D. Day one of his horses was badly injured and he had to shoot it.

Another story that later in life amused Hans was that when they started send over the V1's (Doodle Bugs), if the wind got too strong they would twist round and head back towards them. Hans however was not involved with the launching of them.

Approximately three months after D Day in September 1944 and after one and half years of almost continuous heavy fighting, Hans was captured by French partisans hiding behind a hedge, or as his wife Edna would later put it, "he didn't run fast enough." Hans found himself with a number of colleagues from numerous different regiments hiding behind a hedge when they were captured.

Many of the partisans surprisingly did not know how to use a rifle and asked Hans and his colleagues to show them how their weapons worked. Instead of helping the partisans they stripped them down and made them non-operational, partly to prevent the partisans from using them against Hans and his colleagues. Not surprisingly, nobody tried to escape simply because they didn't want to risk getting shot.

Hans and his colleagues were taken to a nearby barn and a local French farmer brought them some food and wine. They were a bit concerned that he might be trying to poison them so he first had to eat some of the food and drink some of the wine to prove to them that it was ok.

Soon afterwards a Catholic priest of all people arrived with a gun and wanted to shoot them all but fortunately before he could do so they were rescued by some passing Canadian soldiers. They were then taken to a nearby field as night time started to close in on them. They were each told to dig a hole in the ground. Hans started to fear the worst and thought it ironic that they had been rescued from a gun wielding priest who wanted to kill them to a group of Canadian soldiers who were going to kill them. Despite his worst fears the holes were purely for them to sleep in.

Eventually the Canadians handed them all over to the British soldiers who put them on a boat and shipped them to England.

Hans remembers arriving in England on the 15th September 1944. The local people who turned out to see their arrival at the docks in Southampton were not very pleased to see him and his colleagues. As they started marching on to the quayside they were spat at and some even tried to hit them. They were then transferred by train but because there was still a blackout in force there were no signs up showing the names of any of the towns so Hans cannot remember where he was initially sent to.

Hans remembers that the first main camp he was sent to was in Sheffield but after that he was moved to many different camps. Hans felt that this appeared to be a deliberate policy by the British authorities to keep moving them about so that they did not get too familiar with the location of the camps or become too friendly with other comrades who they were imprisoned with.

One of the camps he can remember was Eden Camp at Malton, North Yorkshire. While he was there the POW's made instruments from old bits and pieces and formed a band. When one of the Officers heard them playing he went and found them some old but workable instruments. The camp is now a museum and Hans has been back a few times, each time hoping he would meet up with this officer to thank him but they have never met.

Also while at the camp Hans and colleagues would be taken in an army truck to nearby farms to work. He remembers on occasions they would be guarded by an old guard (Hans would refer to him as being a relic from Dad's Army). This old soldier for some reason wanted to earn more money so he would arrange with the POW's and the farmer to do some work on the farm. He would leave his rifle with the POW's and if an Officer turned up to check on them one of the POW's would take the rifle and go and find the old guard who would return saying the POW was taken bad and needed the toilet. Hans is convinced there weren't any bullets in the gun. He found the Yorkshire Farmers very friendly.

Hans visiting the Eden Camp. Photograph with kind permission of Edna Baldes.

Hans said that he and most of his colleagues were totally unaware of the atrocities which the Nazi regime had carried out across Europe, until they were shown films about the concentration camps. It was a complete shock to him and like many of his comrades, at first he did not want to believe that these atrocities had occurred. They thought it was some kind of grotesque propaganda film designed to discredit Germany and make them out to be some kind of monsters.

In the POW camps that he stayed in there was a mixture of different military personnel, from the Army, Air-force, Navy and the SS. Unfortunately many of them were Nazi fanatics and would try and force the non-Nazis amongst them to celebrate Hitler's birthday. As would be expected, there were men in the POW camps with all different kinds of trades and skills, including chefs, film stars and entertainers who would put on shows for the POW's and after the war for the local population as well. There was some talk about escaping but Hans did not take too much notice of this talk when it came up and was quite happy just keeping himself to himself. Many of the prisoners made a selection of wooden toys for the local children. When the mood took him, Hans would make string bags. When they were sent out to do agricultural type work on the land, Hans recalls that it was always under armed guard. There were regular religious services that took place in the camps, but Hans said that he did not attend any. He gave no explanation as to why, but then maybe for some soldiers it was difficult for them to reconcile whatever their faith was with having fought in a war and seen friends and colleagues die as well as having had to kill enemy soldiers as well.

By the end of the war Hans was at camp 286 in Purfleet in Essex and to enable him to get to work on the various farms he was allocated a bicycle. He worked for five and a half days a week for a princely sum of eight shillings (That would just about buy a newspaper in today's money). Hans and some of his colleagues were later sent to a small camp at Orsett. They got on very well with the few soldiers who were there to guard them. There was also an Army Camp nearby just off the old A13 east of the Orsett Cock Hotel and Hans was often allowed to drive a truck around the camp and out on to the fields nearby. He was not allowed to drive it on the main highway though. On many occasions while in the camp filling up with diesel, soldiers would hide in the truck and jump out when he got top the fields just to get few extra hours of free time.

When restrictions were eased in 1947 they were allowed to go to people's homes, go to church but they were not allowed to fraternise with the locals, although this was something that had been regularly flouted for a long time. To distinguish the German POW's from the local population they wore old army uniforms that had been dyed maroon with a large patch of green or yellow on the back. They also had to make sure that they were back at camp by 10pm.

Hans and some of his comrades went to work for a Mr Pinkerton a local farmer, who had farms at both Bulphan and Orsett. Hans was given the job of ploughing the fields as he was the only one who had any real experience of farming. This suited him as he preferred to work alone.

Hans back row with his colleagues at Pinkerton Farm, Bulphan.
Photograph by kind permission of Edna Baldes

Mr Pinkerton also had several green-houses that were heated by coal and Hans remembers that he would go with his lorry driver, Darky Lowe, to West Horndon Station and shovel coal from the railway trucks into the lorry. They both worked well together and on their return Hans would wash and soap down in a barrel of cold water. As soap was still on ration Hans would give the remainder of the soap to Darky as he had a wife and three children. It was at Pinkerton farm that Hans met Edna his future wife. Edna lived in a plot land bungalow near where the Langdon Hills Tesco's store is today. She was working in the farm's greenhouses looking after tomatoes, cucumbers etc. She used to cycle to work, and one day in early 1946 she got a puncture, Hans offered to mend it for her, surprisingly this happened again the following day and the day after that, with Hans mending her puncture on all three occasions.

Mr Pinkerton would once a year arrange a coach outing to the sea for his English workers, on one such day with only the German's working Han's had finished his work for the day so he went into one of the greenhouses where the other POW's were working to see if he could help. They were picking off the side shoots of the tomato plants. Simple enough, but Han's instead of picking off the side shoot he picked out the middle resulting in half a greenhouse of tomatoes coming along a lot later than they should have been. Han's was banned from the going into the greenhouses. He was however caught on another occasion when

he had gone into the greenhouse where Edna was working. He explained he had a splinter and was getting Edna to remove it, but as Edna says, 'we were cuddling.'

Although the POW's were not supposed to fraternise with the local women, Hans and Edna started meeting each other on Saturdays and going for bicycle rides around the Essex Countryside. At the time Edna was going out with a local lad but despite this, decided to take Hans to the Kurzal in Southend for a day out. She got an overcoat for him to wear to cover up his uniform which had yellow patches on so that people did not realise he was a POW. When they got there Edna wanted to go on the scenic railway (The Big Dipper). Her boyfriend had never wanted to go on it but Edna thought a big strapping German most definitely would, but no, Hans did not want to go on it either. So she took him on the Tunnel of Love and cuddled up to him. This was where Hans said that they captured each other's hearts.

Friends & colleagues of Hans at Pinkerton Farm.
Photograph by kind permission of Edna Baldes.

Edna was living in Dunton at the time near the Working Colony and it was outside the Colony offices watching the clock they both would stand and chat because Hans had to leave by 9pm to enable him to cycle back to the Purfleet Camp by 10pm. The camp was where the Circus Tavern is just off the A13.

It was his quiet, reserved nature and of course handsome features that had attracted Edna to Hans in the first place. In all their sixty years of married life they never argued or raised their voices to each other, he was to Edna, the complete gentleman.

Hans last Prisoner of War Camp was at the Langdon Hills Camp where he spent just two weeks before being released. After his release he still had to report to the Police at Laindon Police Station once a week but within a short period of time the local detective at Laindon told him not to worry about keep calling in, he knew where Hans was if he needed to speak to him.

Hans had never bothered to learn how to speak English until he met Edna and even then he only picked it up as he went along, he never attended any formal lessons. Whilst a POW in the camps there was no need, as all of the camps had interpreters in them.

In 1947 the process began of sending the POW's back home to Germany but because he had by now met Edna he did not want to return home. He took up the offer to stay in England for another year and work for the Agriculture Committee. He was sent to High Garret near Braintree where he had to live for the year. Although basically free, ex-POW's who were sent to High Garret still had to live in huts, similar to the ones that they had lived in as POW's.

On his day off Hans used to travel back to Dunton to see Edna on a Green National Bus, often with other colleagues who were also visiting their English girlfriends. They were Johnny and Ernest Stryczek both from the Langdon Hills camp. Ernest was a Taylor by trade and Johnny and Ernest were both to marry they English girlfriends and stay in England.

Hans was surprised that many of the ex-POW's were being allowed to go home from High Garret before the year was up, when Hans question the foreman about this, his reply was that they were married or had children. So within three weeks Han's and Edna were married.

Hans always said the Queen was allowed to marry her Greek Prince, so King George allowed the German ex-POW's to marry their English girlfriends.

Edna and Hans were married on the 14th June 1948. They caught a bus from Dunton to Brentwood, and were married at the register office there. After the ceremony they caught a bus back home, had a cup of tea, a piece of cake, and then caught the train to Southend for a five day honeymoon in a B&B.

Edna's father allowed them to set up home with him in Western Avenue, Dunton, at the rear of where Tesco's is today. Peter Lee a farmer at Horndon on the Hill employed Hans, so he was allowed to stay and work in England but in theory he still had to report to the local Police once a week.

For the next year they moved around the district, first to Pitsea, then in a caravan near Laindon Station before renting a bungalow in Colony View Road, Dunton, south of the railway line in 1949. Hans was back working at Pinkerton's farm.

Friends of Hans and Edna, Winnie and John a soldier from the Langdon Hills Army Camp were living in the foreman's bungalow at the Dunton Colony (later to become a residential caravan and mobile home site), which was just the other side of the railway line.

If Hans had been carting coal for heating the greenhouses at the farm during the day he would call on his friend's house on the way home to have a bath. All they had in the bungalow 'Loraine' was a bowl and rain water from the rain tank.

Hans was well liked by Edna's family and none of them ever had any problems with their relationship. Neither of them can even recall ever having any issues with any of the neighbours either.

Hans appreciated that his parents must have been hurt by his decision to stay in England and not to return to Germany but they had adopted a female cousin of his as a baby, so he knew that they were not alone and that they loved her dearly. The only real problem with Hans family about his marriage to Edna was not so much that he was marrying an English girl but the fact that she was not a Roman Catholic. But as Hans put it, "I wanted to stay and marry Edna the English rose had got her thorns into me."

After a few years of married life Edna persuaded Hans that he should go back home and see if they could make a life in Germany. Hans did not want to go back at first but agreed when his father informed him that he had started up a haulage business with his brother Clements, who was Hans's uncle.

So Hans, Edna and their baby daughter left England for a new life in Germany. However, Hans soon became disillusioned at how the business was being run financially, so he went to work lumbering in the local forest to save up sufficient funds having decided that he wanted to return to live in England.

While Hans was out working, Edna helped out where she could. In the fields planting potatoes, sewing for the family and spring cleaning the home, this gave Hans's mother the opportunity to look after her granddaughter. It also meant that Edna this English protestant girl could gain some brownie points with Hans parents.

Whilst living back in Germany Hans still refused to go to church, it turned out that the reason why he had lost complete faith in religion went back to when he was captured by the French partisans and the incident where the French Priest threatened to shoot him and his comrades.

Within three months Hans had saved enough money to return to England with Edna and their daughter. However, the problem now was would he actually be allowed back into England? Edna's stepmother contacted her local MP and the advice eventually given was to travel and just see what Customs had to say, so that's just what they did. Well, whatever it was they said at Customs worked because they allowed Hans back in to the country. Han kept in touch with his family back in Germany and over the years they visited each other as often as they could.

He was finally demobbed from the German Army in 1948 at Laindon Police Station by the local detective. He became a British citizen in 1952 and a British Subject in 1970 when he swore an oath on the bible to the Queen and Country.

When looking back on his life he often said it took a war to find love and happiness. Edna and Hans were married for 61 years. They had two children, two grandchildren, two great grandchildren, a wonderful family and a wonderful life."

Hubert Heeman -The Bottle

When researching the impact that Scottish farmers had on farming following the Agricultural Depression of the 1880s I contacted Janet McCheyne of Noke Hall Farm, Doesgate Lane, Bulphan and she told me the story of Hubert Heeman and his bottle.

Hubert was a prisoner from 1944 to 1948. He was not from the Langdon Hills Camp but from the Purfleet. I have included his story because it just highlights the type of emotional relationships that were formed.

Hubert was born in St Tonis in 1924 and attended the local Catholic Boys' School in School Road for eight years. He was captured sometime in 1944 and eventually ended up in at the Purfleet POW camp. He was sent to work with several other prisoners on the Brown's family farm at Noke Hall, Bulphan, Essex. Ten prisoners helped to set up a chicken farm there. After completion, Hubert and another prisoner stayed on the farm, doing field work. Despite a stringent ban on contact with the POW's Mrs Brown supplied them with coffee, sandwiches and even cigarettes. In gratitude for the good treatment they had received for nine months Hubert crafted a painstaking miniature model of the Farm. He was able to place the model in a glass bottle and presented it to the Brown family when he left for home.

In 2000 Thomas Barber arrived at the German Embassy in London with the following story: "Perhaps you can help me regarding a model of a farm in a bottle. This bottle originated from a former prisoner of war, who worked sometime between 1944 and 1948 on Mr Brown's farm in Bulphan, Essex who presented the bottle to the Brown family shortly before he went home to Germany.

I received this bottle some years later, after Mr Brown's death. I simply cannot keep this bottle, especially as I was also a former soldier and I realise that this bottle must be very important to the family in Germany, just as it would have been to me. Can you therefore, please try and discover the maker or his family, because I would like to return it to the maker or his family. Also, it would help me find peace of mind if I knew that the bottle found its rightful home."

On the 6th July 2000, Hubert now 76 and who had lost his sight in 1999, received a 'phone call from the German Embassy in London;' a Mr Miller enquired whether he had been a prisoner of war in England and, if so, when and where.

Following the telephone call, Hubert Heeman received the following letter from the German Embassy in London:

Dear Mr Heeman

I am sending you, as arranged with Staffboatman Miller, the handicraft masterpiece which you presented to Farmer Brown during your time as a prisoner of war in the 2nd World War. I am very happy that we have been able to work together to bring your unique work "home". It's perfect condition after over 50 years proves on one hand, the excellent handiwork and on the other hand, how carefully this souvenir has been handled over all those years. It must have had great significance to the owner. Also, the German Embassy in London are very interested to hear your story with admiration, nominate yur art work in eye-shine (mit Bewundernung Ihr Kunstwerk in Augenschien genommen).
We would be grateful if we could perhaps telephone you to find out more aspects of your time in England.
With friendly greetings
Hass Kortge, Colonel and Air Force Attache.

The bottle with the model farm reached Hubert undamaged in August 2000. Hubert, with his old schoolmates helped him to produce a thank you letters to Mr Barber and the Germany Embassy in London. And over time, a lively correspondence developed. Although Hubert and his family are overjoyed to have it in their possession after more than 50 years, he is naturally disappointed that he can no longer see the model in the bottle. It, however, brought back many memories of his three and half years as a POW in England.

Hubert and his colleagues with the bottle. Photograph by kind permission of Janet McCheyne.

Ernest Stryczek

Sometime during the late 1940s, Albert Banks and Ernest Stryczek used to pass each other walking along Laindon High Road and as polite people do would acknowledge each other. After a while the pleasantries turned into conversation and this then turned in to a lifelong friendship.

Ernest was a Polish born German POW from the Langdon Hills camp and was a tailor by trade (possible the tailor referred to in Ivy Powell's memories). Ernest and Albert would meet up for a quiet drink and a chat in the Laindon Hotel or the Fortune of War public house. Ernest also became friends with the rest of Albert's family and would often drop in for cup of tea or for meals if he was not working. Ernest was born in 1921 in the Polish district of

Siemianowice-Slaskie which had been under German (Prussian) control since the late 1790s. By 1922 following several short lived uprisings the Siemianowice area found itself within the borders of a 'reborn' Poland. Only to be reoccupied by Germany in 1939.

Ernest like most of his compatriots was given the option of joining the Germany army or going to work in a Labour camp. Ernest decided to join the army, although not appreciating that Germany was on the brink of the Second World War.

Little is known of Ernest's war service other than at some stage he was shot through the arm as he ran across a potato field in France. The force of the shot knocked him over. As he fell there was a hail of bullets and the poor chap next to Ernest was practically shot in half. (Ernest was fortunate that he fell otherwise he would have met the same fate! It makes you realise what awful things these men witnessed no matter what country they were fighting for).

As soon as he recovered he was sent back to his regiment. His only hope then was to be captured by the British as he did not want to fight for the Germans. Soon after his capture he was shipped off to England and found himself at the Langdon Hills Camp. He became known as the camp tailor and it is understood that he made many clothes for the British Officers and Guards. He was also called upon on several occasions to make costumes for the various shows the POW's put on at the camp.

At the end of the war what had been his home became part of the Russian Zone, so like many other German prisoners he decided to stay behind in England and make a life for himself here. It would be nearly 30 years before he saw his family again, although they were able to write to each other during those intervening years.

German POW Camp 266 – Langdon Hills

Ernest met up with a young girl Doreen Runnacles, (known by her family as Dean,) who lived in Suffolk Road, Laindon. It was possible that they met through Albert who was a friend of the family. Like other POW's from the camp who decided to stay behind, he was sent to High Garrett, north of Braintree to work on the farms for the Agriculture Committee. This is how Edna (refer Hans Baldes story) got to know him and Dean as they waited at the weekends for Hans and Ernest at the bus stop in Laindon.

Ernest and Dean got married at St Nicholas Church, Laindon on the 31st July 1948. Ernest's abode was given as the YMCA Hostel, High Garrett. When he eventually left there he returned to Laindon and got himself a farm job working for the Pilkington's at Bulphan alongside Hans Baldes and other ex POW's.

He was living at the time in a cottage opposite Orsett Hospital. He was possibly renting it from the Pilkington's. Unfortunately the farmer one day spotted him taking it just a little bit too easy and immediately sacked him. Hans who was there at the time retorted if you can sack one German you can sack another and immediately resigned.

Hans and Edna who were also married were living in a cottage on Bulphan Fen owned by the Pilkington's. So both Ernest and Hans found themselves homeless. Hans and Edna went back to live with her parents. We are not sure where Ernest and Dean went but they soon ended up in a flat in Billericay in the South Green area. He managed to get himself a job with Marconi's in Chelmsford but from his flat he also ran a tailoring business part time for a few years. The tailoring business eventually failed because he had difficulty in getting his customers to pay on time.

He had several other jobs over the years, working for Brown and Tawse. He was also a Bus conductor on the 241 and 244 route which ran from Laindon railway Station, down the High Road, along St Nicholas Lane, Ballards Walk to Basildon and Back. He eventually ended up working at Yardley's which used to be off of Cranes Farm Road.

Ernest had three children, Paul, Alan and Lorraine (known as Lee). As soon as he could, which was twenty five years later he eventually managed to take out British Nationality which enabled him to return home to Germany for a visit with his family. If he had gone back to Germany before then he risked never been allowed to return to England.

The family moved back to Laindon in the early 1960s, and then in the late seventies with the children off hand, Ernest and Dean moved to Cross Green in Basildon near the Castle Mayne Public house in Lee Chapel South.

His sister Anna who he had never seen, because she was born after he had left home to join the army, managed to come and visit him in the early 1970s. Ernest, eager to introduce her to his friend Albert went off to the Fortune of War Public house to find him. Initially they could not see him but when Ernest went to the toilet Anna could feel this man at the bar watching her. When Ernest returned she pointed the man out to him. It turned out to be Albert, the very person they were looking for.

In the pursuing conversation Ernest turned and jokingly said to him 'I will sell my sister to you for a Goat'.

Ernest returned home to Germany for the first time in 1974 to be at his parents Golden Wedding Anniversary celebration. Albert had corresponded with Anna following her return and when he eventually went with Ernest to Poland he asked her to marry him. Anna got permission to leave Poland and they got married on the 2nd August 1975. I wonder what happen to the Goat?

German POW Camp 266 – Langdon Hills

Ernest, Sister Hilda, Albert and Anna. Permission of Lee Jenkins.

One amusing story when Ernest first met Dean's mother for tea, is when she asked him if he would like any "ice cream?" He jumped up saying "why, why, what did I do?" Ernest thought she had said "I scream!"

Ernest and Dean passed away in 2006 and 2009 but Lee still lives in Basildon, Paul in Manchester, Alan, Albert and Anna in Laindon. Ernest could speak five languages Polish, German, Austrian, Dutch and English.......................

Ernest and Deans wedding at St Nicholas Church, Laindon.
By kind permission of their daughter Lee Jenkins.

Eberhard Fischer

Eberhard Fischer was a crew member of U-boat, U-825 when Germany surrendered on the 6th May 1945. The German Navy had ordered all U-Boats to cease operation on the 4th May and return to Norwegian posts. On the 8th May the Admiralty ordered all U-Boats to surrender, and those still at sea to go to designated reception posts. Following these instructions the U-Boat commander Gerhard Stoelker surrendered at Portland Bill on the 10th May 1945. It then transferred to Lock Eriboll, Scotland on the 13th May 1945.

U-825 had been launched on the 16th February 1944 and commissioned on 4th May 1944. It carried out two patrols the first 4th May 1944 to 30th November 1944 which was a training mission. It's second which was an active patrol from the 1st December 1944 to 8th May 1945 and during this patrol it damaged, on the 27th December 1945, the American Merchant ship 'Ruben Dario', 7,198 tons. The Ruben was hit by a torpedo on the starboard side. The explosion destroyed the bulkhead between I and 2 holds which caused flooding of both holds but following a survey the ship was able to continue at 9 knots. There were no casualties.

On the 27th January 1945 a torpedo from U-825 hit the Norwegian Motor tanker 'Solor' on the port side in the engine room. The tanker was abandoned at 1.25 pm an hour after it was struck. Four crew members died, 40 remaining crew including seven injured were picked up by the British rescue ship Zamalek. The Solor was taken in tow and beached at Oxwich Bay, half the cargo and 17 gliders were unloaded before she broke in two and declared a total loss.

U-1003. Photograph by kind permission of Eberhard Fischer.

Previous to the U-boat 825, Eberhard had been a crew member of U-1003, which unlike the 825 did not have any successes. It was in fact spotted by HMCS New Glasgow (Frigate) but as she prepared for a depth charge attack she herself was damaged as the U-Boat collided with her. U-1003 sat at the bottom for 48 hours as 14 Allied Ships hunted for her. The damages were however so severe the commander, Werner Strubing, scuttled the U-Boat. The Commander and 14 crew members were lost. HMCS Thetford Mines picked up the remaining 33 crew members but two died later and were buried at sea.

It would appear that Eberhard had already transferred to U-825.

U-825 was transferred to Lisahally, Northern Ireland as part of Operation Deadlight and sunk on the 3rd January 1946. As part of this operation 116 U-Boats were sunk.

Photograph by kind permission of Heritage Images.

Eberhard did not really see himself as a POW because he had surrendered after the war was over but unfortunately for him he was treated as one until he was repatriated on the 14th July 1948.

His first camp was camp 19, Happenden, Douglas, Lanarkshire, Scotland until 20th August 1945 when he moved down to Camp 266, Langdon Hills. He became one of the camps Lorry Drivers and he believes he was the last to leave the camp on 29th June 1948 when he had to deliver a Bedford 15 cwt to Staines. He then went by train to camp 186 at Bury St Edmunds then approximately a fortnight later on the 8th July he transferred to a camp in Germany before going home on the 14th July 1948.

Eberhard was born on the 6th March 1924 in Aschaffenburg, the family lived a few miles away at Lanfach where his father was a manager in an iron foundry. He was from a protestant family. He travelled by train to his secondary school in Aschaffenburg where he was taught English and French. He enjoyed school and had a very happy childhood.

He joined the Hitler Youth and had a great time, as he said 'it was the best thing that could happen to us at this time, we had a lot of fun', they had no idea what was happening in other places. He explained that every young boy whether you were English, French or German would have done the same and enjoyed their youth. 'What happened later was another problem'!

His fascination was always the water and ships and his exercise books at school were full of drawings of ships and it was his intention to join the

Merchant Navy when he left school. He contacted a shipping company in Hamburg but they told him to come back after the war.

That was going to be too long for him so in 1941 at the age of 17 he volunteered and join the Navy where he trained to be a wireless operator. Initially he was on minesweepers working in the Channel and around Finland; he then transferred to U-boat 1003. He was a Funkmaat (NCO) and U-1003 was operating in the Irish Sea. The Royal Navy were dropping depth charges day and night, they just appeared to have millions of them, fortunately they were not hit and they returned to Norway (Bergen).

The crew of U-1003, Norway December 1943.
Eberhard is 3rd from the left with a cigarette in his Mouth.
Photograph by kind permission of Eberhard Fischer.

Eberhard was then transferred to U-boat 825. The area it patrolled was between Shetland and the Faro's, south on the West Coast of Ireland and the channel. With the war over the U-Boat Commander was ordered by the British to take the boat to Scotland, Loch Eriboll and then to Loch Alsh. This is where he became a POW, being transferred to London by train and then a few days later back to Scotland at Camp 19.

Eberhard's job as a driver was to transport other POW's to places of work or act as a chauffeur to the camps officer's. He had been issued by the Secretary of State a War Department Driving Permit allowing him to drive vehicles on Military Service, not privately. He still remembers clearly what

Major Gill used to say every evening after returning from a trip, "We are back alive, have a good night and please don't forget to wake up tomorrow morning."

He was obvious a very good driver and therefore appreciated by the camp officers. When he left the camp in June 1948 the camp commandant gave him the following reference,

'The bearer FISCHER Eberhard (990592) has been in this camp as driver from August 1946 until to-day (28th June 1948). He is an excellent driver and kept his vehicle always in very good order. He is trustworthy, diligent and may be recommended for any position.'

However he did have one or two narrow escapes. In early August 1947 he was driving along Orsett Road, Grays with other POW's in the back of the truck when a small boy stepped in front of him and was knocked over. Fortunately he was not seriously injured. The father of the boy, Edward M Neatham wrote to the camp and enclosing a letter to Eberhard thanking him for his very careful driving and the kindest and consideration shown by the other POW's to his son.

In the letter to the camp which was dealt with by Lt Colonel Hobby he wrote that the Police on request had given the family an excellent report of the way that Eberhard had conducted himself. This was confirmed by his sisters who also witnessed the accident, that it was not the fault of the driver. At the end of the letter he goes on to say, 'I trust therefore that no reflection upon Fischer will be made in any official reports but rather that he be commended for his carefulness and considerations.

In the letter to Eberhard he starts off by saying, 'Dear Eberhard, Greetings to you. It is my hope that you can read this writing of mine, so that you may receive my thanks and my blessings.' He then goes on to explain that the Police have given him a fully report on the accident, the contents of which are confirmed by his sister and therefore absolves him from any blame.

He then goes on to say, 'It is a pleasure to write to you, who was born in another land and taught things so alien to me and to say, 'thank you Eberhard, for your careful driving.'

He also requested that Eberhard conveys his thanks to his comrades in the lorry and finally wishes Eberhard well and that he will soon see his homeland again.

The next incident was in January 1948 when he was on his way to Andrew's post office in Laindon with Col. Patmore, presumably to pick up post. It would appear that he was going a little too fast when he entered the post yard and he knocked over a dustbin. The Colonel complained that he nearly broke his neck.

One of Eberhard's many sketches. By kind permission of Eberhard Fischer.

A few days later the camp received the following postcard from Mrs Andrews;

'This is to certify that I have accepted a dustbin from POW Fischer. A driver from 266 POW Camp, Laindon, to replace one accidentally damaged by his lorry on Saturday Jan 31st. in the yard of the Post Office. I am perfectly satisfied with the exchange of this utensil and make no further claim what so ever.

Like the other POW's Eberhard found work in the local vicinity. He went to work for Finches who had a Greengrocers store in the high Road with two other comrades. Refer to Peter O'Rorke and Joan Wilkins (nee Finch) memories of him. They got on extremely well with the family and Eberhard and his family have stayed friends to this day.

In October 1947, Joan's sister Winifred married William Rossiter at St Nicholas church. Eberhard and his comrades attended. Other guests included Dr and Mrs Chowdhary whose daughter Shakuntala was one of the bridesmaid. Eberhard had carried a camera with him throughout the war but it had been confiscated when he surrendered. However, because he was going to the wedding he asked for his camera which was returned to him. He was able to keep it for the rest of the time he was in England. Photography was one of Eberhard's passions and has taken many of the photographs you will find in this book.

That Christmas (December 1947) the family asked permission for Eberhard to be allowed to spend Christmas with them. Permission was granted by the Camp Commandant.

The next piece is written by Eberhard in his own words;

On the 21st August 1945, a number of us transferred from Camp 19, which was somewhere up in Scotland to Laindon (Langdon Hills Camp was frequently referred to as the Laindon Camp).We moved from a camp with barbed wire round it to one with no fence, it gave us the feeling of being free. Within a few days we were sent out with a small group in Lorries to work on the farms. I was employed first by Stambridge Thrashing Co, a very dusty job. Then at Oliver's farm at Barling near Southend. I later moved onto working on the roads and houses in Aveley with Hipperson and Son, London. On the Lorries we had written, Hipperson and Sohne, grosse schulerin, Kleine Lohne....Which means in English- Hipperson and Sons, great big schools, little wages.

One day the foreman for some reason was very annoyed with us. The next day a lot of the tools went missing. There was great excitement; we had buried them in the concrete in last section of road we were working on.

In the evenings we would sit around the stove in the huts telling each other stories, drinking coffee and placing bread on the stove to go brown (toasting) We would often burst into song and one of our favourites was :-

'Got no matches
Got no Fags
Got no girls with lovely legs
But we got the sun in the morning
And the moon at night'

(This was sung to the tune of 'I got the Sun in the Morning' words and music by Irvin Berlin 1946)

At the weekends we were often entertained by our band in the camp or a theatre performance. In other spare time we used to make toys out of wood such as Lorries and Cranes. Our foreman would take most of them and sell them for us. So I always had some money.

German POW Camp 266 – Langdon Hills

In the autumn of 1946 the camp was looking for some drivers, I volunteered and I was sent to Brentwood and took a test on a 5 ton Dodge. I passed and received a licence. From then on I drove nearly every day in all sorts of vehicles often taking the officers to Cambridge, London and various hostels at Chelmer Road, Hylands Hall, Toby Priory, Harold Wood, Purfleet, Tilbury Transit Camp, Horndon, Rawreth, Tillingham, Great Wakering, Southend and Shoeburyness.

Drawing reproduced by kind permission of Eberhard Fischer.

One day I received a letter from my mother telling me that she has a girlfriend married to a lawyer (German) living in London. So on one occasion I had to take the camp commander from Langdon Hills to London, and being aware I had 3 hours to spare, requested that I go and see him in the car. I found the house a girl came to the door and said 'good morning sir, your card please'. I replied 'sorry', 'I'm a POW and I would like to see Mr Nathan. I had a long chat with him and his wife. On his writing table was all his decorations from the First World War, he was a German Officer who spoke with swabian dialect (Prussian). He came to England in 1923. After this I often called in for a cup of coffee when I was in London. In 1948 when Werner Heimans and Lousie (refer Petter O'Rorke story) were talking about getting married, I introduced them to him and he helped them sort out all the legalities.

On the 17th April 1947 I was out and about in a Chevrolet around Tillingham and Bradwell. I spotted on the shore a lot of big bags of flour from a sunken ship. I took as much as possible and our camp bakery had a find time making plenty of good bread and cakes.

By 1947 we could walk out of the camp when we wished and on the 18th April 1947 in the morning I was walking along Manor Road in Laindon with Erich and Werner. We heard a man grumbling and having problems with a motor plough. I said excuse me sir can we help you? Werner was a car mechanic so he was happy for us to try and get it going. We came back the next day and spent all day on it without any luck. We returned on the fourth day, a Sunday and managed to get it running.

This was the beginning of a good friendship with the Finch family. On the 14th May Joan had a birthday and we had a nice birthday, then on the 27th May, Sonny was 14 years old.

I liked to drive Major Gill on his farm visits. He liked eggs and whenever we stopped at a farm he went and saw the farmer for a drink and I went and collected eggs. We usually collected six eggs from each farm. We must remember food rationing went on well after the end of the war in fact meat rationing did not come off until 1954.

Werner, Rudi and I often spent Sundays with the Finches in Manor Road and on occasions we would go to Billericay to have a game of mini golf or to fish. With the boys Sonny and Peter (refer Peters Story) who were two very good friends we played darts; they were always ready for a joke. We got on very well with them and liked them very much. Sometimes Dr Chowdhary's children also came to play.

We often went to the cinema in Laindon but we had our own operator with German Films, though most of the time I took him and his equipment to the other hostels' and camps nearby.

On the 31st August 1947 I was driving our Doctor to the Tillingham Camp when we stopped by the River Blackwater for a bath. Then on another occasion I stopped in Burnham on Crouch so that Major Gill could go to a barbers shop for a shave. As I sat in the car reading a paper a car with nobody in it came rolling down the road backwards and crashed into my front bumper. Major Gill came out of the barbers with soap all over his face 'what's going on here!' He looked at our 'Chevrolet', only the car was damaged. The driver came running down the road to see what had happened. Major Gill had a few words with him and went back into the barbers.

The 30th November 1947 was the wedding of Win and Bill at St Nicholas Church in Laindon. After church we went to the British Legion Hall. On the door before we went into the hall were Win and Bill. The ladies got a kiss from Bill and the gent's got a kiss from Win. We Germans passed and had our kiss from Win. I said 'let's go round again'. (We said as POW's we never get a kiss) We did and got another kiss, which had other guests laughing. Later the best man Norman gave a toast to us three

244

Germans, Werner, Rudi and I. I had also promised that if I was allowed to go to the wedding I would wear a top hat. I did and looked like Charlie Chaplin.

On the 20th February 1948 there was so much snow that when I came back from a trip from London in the Chevrolet I had to put snow chains on the wheels to get up the hill to the camp.

We went to many dances; in early 1948 it was nearly every week either in the Langdon Hills Parish Hall (Rev. Hickson), the Memorial Hall in Laindon or the hall at the back of the Crown Hotel. Our band often played in the Crown Hotel hall. I particularly remember a U.N.A party held in the Laindon School.

At the end of 1947 into 1948 repatriation started and I would transport those being repatriated to the station. As previously mentioned I often drove British Officers into London and would have six hours to spare. With all this time on my hands, I would go off and have a cup of tea or coffee, go to the cinema or just walk the streets of London.

Our last dance at the Crown Hotel with our band was held on the 15th April 1948. On the 6th June on the way back from Romford, Police stopped us and other vehicles. For a moment we did not know why but then came along a procession of cars one with an open top and sitting in it was the present Queen and Prince Phillip. They came quite close and I had forgotten my camera!! Later I heard that they were on the way to the Essex Show at Orsett.

On the 26th June 1948 I transported the last fifteen men to the station for going home. The following day I went to the wedding of Werner and Louisa in Brentwood. Visited them in Fobbing the following day to say goodbye! On the 28th Shell took over the camp and that evening I spent time saying good bye to the Finches.

On the 29th at 7am I took the last vehicle out of the camp, a 15cwt Bedford, Nr.Z-1850778 and with Lt. Crees I went to London. I said goodbye to him and delivered the truck to Staines. I received my papers and ticket for a train back to London. I spent a day visiting several pubs and saying my farewells to London. In the evening I took the train to Bury St Edmunds, Camp 186 and moved into hut 63. On the 7th July Mr and Mrs Finch came up and visited and we spent a nice day together in Bury St Edmunds. In the evening we said our goodbyes and the Finches went back to Laindon.

Unloading at Laindon Railway station.
Photograph by kind permission of Eberhard Fischer.

On the 8th I left the camp for Harwich boarded the ship 'Biaritz' for the Hook of
Holland. It was heavy going and nearly all the passengers were sick. I did not have a
problem and spent most of my time in the bar.

We arrived at the Hook of Holland at 7.30 in the evening and took a special train
to Minster-lager in Germany arriving next day at 9.30am. On the 14th took a train to
Hammelburg. 15th, I was met by my two sisters at the station and then home to my
mother. My father had died in December 1944.

The first thing I did was to write a letter to the Finches – I'm at home! We kept
in touch and Mr and Mrs Finch came twice to Germany to see me, March 1959 and
August 1962. In June 1991 we spent our holiday in England with Joan and her
husband Reg and visited many old haunts. And in June 1993 Joan and Reg visited us
in Germany. We are still in touch with cards and the occasional telephone call.

Besides Eberhard's remarkable wartime exploits and his stories of his
time spent being a POW, he was also somewhat of a budding artist and
recorded some of his memories by drawing and sketching them. The next
couple of pages include some of his artistic works which go some way to
recording what life was actually like in the camps for the prisoners.

Eberhard unfortunately reversing a lorry in to the camps toilets

Prisoners on their way back into Camp. Notice that one of the guards is one of the German POW's

Another accident? Although we are not certain what part if any that Eberhard played in it.

The above sketches have been reproduced with kind permission of Eberhard Fischer. See if you can translate them.

Eberhard somewhere off of Norway December 1944.

Eberhard at the wedding of Winifried Finch and Bill Rossiter at St Nicholas Church, Laindon. As Charlie Chaplin, 30th November 1947.

Eberhard was very fond of cats. He had one at the camp.

Eberhard driving a Chevrolet lorry out of Camp 266 at Langdon Hills, sometime in 1947.

A picture from inside the camp sometime in 1947

CHAPTER
(Camp Closure)

German POW's getting ready to move out of camp 266 in June 1948.
Photograph by kind permission of Eberhard Fischer.

The last of the German POW's moved out of the camp in June 1948 although many were still not repatriated until later in the year. Soon afterwards Shell Oil Company leased the land and the buildings turning it into a hostel for up to 400 of their employees who were working at the Coryton oil refinery plant at Shell Haven.

Shell had upgraded the buildings and all the huts had central heating, cosy cubicles, large kitchens and recreation rooms. From reports it would appear that the workmen lived in relative comfort.

The company had a program of work that was to last for at least five years but unfortunately after only two and half years into the program the company had to make cuts in both the program and the work force. Fortunately the majority of the work force was able to find lodgings in London, whether they continued working for Shell is unknown.

Officers of the Billericay Council Housing committee inspected the buildings as a possibility of converting the camp into housing units for desperate people who were on their housing list. However after careful consideration the council decided that it was not economical to do so.

Factory Restaurants Ltd who were the catering contractors on site for Shell were surprised when they were given notice to quit immediately with no explanation. Their spokesman commented that they were sorry this had happened for it was a very comfortable hostel. He also agreed to convert the hostel into quarters for housing needs would indeed be an expensive task.

In December 1965 I joined Bateman's Catering Organisation and one of its subsidiary companies was Factory Restaurants Ltd. What do they say, funny old world!

The Basildon Corporation had also notified the authorities that they were not interested in the site, however it was different back in June 1948 prior to the camp becoming vacant and Shell taking over. It had expressed some interest in the site to house its officials, however they could not make any firm proposals until the proposed Basildon New Town Public Inquiry had been held which would probably not be until the middle of October of that year.

By October agents working for the Corporation had located four possible properties to house officials of the Corporation.

1. Small compact modern detached house in Pound Lane, Bowers Gifford.

2. Gifford House, Bowers Gifford, with one acre of land and other available.

3. The Old Rectory Basildon with 20 acres of land

4. Pre-war built military camp, Church Hill, Langdon Hills.

The agent Colonel S. Archbold Smith recommended the camp for the following reasons: -

1. The whole of the Corporation Staff with a large works depot could be accommodated on this site.

2. Ample office room, large garages, several large well-constructed NAAFI entertainment halls, Regimental offices etc.

3. The commanding Officer's quarters together with Regimental Offices' houses would solve the housing of the New Town Chiefs of Staff at once with very little adaptation required.

4. All services are laid on and many of the huts are centrally heated.

Smith concluded his report by saying 'Here we have in this camp the opportunity to house the whole of our staff and to bind them together into a really efficient team; if I was given the job to build this town as a ordinary civil engineering contract, I could wish for nothing better'.

He also stated that the if the Corporation were interested they would have to move quickly because both Billericay and Thurrock will want it for housing and was also aware of other Government Departments having an interest.

The reply two days later on the 28th October 1948 indicated that the Corporation were going to try and get they hands on the camp and did not think they would have any problem.

Well they failed because by early November it was in the hands of Shell who informed the Corporation that there was insufficient room in the camp for them. The Corporation eventually took over Gifford House.

Following the demolition of the camp the field was acquired by the South Essex Waterworks who named it Tower Sports Ground. They rented it out to a newly formed cricket club 'Westley Cricket Club' and on the 13th May 1956 the ground for cricket was officially opened by the Essex and England all-rounder Trevor Bailey. After only a few years the club vacated the ground and it became part of the Langdon Hills Country Park. As indicated previously the field is now known as 'Beacon Field'.

Finally

Below is an extract from the Camps newsletter issue 41 dated 1st December 1947 from an article written by Heinz Hermel in response to a letter from a German Student who had come over after the war to England with friends to familiarise themselves with the customs and traditions of this country and to see the plight of the German Prisoners of War.

Heinz had this to say;

'I am convinced that over 80% of the comrades in camp have initiated contacts with the British population which not only worked but led to friendly relations which had a lasting impact and many friends. We therefore do not live in isolation in the middle of a foreign nation, nor are we dissatisfied because of our cohesion.

On the contrary, in weak moments of despair by the Germans, an Englishman, just by using encouraging words and displaying fairness and diligence to his fellow man, will listen to the Germans and find solutions which are acceptable. Many of us will take back truly warm feelings for our English friends opposite who have looked after us in captivity, which is just as important. These facilities were only made possible by their adoption by the English Government but are more or less at the insistence of the British population, with the backing of the Church of England.

Let's hope that this bond which has developed between our two nations in the three years following the war will last for "A Thousand Years" and beyond.'

In closing we both hope that you have enjoyed reading this book as much as we have had writing it. Just like some of the people whom we have written about amongst these pages, we were strangers when we started our journey. We didn't know each other or hadn't even heard of each other when we started putting this book together. We only became friends because of it, which in turn adds a certain nice irony to the story.

We would like to thank everybody who has helped us with the compilation of this book by providing us with their own personal stories which have helped us bring this book to life. If we have missed anybody out in our thanks and acknowledgements then we humbly apologise as it was certainly not done intentionally.

We are sure there are many more worthwhile and memorable stories out there which could have been included in the book but we just never found them. Hopefully this account will help bring more of them to light.

Let's also hope that the bond that developed between our two nations in the three years following the war and since will last for "A Thousand Years" and beyond.

Lightning Source UK Ltd.
Milton Keynes UK
UKOW051902241012

201149UK00017B/150/P

9 781849 44173